MADAME FAVART BY FRANCOIS H. DROUAIS. 1757. Courtesy of the Metropolitan Museum.

COSTUME
THROUGHOUT
THE AGES

by
Mary Evans

J. B. LIPPINCOTT COMPANY
Philadelphia and New York

Library of Congress Catalog Card Number 50-8475

To
KATHERINE EVANS

PREFACE

THE history of the development of dress throughout the ages is one of very absorbing interest to the student of costume in any of its phases, and is the subject of Part I of this book. Many happy hours can be spent in the reading and study of this subject which has such close associations with history, literature, art, and ethnology. In the average school or college courses, however, time does not permit of very intensive study in this far-reaching field. With this condition in mind, an attempt has been made to gather together for the student of costume, merely the high lights of that fascinating story which has been created and bequeathed to future generations by peoples of diverse ages and countries in their attempts to satisfy their innate love of adornment, attempts that have been modified in the case of different peoples by the different social, political, religious, economic, and geographic conditions which surrounded them.

For the guidance of those interested in pursuing the subject more thoroughly and deeply than attempted in this book, the references at the end of each chapter and the classified bibliography will be found to cover a wide range of the literature available. It is suggested that the interested reader familiarize himself thoroughly with the reproductions, where originals are not available, in museums, in private collections, or through travel, of paintings, tapestries, sculpture, textiles, and examples of the minor arts which shed light on the subject of costume. Wherever possible in this Outline photographs of original sources have been used.

In Part II, dealing with national costumes, no attempt has been made to record the history and development of national and peasant costumes, but rather to direct the attention of the student to those rich sources of inspiration for designs which exist today but which, in so many instances, are fast disappearing.

For the many courtesies which have been invariably extended by the authors and publishers of the books drawn on for authentic material most sincere acknowledgment is made, particularly to the following who have been most gracious and generous in granting their permissions:

His Britannic Majesty's Stationery Office; Methuen and Company Ltd.; John Murray; A. C. McClurg, and Company; The Macmillan Company; Macrae Smith and Company; Eveleigh's Nash and Grayson Ltd.; Allen and Unwin Ltd.; The Encyclopaedia Britannica Company; Fairchild Publishing Company; Ernest Benn, Ltd.; Brentano; Cassell and Company Ltd.; Benziger Brothers; The Century Company; Chatto and Windus; Dodd, Mead and Company; George H. Doran Company; Sampson Low, Marston and Company Ltd.; L. C. Page and Company; G. P. Putnam's Sons; Charles Scribner's Sons; Arts and Decorations Company; Scott, Forsman and Company; Doubleday, Page and Company; The National Geographic Society; Duffield and Company; The Field Museum; Skeffington and Sons; The Studio Ltd.; Harper and Brothers; The Johns Hopkins Press; Longmans, Green and Company; Mr. E. H. Mackay; E. P. Dutton and Company; J. B. Lippincott Company; the American Museum of Natural History; the Metropolitan Museum; Thomas Nelson and Sons; J. M. Dent and Sons Ltd.; and Chapman and Hall Ltd.; Miss Estella Canziani; The Druid.

For the careful reading and helpful criticism of the manuscript by Miss Helen D. Wicks, Professor W. H. Spohr, and Mr. Louis Harmuth I am very deeply indebted and extremely grateful.

MARY EVANS

CONTENTS

ILLUSTRATIONS

PART I

THE HISTORIC DRESS OF THE ANCIENTS, THE
FRENCH, THE ENGLISH, AND THE AMERICANS

COSTUME THROUGHOUT THE AGES

CHAPTER I

COSTUMES OF THE EGYPTIANS, ASSYRIANS, PERSIANS, AND HEBREWS

Old Kingdom, 2830–2530 B.C., development of stone architecture
Middle Kingdom, 2130–1930 B.C., Dynasties XI–XIV
    Hyksos period, 1700–1580 B.C.
New Kingdom, 1580–945 B.C., Dynasties XVIII–XIX
Late period, 945–525 B.C., building of Carthage
Persian period, 525–332 B.C.
Ptolemaic period, 332–330 B.C., founding of Alexandria
Roman period, 30 B.C.–395 A.D.
    Christianization of Egypt; Cleopatra, 69–30 B.C.
Byzantine (Coptic) period, 395–638 A.D.

Egyptians.—When carefully preparing their mummies for burial, placing beside the embalmed body vessels filled with food and various ointments for the spirit in the other life, or when engraving scenes from the daily life of the deceased upon the walls of the tombs, the ancient Egyptians little thought that they were creating records of customs and costumes which would be eagerly scanned by strange peoples in centuries and countries far removed. For it is from the funeral statues and tombs that our knowledge of the dress of the Egyptians is derived; from the mummy wrappings we learn of the materials which rival in fineness the cobweb-like fabrics of our modern power looms; from the number and variety of the bottles, vessels, and boxes found beside the mummies we realize the great amount of care that was expended upon the body. The crude, angular drawings of the early artists are authentic representations not only of the daily life and customs of the people, but of their manner of dress during the various periods of their history.

Although simple in comparison with the intricacies of modern

3

costume, Egyptian dress underwent rather frequent changes during the Old, the Middle, and the New Kingdoms, and strange as it may appear to us, it was the costume of the sterner sex which was varied, elaborate and interesting.

Attire for Men.—In the Fourth Dynasty of the Old Kingdom, the fashionable attire for men consisted of a loin cloth or short skirt of white linen wrapped rather loosely around the waist and hanging to the knees. It was a straight piece of cloth wrapped, as a rule,

around the body from right to left with ends coming at the center front and the upper, outer corner tucked into the bow of the girdle which held the skirt. In the Fifth and Sixth Dynasties the skirt became longer and wider, the fulness being gathered together in the front and by some artificial means made to stand out in a triangular erection. During the Middle Kingdom it became fashionable to wear the skirt narrower and slightly longer in front than in back. Frequently the outer edge was decorated with an embroidered border. The skirt, like that worn in the Old Kingdom, was at first of heavy material, but later men of high rank wore it of fine white material so transparent that an inner skirt was adopted.

FIG. 1. EGYPTIAN STELA SHOWING THE TRIANGULAR ERECTION, WIG, AND COLLAR. Courtesy of the Metropolitan Museum.

It is in the time of the New Kingdom that we find evidences of the most radical changes in the clothing of the men. The rapid development of the country and contact with other peoples brought with them attendant changes in dress. With the New Kingdom came the introduction of a new garment, the shirt. This cover for the upper part of the body was tucked into the girdle, open at the right side, and possessed one short sleeve for the left arm, the right one remaining uncovered for greater freedom of movement. During this same period the skirts were arranged in many different ways. At first the outer was shortened in front and lengthened in back, and toward the latter part of the Eighteenth Dynasty was looped up in puffs to show the lengthened and frequently plaited inner skirt. With a full, plaited skirt the king in the Nineteenth Dynasty wore a large, loose mantle which fastened in front at the chest. As we find in European history, it was the king who set the fashion in dress, his lead being quickly followed by men of high rank who in turn were imitated by subordinate officials of the court. The peasant, in all periods appar-

FIG. 2. INI AND HIS WIFE. XIXTH DYNASTY. NOTE THE ENDS OF THE HAIR. Courtesy of the Metropolitan Museum.

ently, was content to wear the skirt which was in vogue during the time of the Old Kingdom.

The Wig.—A most important adjunct of the costume of the Egyptians was the wig. Always an extremely cleanly people, they cut short the hair, shaved the beard, and wore artificial hair. The wigs, usually black, were made of human hair or of sheep's wool. One style was made in imitation of short, curly hair, and another

popular style in imitation of straight hair, both forms being worn
by men of rank until the Eighteenth Dynasty. Then it was considered correct for the wig to cover the neck, or to fall over the
shoulders with its ends twisted into small curls.

FIG. 3. RELIEFS FROM AN EGYPTIAN TOMB SHOWING THE
USE OF TRANSPARENT MATERIAL. Courtesy of the Metropolitan
Museum.

With these wigs were worn very interesting head-dresses which
were indicative of the wearer's rank; the pharoah, of course, wore
special head coverings, the folded kerchief, the helmet, or the crown
of that part of Egypt over which he ruled. The king of Upper
Egypt wore a red crown, of Lower Egypt a white one, and when the
same king ruled over the united country he combined both crowns
into one head-dress. The king's sons wore diadems or kerchiefs

bound over the forehead and top of the head. At festivals or on gala occasions the common people entwined wreaths of flowers or bands of coloured ribbon in their hair.

In order to conform to his standard of cleanliness the Egyptian shaved his beard, but on solemn occasions when he wished to

FIG. 4. THE VULTURE HEAD-DRESS OF AN EGYPTIAN QUEEN. Courtesy of the Metropolitan Museum.

command respect he wore an artificial appendage on his chin. This symbol of manliness and dignity was a short piece of hair tightly plaited and held in place by means of straps which passed behind the ears.[1]

---

[1] WILKINSON, SIR J. G., THE MANNERS AND CUSTOMS OF THE ANCIENT EGYPTIANS, Vol. II, p. 333. Dodd, Mead and Company.

Footwear.—Although the head covering received from earliest times great care and attention, but little at any time was expended upon the footwear. Even when clad in his richest garment the Egyptian preferred to go barefooted, wearing sandals only when necessary out of doors; while women, apparently, wore none at all until the late period. In the early periods sandals were of the simplest form—soles of leather, palm leaves, or papyrus reed, with straps of the same material, one passing over the instep, the other between the first and second toes. "Those worn by the upper classes and women were usually pointed and turned up at the toe."[2]

Women's Dress.—One can scarcely fail to notice that with the people of Egypt it was the men rather than the women who were keenly interested in the subject which is to-day one of woman's greatest delights. Throughout the Old and the Middle Empires when men were caught in the toils of changing fashions, the woman's dress consisted of a simple, exceedingly narrow, straight garment which reached from the breasts to the ankles, and was held up by two straps or braces over the shoulders. This simple chemise-like dress was worn by princess and peasant alike; it had an embroidered hem at the top and occasionally at the bottom as its only decoration. At the beginning of the Eighteenth Dynasty the left shoulder was covered by the dress, and a large cloak fastened in front and finished with an embroidered hem formed a fashionable addition to the woman's as well as the man's wardrobe. Decided innovations were made during the next dynasty when a left sleeve was placed in the dress and a thick under dress was worn beneath a semi-transparent outer one.

Wigs of artificial hair were worn by the women as well as by the men in this hot country, the styles of hair dressing changing, apparently, as infrequently as did that of the dress. Until the Eighteenth Dynasty the woman's coiffure was of straight hair worn hanging to the breasts in two tresses, the ends of which in the Middle Empire were twisted to form a fringe. It was but natural that the innovations which occurred in dress during the Eighteenth Dynasty should affect the hair dressing also. From that time throughout the New Empire there were many variations in the

---

[2] *Ibid.*, Vol. II, p. 337.

arrangement of the hair; in one the hair of the wig stood out from the head like the bobbed locks of the flapper of 1923; in another, the hair was long in both back and front, but short over the shoulders.

The jewelry of this highly civilized people was exceedingly rich and beautiful, showing choice designs and expert craftmanship. Carnelian, turquoise, lapis lazuli, green feldspar, glass, and faience were combined with delicate bars and balls of gold to form broad necklaces and wide bands for the upper arm and ankles of the beauties of those ancient days. Ear-rings, first in the shape of broad disks, later of large rings were probably introduced into Egypt when that country

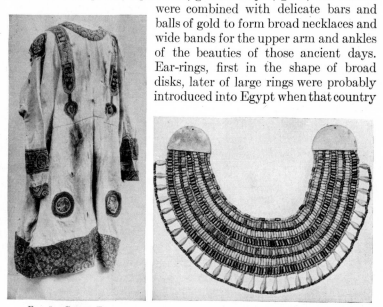

FIG. 5.   COPTIC TUNIC.   FIG. 6.   FAIENCE COLLAR.
Courtesy of the Metropolitan Museum

was thrown open to the foreigner in the seventh and sixth centuries B.C. Fans of feathers or papyrus were very useful accessories of costume in that warm climate whose dryness made the rubbing of oil on the body a daily necessity. Imported fragrant oils were rubbed freely into the body and on the head. Cosmetics were as popular with the Egyptian beauty as with the modern woman. Wall paintings show women with carmined lips, finger nails touched with yellow or orange stain, eyes made more brilliant by lines of green below the lids, and eyebrows painted black.

Materials.—The dress worn in the earliest period by both sexes seems to have been of thick material but in the New Empire thin, transparent materials were fashionable for dresses and cloaks. Bright colours, such as red, green, and blue were common. Linen was the principal fabric used and was woven on crude hand-looms in textures of wonderful beauty and fineness. While wool garments were worn by laymen, that fibre was never found in the clothing of the priests as it was considered unclean and therefore unfit for service in the temples. Later, wool thread was much used in the decorative bands (*clavi*) at the shoulders and in the four medallions (*roundels*) at the hem of the linen tunics of the Copts, the native Egyptians who embraced Christianity. The tunics with their tapestry woven decorations, originally badges of rank with the Romans, were adopted and worn by both sexes during the period of Roman dominance.

Assyrians.—Two garments apparently answered the costume needs of the ancient Assyrians, men as well as women. Old stone reliefs and statues show the simple body garment of both sexes as a straight, ankle-length tunic with fringe at the bottom and further decorations of embroidery in the form of dots, rosettes, and hexagonal motifs in border and allover patterns. A broad belt with pendant tassels bound the tunic about the waist. The chief difference between the tunic of the men and that of the women seems to have been in the greater length of sleeve of the latter. The second garment common to both sexes was a large shawl edged with fringe so draped that it crossed the chest and back in a diagonal line from the left shoulder, where it was fastened, and under the right arm.

The feet were shod in sandals that protected the whole of the heel like the counter of the modern shoe. In common with many of the ancient peoples of Asia Minor the Assyrians shielded the legs with wrappings of narrow strips of cloth.

Some figures of men on the reliefs are represented with close caps that resemble the fez worn so commonly in Asia Minor today; others with fillets binding the curled hair that hung free over the shoulders. Their beards were cut square and their jewelry, like that of the women, consisted of very large hoop-like ear-rings, and massive bracelets and armlets.

Persians.—Most typical of ancient Persian costume were the long trousers worn by both sexes. They were of moderate size and at the ankle met sandals or shoes of leather.

Another distinctive garment was the long coat with its full-length sleeves set into small armscyes. Beneath this was worn the girdled tunic that extended below the knees and was probably made of the same linen or wool that was used for the coat and trousers, though the latter were frequently made of leather.

FIG. 7. AN ASSYRIAN RELIEF INDICATING THE USE OF FRINGE.

FIG. 8. PERSIAN MINIATURE ILLUSTRATING THE COAT AND TROUSERS AS WORN BY THE ANCIENT PERSIANS.

Courtesy of the Metropolitan Museum.

Hebrews.—The loose, roomy garments of the East were common to the ancient inhabitants of Israel. The chief article of the men's dress was the long, girdled coat, *kĕthôneth*, that opened down the front,[3] beneath which were worn a simple shirt of linen, *sădîn*, and long, loose linen trousers, *mikhnĕsê*. Over the *kĕthôneth* was placed an ample cloak, *simlah*, that in cut resembles very much the Arab *aba* of modern times. Fringe, tassels, and embroidery were

---

[3] MACKIE, G. M., Article on "Dress" in the DICTIONARY OF THE BIBLE, Vol. I, pp. 623–628. Charles Scribner's Sons.

employed in the decoration of this wrap of wool striped with a variety of strong colours. It is generally believed that the head-dress was in all probability similar to that of the modern Bedouins,—a striped, coloured kerchief so arranged over the head that the long hair was practically concealed and ears, forehead, and neck were effectually protected from the hot sun. (See page 265.)

The prohibition of the interchange of men and women's clothing in Deuteronomy 22:5 leads authorities on this subject to believe that there must have been great resemblance in the garments of the two sexes. Dr. Mackie describes the feminine costume as consisting of an inner garment, a long, girdled tunic, *kethôneth*, and a second tunic, *me-îl*, that fell straight to the feet unconfined by any form of girdle, and enriched about neck and loose sleeves with colourful silk embroidery. These loose, flowing vestments were doubtless of the natural white material broken with patterns of various colours, the costly purple favored by those of great wealth.

The third chapter of Isaiah bears witness to the love of the daughters of Zion for rings, nose jewels, chains and necklaces, ear-rings, bracelets, and anklets. From a similar source [4] we learn that they employed in their toilettes cosmetics for cheeks, eyelids and nails.

REFERENCES

ERMAN, LIFE IN ANCIENT EGYPT, Chap. X.
WILKINSON, THE ANCIENT EGYPTIANS, Chap. X.
HOUSTON AND HORNBLOWER, THE ANCIENT EGYPTIANS, ASSYRIANS, AND PERSIANS.
RACINET, HISTOIRE DU COSTUME, Vol. II.
FALES, DRESSMAKING, pp. 3–5.
LESTER, HISTORIC COSTUME, Chap. II.
SAGE, A STUDY OF COSTUME, Chap. I.
BUSZ, DAS KOSTÜM IN VERGANGENHEIT UND GEGENWART pp. 1–11.
ENCYCLOPAEDIA BRITANNICA, "Costume."
PEROT AND CHIPIEZ, HISTORY OF ART IN PERSIA.
DICTIONARY OF THE BIBLE, "Dress."
ZUR GESCHICHTE DER KOSTÜME, plates 538, 566, 627, 635, 722.
HOTTENROTH, TRACHTEN DER VOELKER.

[4] II Kings, 9:30; Ezekiel 23:40.

CHAPTER II

GRECIAN COSTUME

Pre-Hellenic Period
    Minoan Period, 2800–1200 B.C.
    Mycenaean Age, 1600–1200 B.C.
Homeric Period, 1200–
Classical Period
    Homeric poems committed to writing, 550–510 B.C.
    Persian Wars, 500–440 B.C.   Sophocles, 495–406 B.C.
    Periclean Age, 454–431 B.C.   Phideas, 490–432 B.C.
    Parthenon built, 438 B.C.   Herodotus, 484–425? B.C.
    Conquest of Greece by the Romans, 146 B.C.   Aristotle, 384–322 B.C.

A COSTUME which offers greater possibilities of adaptation to modern dress than that of Egypt is that of her neighbor to the northwest, Greece, and it is from rather similar sources we derive our knowledge of Greek costume. The wall frescoes of the houses, grave reliefs, vases, together with records of travel, and poetry form most authentic sources of information relating to the clothing worn by that ancient race to which we trace much of our civilization. These artistic and literary records also indicate that the costume of the Greeks was quite different in the early and later periods of their political development.

Pre-Hellenic Period (Crete).—The excavations conducted by Sir Arthur Evans in the island of Crete and those by Heinrich Schlieman on the sites of ancient Troy and Tiryns revealed a costume which in comparison with that worn during the Golden Age of Grecian history, appears strikingly modern and familiar. The dress of the men of the Pre-Hellenic Period was extremely simple, consisting normally of a loin cloth of gaily coloured and patterned material hanging from the waist or drawn into short drawers, and a broad belt. Some men wore a short mantle fastened with a jewelled pin on one shoulder. The Cretans apparently indulged in fine footwear, as shoes and half boots with embroidered bindings are represented in the wall reliefs. There are also indications that shoes with heels of moderate height were worn by women.

The dress of the Cretan woman consisted of a short sleeved bodice extremely low cut at the neck, and so small in the waist as to suggest the general use of some form of corset at that period.

FIG. 9. CUP BEARER OF KNOSSUS. MEN'S COSTUME OF THE CRETAN PERIOD.

FIG. 10. CRETAN WOMAN IN ELABORATE SKIRT AND LOW-CUT BODICE.

Courtesy of the Metropolitan Museum.

Chemisettes were frequently worn with the low neck gowns. The bell-shaped skirt with its tucks or flounces reminds one of the ruffled skirts worn over the crinolines in 1860 in France, while a small statue of a votaress of the Snake Goddess indicates that a form of the modern apron was not unknown. Several strands of curled hair were allowed to hang free to the waist, while the remainder was elaborately knotted at the back of the head. The head covering was evidently an important item in the costume as many of the figurines wear tall crowned, narrow brimmed hats.

FIG. 11. EIRENE. DORIC CHITON.
Courtesy of the Metropolitan Museum.

FIG. 12. IONIC CHITON

Both men and women counted in their articles of personal adornment necklaces, and bracelets for the wrist and upper arm, as well as rings of surprising beauty and fine workmanship. Long strings of beads hung from the women's necks, while daggers inlaid with golden figures were thrust in the belts of the men.

Classical Period.—The writings of Homer describe for us the costume of his fellow countrymen who wore practically the same type of garments as did the Greeks of the later classical period. Similar in shape and method of adjustment for both men and women, the dresses and wraps were woven as distinct garments, draped on the person, and held in place by means of pins. They were woven in the houses by the women and servants of the household, and formed part of the family treasure. The dress or *chiton*, was the principal garment and of two types, the Doric and the Ionic.

The Doric chiton, the simpler of the two styles, was a rectangular piece of material, wool usually, which measured generally one foot more than the wearer's height, and equalled in width twice the distance from finger tip to finger tip with arms outstretched. The extra foot or more in length was folded back, then the long rectangle was folded in half and placed around the form with the fold at the left hand side, the back and front of the dress were then caught together at the shoulders with pins, *fibulae*, and held in at the waist by a girdle. The desired length of the dress from the floor was adjusted by pulling the dress up above the girdle, forming a blouse which was known as the *kolpos*. No attempt was made to form a covering for the arm. This type of *chiton* somewhat longer and fuller for the women than for the men, was the one in which all Greek women were garbed until about the sixth century B.C.[1]

The Ionic chiton differed from the Doric in material, size and arrangement over the arms. This considerably larger rectangle was of finely woven linen or, after the conquest of Greece by Alexander and the introduction of cotton from India, of fine cotton material which hung in many soft graceful folds from the shoulder and the waist. It was sewn from the waist down and sleeves were formed by holding the front and back of the *chiton* together at intervals along the arm with beautiful small pins. In general the Ionic *chiton* did not have the overfold, or *apotygma* but occasionally there is seen a blending of the two styles of dress when the *apotygma* is found in the *chiton* with sleeves. Worn originally by "the Ionians of Asia and quite generally adopted on the mainland, the Ionic

---

[1] ABRAHAMS, E., GREEK DRESS, p. 42. John Murray.

dress was probably discarded by the Athenians after the outbreak of the Persian War when a reaction set in against Orientalism and a tendency towards greater simplicity began to manifest itself."[2]

Besides the girdle, which was frequently quite elaborate, a cord or strip of leather gold-embossed, straps passing over the shoulders and under the arms were sometimes worn with the Ionic *chiton*. The position of the girdle varied: at times it was placed low on the hips, then gradually higher, until it was eventually worn under the breast.

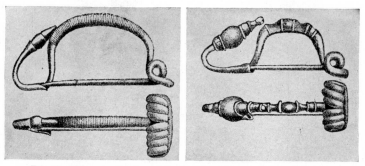

FIG. 13. FIBULAE. Courtesy of the American Museum of Natural History.

The out-of-door garment of the Greeks was also of two styles: the *himation*, worn by both men and women, and the *chlamys*, a smaller mantle used by men when travelling and riding. This latter wrap measured about two yards by a yard and a half, and was fastened by a *fibula* on the right shoulder or in the front. The *himation* was as significant to the Greek as was the *toga* to the Roman; without it he never appeared beyond the portals of his own house. It consisted of a large rectangle of white woollen material draped over the left arm and shoulder, across the back, and over or under the right shoulder, a weighted end being thrown over the left shoulder or over the left forearm.

Materials.—Wool, linen, either heavy or fine in texture, and later silk, were the materials from which the Greeks fashioned their clothing; the wool being used chiefly by the Dorians, and the linen by the Ionians. As in northern countries, changing seasons called

[2] *Ibid.*, p. 58.

for materials of varying weight and thickness. Cotton, a costly fabric at that time, was used chiefly in veils. The fine spray designs and delicate borders of their patterned fabrics may have been woven on the loom or embroidered by hand. The *chitons* were usually colourful, purple, red, blue, and saffron being the favorite hues. The *himation* was generally white.

FIG. 14. GRECIAN HEAD-DRESSES. From *Costume of the Ancients,* Hope.

Head-dress.—On her rather infrequent journeys from home the Greek woman drew up a fold of her *himation* as a head covering or enveloped her head with a shimmering white veil. Hats were not common though some Tanagras-terra-cotta figurines found in Tanagra, Boeotia—show a form of such head-gear. When travelling, riding, or in the country the men wore the *petasus,* a broad brimmed hat with ear flaps.

As the dress followed the natural lines of the body, the hair dressing of the Greek woman revealed the contour of her head. In general the hair was drawn back in soft waves from the forehead, gathered into a knot at the back of the head and held in place by pins of bone or ivory. Fillets, hair nets, or a broad band of cloth also helped to keep the hair in place. During Homeric times the men's hair was worn long and held back by metal clasps, but after the Persian wars it was worn considerably shorter.

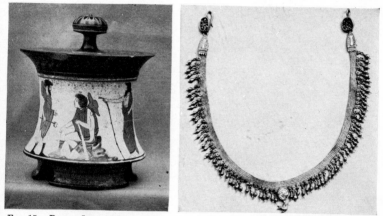

FIG. 15. PYXIS, JUDGMENT OF PARIS. SHOWING THE CHLAMYS AND PETASUS.

FIG. 16. A GRECIAN NECKLACE.

Courtesy of the Metropolitan Museum.

Jewelry.—Grecian jewelry lacked the colourful quality of Egyptian ornaments as stones and precious gems were but little used, engraved gems being found only in rings. The combs, pins, and nets which confined the hair were ornamented with mountings of gold, and this same metal, with silver, formed the bracelets, necklaces, and rings. After Alexander's eastern conquests coloured stones became popular and as a result, the fine quality of gold work deteriorated and the jewelry became more showy.

The Grecian costume was completed by the addition of a very unpretentious foot covering in the form of a sandal with sole of leather and straps of the same material around instep and ankle. Boots of soft leather were worn at times by both sexes.

REFERENCES

ABRAHAMS, GREEK DRESS.

EVANS, GREEK DRESS.

HOPE, COSTUME OF THE ANCIENTS.

HAWES, CRETE THE FORERUNNER OF GREECE, pp. 27–30.

GULICK, LIFE OF THE ANCIENT GREEKS, pp. 153–178.

RACINET, HISTOIRE DU COSTUME, Vol. II.

METROPOLITAN MUSEUM OF ART, THE DAILY LIFE OF THE GREEKS AND
ROMANS, Chap. VI.

BUSZ, DAS KOSTÜM IN VERGANGENHEIT UND GEGENWART, pp. 11–20.

FALES, DRESSMAKING, pp. 5–9.

LESTER, HISTORIC COSTUME, Chap. IV.

SMITH, ANCIENT GREEK FEMALE COSTUME.

ENCYCLOPÆDIA BRITANNICA.

HEUZEY, COSTUME ANTIQUE.

NORRIS, COSTUME AND FASHION, Chap. II.

SAGE, A STUDY OF COSTUME, Chap. II.

BLÜMNER, HOME LIFE OF ANCIENT GREEKS, Chap. I.

TUCKER, LIFE IN ANCIENT ATHENS, Chap. VIII.

GUHL AND KONER, LIFE OF THE GREEKS AND ROMANS.

ZUR GESCHICHTE DER KOSTÜME, plate 531.

BARKER, A. W., COSTUMES OF ATHENIAN WOMEN, *American Journal of Arche-
ology*, No. 4, 1922.

HOUSTON, ANCIENT GREEK, ROMAN AND BYZANTINE COSTUME.

CHAPTER III

COSTUME OF THE ROMANS

Kingdom, 753–509 B.C.
Republic, 509–31 B.C.
Roman Conquest of Greece, 146 B.C.
Empire, 31 B.C.–476 A.D
Cicero, 106–43 B.C.
Caesar, 102–44 B.C.
Cato, 95–46 B.C.
Roman Empire at its greatest extent, 117
Constantine, 306–337
Justinian, 527–565
Early Christian art, 313–800
Establishment of Byzantium as capital of Western Empire, 330
Sack of Rome by Goths under Alaric, 410
Sack of Rome by Vandals, 445

Rome.—On account of the mild climate of Italy, close fitting garments were unnecessary for the Romans; and because of their interest in attaining physical perfection for the benefit of the state, their clothing from the earliest times to the Empire remained very simple.

The tunic and toga were the chief and the most important articles in the wardrobe of the Roman citizen, the former consisting of two pieces of woolen material sewn at the sides and top to form a shirt-like garment with very short sleeves. The tunic reached to the calf of the leg or half way down the thigh and was drawn up under a girdle. During the latter part of the Republic (509-31 B.C.), ankle-length tunics with sleeves to the wrist were fashionable but considered quite effeminate. Purple stripes, *clavi*, woven or sewn to the tunic were indicative of the wearer's rank, a wide band down the center front being reserved for senators, and narrow ones extending from shoulder to hem, both front and back, for the knights.[1]

The other important article in the man's wardrobe was the *toga*, a cumbersome white woolen wrap expressive of the dignity and formality of the Roman citizen who jealously guarded against its use by foreigners and subject peoples. At first small and semi-

[1] Hope, T., Costumes of the Ancients, Vol. I, p. 42. Bulmer and Company.

21

circular in shape, the *toga* under the Empire (31 B.C.-476 A.D.), became elliptical, measuring about eighteen and a half feet in length and seven feet in width. It was folded lengthwise and draped around the body in a manner that was graceful but not conducive to swift motion of any kind. With one end touching the left foot, the folded edge was drawn up over the left shoulder,

FIG. 17.   A DETAIL FROM THE ARA PACIS.   SHOWING THE COSTUME OF ROMAN MEN, WOMEN, AND CHILDREN.   UFFIZI, FLORENCE.

across the back and either under the right arm or over the right shoulder. From there it was carried across the front of the body and the weighted end thrown over the left shoulder or the left forearm as the wearer desired. In the *toga* of the Republican and Empire periods the upper edge was loosely draped to form the *sinus*,[2] a deeply curved drapery falling to the right hip, allowing greater freedom of movement to the right arm and many times serving as a

---

[2] WILSON, L. M., THE ROMAN TOGA, p. 44. Johns Hopkins Press.

pocket in which to carry small possessions about the person. The *umbo*, a further elaboration of the drapery of the large *toga*, was made by pulling up the edge between the waist and shoulder on the left hand side and letting it fall in a deep loop over the fold forming the *sinus*.[3]

The *toga prætexta* with its purple border was worn by magistrates and priests,[4] also by the chief officers of free towns and colonies, and young boys, while the *toga picta*, entirely of purple cloth with embroidery of gold, was reserved for the use of victorious generals and emperors. The *lacerna*, the dark colored-mantle of both poorer classes and soldiers, was adopted by citizens as a protection for their *togas* from the vagaries of the weather. This was a short, sleeveless mantle open at the sides, sometimes possessing a hood, and fastened at the right shoulder with a brooch.[5] For comfort when traveling both men and women donned a thick, woolen cloak, *pænula*, that was closed at both sides, the only opening being at the neck. That children at a very early age were wrapped in tiny *togas* is evidenced in the reliefs of the Ara Pacis which contains the figures of boys and girls in diminutive *togas* and tunics.

In early times the hair and the beard of the Roman citizen were both long, and were kept in a state of perfect grooming by slaves of the household until the advent of professional barbers in 300 B.C. Ordinarily the men of the upper class wore no head covering except in the country or for traveling when the broad brimmed *causia* gave the necessary protection. At times the back of the *toga* was drawn up over the head.

As citizens and men of rank never appeared in public with bare feet, considerable attention was paid by the Romans to the foot covering. Slippers known as *soleæ*, of leather or matting with straps of various forms, were worn with the tunic in the house, and replaced for wear in the street by the shoes, *calcei*, which covered the upper part of the foot and were fastened with laces and straps. The shoes of senators were higher in cut than those of less exalted rank, while those of patricians and some magistrates were of rich

---

[3] *Ibid.*, p. 49.

[4] HOPE, T., COSTUMES OF THE ANCIENTS, Vol. I, p. 42.   Bulmer and Company.

[5] JOHNSTON, H. W., THE PRIVATE LIFE OF THE ROMANS, p. 166, 1903 Edition. Scott, Forsman and Company.

leather with ornaments of gold and silver.[6] The shoes and slippers of the women were similar in cut to those of the men but of finer leather. The Emperor Aurelian forbade the wearing of yellow, white, and green shoes by men, reserving those colors for feminine footwear alone.

The dress of the Roman woman was quite similar to the Ionic *chiton*. This *stola*[7] was fastened along the upper arm by costly brooches, thus forming a sleeve. A distinctive feature of the matron's *stola* was the *instita*, a wide flounce at the bottom. The dress was pulled up under a girdle, *zona*, at the hips.

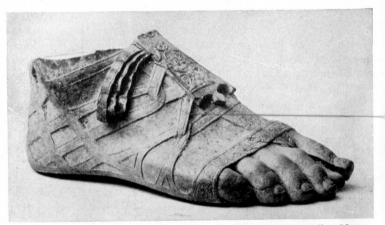

FIG. 18. ROMAN SANDAL OF THE IMPERIAL PERIOD. Courtesy of the Metropolitan Museum.

In early times the *toga* probably served as a wrap for the women, too, its place being taken eventually by the *palla*, a shawl-like wrap composed of a rectangular or square piece of wool material and worn in much the same manner as was the *himation* of the Greeks.

Materials.—Wool and linen were the materials in general use until the latter part of the Republic when silk, alone or mixed with wool, became the fashionable fabric for the tunics of the women, a mode which was later, in the Empire, adopted by the men. That

[6] *Ibid.*, p. 168.

[7] HOPE, T., COSTUMES OF THE ANCIENTS, Vol. I, p. 44. Bulmer and Company.

silk gradually became the material par excellence is shown by Tacitus who recorded an order of the Roman Senate in 16 A.D. prohibiting the use of silken robes by the men in Rome. In 409 Alaric demanded 4000 silk tunics as a ransom for the protection of the Eternal City against the invading Goths. The undergarments of the women were made of the finest linen brought from Egypt.

The *toga* was white by law; the dress or tunic also was probably white in early times but under the Empire tunics of scarlet, purple, and violet were worn by both men and women. Brown and black were restricted to the use of the lower classes.

While the Roman had a signet ring, often of gold set with precious stones as his only personal jewelry, the women of his household indulged in quantities of costly ornaments, rings, necklaces, bracelets, and diadems set with diamonds, sapphires, emeralds, garnets, and opals. Elaborate pins, nets, fillets, and combs confined the hair in a knot at the back of the head. The umbrella (*umbraculum*) and the fan were two accessories much used by the Roman beauty.

Byzantium.—With the collapse of the Roman imperial system in the west, the fashion center of the Empire was transferred to Byzantium which city the Emperor Constantine chose for his new capital (324) and designated Constantinople. The rich and stately court maintained by the various emperors required correspondingly fine costumes whose cut, texture, and decoration were reflected in the *moyen âge* costume of France and in that of the Russian court. The encouragement of the manufacture of silk fabrics within the borders of the eastern empire, particularly by the Emperor Justinian (527-565) did much toward the gradual spread of the use of that material throughout the west. Skilled workers in Damascus, Constantinople, and other centers employed the floral and animal motifs of the Persian designs in their silken tissues, while goldsmiths wrought rich ornaments for head, arms, and neck, and embroiderers combined pearls and precious stones with their colorful threads.

Similarity—Men's and Women's Dress.—A very clear idea of the general richness, detail, and similarity of masculine and feminine dress during the Byzantine period may be secured by a study of the mosaics in the church of St. Vitale in Ravenna, which portray the Emperor Justinian and his stately consort Theodora with a few of their court attendants. These mosaics show that three types of garments were used alike by men and women, individuals varying the length, fullness, and color according to their rank. The tunic worn by the men reached slightly below the knee and was caught

Fig. 19.   Empress Theodora and Her Ladies in Byzantine Costume of the VIth Century.   Courtesy of the Metropolitan Museum.

at the waist by a girdle. When worn by women, the tunic extended to the ground. The sleeves for both were long and close at the wrists. During the fifth century the *clavi* became short shoulder bands ending above the waist in *orbiculi*, somewhat circular shaped motifs like the *clavi* in tapestry weaves. *Roundels* of the same embroidery were placed at each knee while bands of similar decoration, *paragauda*, edged the bottom.

The second type garment was the *dalmatica*, introduced from Dalmatia about 300, a loose, straight garment that was put on over the head, like the tunic, and was distinguished by its large, loose sleeves. Of cotton, linen, or wool, it too, had the *clavi* but in this case extending the full length of the garment, front and back, and was generally worn beltless. In the sixth century the *clavi* on the

FIG. 20. EMPEROR JUSTINIAN. MOSAIC OF THE VITH CENTURY SHOWING BYZANTINE COSTUME. Courtesy of the Metropolitan Museum.

women's *dalmatica* were replaced by the fichu, a band of embroidery or patterned material that encircled the neck, extended in a band of about six inches in width down the front and in a somewhat broader one at the bottom.

The wrap was the third garment. A straight length of cloth or heavy silk with its lower edge longer than its upper one, it was wrapped around the shoulders and fastened with an ornamental clasp or *fibula* on the right shoulder. It was distinguished by richness of material; its decoration was centered in two embroidered squares, *tablion*, one on each side of the front and back edges. While stately and long, this wrap had none of the inconvenient features of the cumbersome *toga*.

The many conflicts of the Romans with the barbarians to the north introduced the former to the trousers of the northern peoples who, because of their lack of spinnable textile fibers, sewed together small skins for protection against the cold and thus originated the art of tailoring, or the making of fitted garments in contrast to the draped garments of the Mediterranean peoples. Their contacts with their neighbors to the east, particularly the Persians, rendered them still more familiar with the long, close nether garments which they adopted during the sixth century and wore under their tunics. From Persia, too, came the soft leather boots that extended well over the ankle.

From the same source, probably, came the elaborate head-dress of the woman with its rolled brim crossed with bands of jewels, and strands of pearls that hung down each side of the head well below the shoulders, a style much affected in western Europe during the twelfth century.

The extreme cold of the Byzantine winters caused both men and women to seek the warmth and comfort of the rich furs that were brought to the city from the countries to the north of the Black Sea.

REFERENCES

RACINET, HISTOIRE DU COSTUME, Vol. II.
JOHNSTON, PRIVATE LIFE OF THE ROMANS, pp. 158–182.
HOPE, COSTUMES OF THE ANCIENTS.
PRESTON AND DODGE, PRIVATE LIFE OF THE ROMANS, pp. 88–104.
WILSON, THE ROMAN TOGA.
NORRIS, COSTUME AND FASHION, Chaps. III, IV.
FRIEDLANDER, ROMAN LIFE AND MANNERS UNDER THE EARLY EMPIRE, pp. 173–185, Vol. II.
MARQUARDT, DAS PRIVATLEBEN DES RÖMER.
ABBOTT, THE COMMON PEOPLE OF ANCIENT ROME, pp. 164–165.
SANDYS, A COMPANION TO LATIN STUDIES, pp. 190–200.
SMITH, DICTIONARY OF GREEK AND ROMAN ANTIQUITIES.
HARPER, DICTIONARY OF CLASSICAL LITERATURE AND ANTIQUITIES.
METROPOLITAN MUSEUM OF ART, THE DAILY LIFE OF THE GREEKS AND ROMANS.
FALES, DRESSMAKING, pp. 9, 10.
LESTER, HISTORIC COSTUME, Chap. V.
SAGE, A STUDY OF COSTUME, Chap. III.
ZUR GESCHICHTE DER KOSTÜME, plates 707, 1144.
RÜCKLIN, DAS SCHMUCKBUCH.

CHAPTER IV

FRENCH COSTUME OF THE MOYEN ÂGE

The Gauls.—The barbaric neighbors of the Romans beyond the Alps presented a strong contrast to the civilized peoples of the Mediterranean countries in costume as well as in customs and modes of life. The ancient peoples were clothed in straight pieces of cloth draped in various graceful arrangements around the form; the Gauls on the other hand, protected themselves from the northern cold with garments that were more closely fitted to the body.

The triumphal arches and columns of the Roman conquerors, the chief sources from which we gather information regarding the clothing of the Gauls before their conquest and Romanization, 255-50 B.C., represent the Gallic man in trousers, tunic, and mantle. The trousers, *bracchae*, were either fairly close fitting or quite loose, and reached to the ankle where they were met by the heel-less leather shoe. The long-sleeved, girdled tunic fell to the mid-leg and was of wool dyed in various bright colors and woven into patterns of stripes and checks. The square, straight mantle, *saggum*, was also of wool, frequently quite small in size, and fastened by a clasp in front or on the right shoulder. A small, close cap covered the long, bushy hair, as worn by all classes of men, while a clean shaven face distinguished the man of rank from his inferior.

The dress of the Gallic woman was as colorful and barbaric as that of the man; the tunic and mantle were similar for both, the woman's differing only in added length. The outer tunic was short, with its elbow length sleeves displaying the long, close sleeves of the inner tunic. Both were girdled about the hips by a rich belt. The shoes were similar in cut and material to those worn by the men. This simple costume was enriched by heavy jewelry in the form of bracelets, necklaces, rings, and girdles. The hair hung in two long braids in front.

The Gallo-Romans.—After close contact with the civilization of their conquerors, the Gauls made several changes in their costume: those who had become Roman citizens adopted the tunic and *toga;* others without the rights of citizenship, added length and fullness to the tunic and *saggum.* The outer tunic of the woman was lengthened, the sleeves fastened along the top of the arm with brooches after the manner of the Roman matron's *stola,* and the long braids were bound up at the back of the head. That the Romans were not unimpressed by the garments of the barbarians is evidenced by the addition to the Roman's wardrobe of knee-length trousers, and the replacement of the honored *toga* by the short, practical *pœnula.*

The Franks and Merovingians, 486–752.—Because of the scarcity of information regarding the Franks, no very detailed account of their costume is possible. Planché quotes an early writer who describes the Franks as wearing close fitting, short tunics with exceedingly short sleeves, a mantle very much like a cape with a hood attached, and sandal-like shoes.[1] After their conquest of the Gallo-Romans the Franks adopted some of the garments of the vanquished people and are said to have worn in the latter part of the Merovingian period knee-length trousers, tunics held at the waist by girdles, leggings over their erstwhile bare legs, shoes with straps at instep, short mantles, and either hoods or small caps.

The Frankish woman was attired in much the same manner as

---

[1] PLANCHÉ, J. R., CYCLOPÆDIA OF COSTUME, Vol. II, Chap. 2, p. 26. Chatto and Windus.

the Gallic woman, her costume consisting of two tunics and a large mantle. In addition, she wore a long veil which was of sufficient size to replace at times the long mantle. Gloves of fur much like

Fig. 21. Carolingian Costume. From an old engraving.

the present day mittens in shape were worn by men and women of the wealthier class.

Carolingian Costume, 752–987.—With their kingdom firmly established in the country that is now France, the Frankish ancestors of the modern French people were free to turn more of their attention to the refinements of life. Dress became richer and more elaborate under the Carolingian rulers, the men adding a new garment in the form of a short linen tunic which was worn beneath a short outer one of wool. This outer tunic was then frequently decorated with bandings and embroidery in bright yarns. Eastern influence is detected in the fitted band or fichu which outlined the neck and extended down the front of the woman's outer tunic. Bands of matching embroidery were used at the bottom of the long, flowing sleeve, and at times edged the large veil. Precious stones set in the embroidery were further indications of Byzantine influence. A rich girdle of gold or silver with a long pendant down the front was worn at a lowered waist line.

Materials had increased in variety of weave and richness of coloring and texture; wool, silk, and linen as well as mixtures of these fibers comprised the garments of both men and women.

Capetian Costume, 987–1328.—During the eleventh century length and fullness characterized most French costume reflecting the influence of the long, flowing garments of the East whence the Crusaders brought back to their homes in France and other countries of western Europe, not only clothes of novel cut, but unfamiliar, gorgeously patterned fabrics and jeweled ornaments of curious shape and remarkably fine workmanship. The introduction of those innovations resulted in a gentleman of the time being attired in short trousers beneath a long inner tunic of linen, and an outer tunic that was quite unlike the one worn in preceding centuries. This transformed tunic, known as the *bliaud*, had fullness in the skirt as a result of the addition of gored sections at the sides. Kimono sleeves were other alterations in this garment which appeared sometime after the first Crusade, 1095. The usual leggings were replaced by stockings, *chausses*, made of cloth cut to the shape of the leg. The shoes showed the slightest indication of points, while the hats were somewhat square in shape. The mantle, hitherto short except for formal occasions, became long and added to the inconvenience of the already restricting costume by fastening on the left shoulder.

Additional length and fullness were found in the woman's tunics also, the outer of which was termed the *bliaud*, and possessed one of two types of sleeves: one a long and flowing sleeve displaying underneath the close, long one of the linen chemise; the other a long, tight sleeve with bands of material hanging either from the wrist or the elbow. A broad girdle confined the *bliaud* at the waist line. The hair was worn flowing, and partially concealed by a small, circular veil.

Twelfth century.—During the twelfth century costume remained the same in general cut, acquiring gradually greater richness in detail and fabric. In summer, silk, in winter, soft furs lined the luxurious silken mantles. The stone effigies of the period which record so naturalistically the costume of the lords and ladies, show that the woman's *bliaud* had become really a bodice and skirt joined together at the hip line, the former of some soft, pliable material fitting the body closely and lacing down the back or under the arm, the latter of a soft textured cloth which fell in fine, soft folds like the Ionic *chiton* of the Greeks. Two belts were used, one at the normal waist line, the other over the joining of the bodice and skirt. The sleeves were long and tight at the hand; the neckline round and close, open a few inches down the front, and fastened at the throat with a jeweled brooch.

FIG. 22. KING OF JUDA. FRENCH, 1150? THE BELT AND NECKLINE ARE CHARACTERISTIC OF THE BLIAUD OF THE TWELFTH CENTURY. Courtesy of the Metropolitan Museum.

Two general styles of hair dressing were in vogue: one in which the hair hung down the front in two long braids, each wound or plaited with narrow strips of colored cloth; the other in which it hung free and flowing. In either case the small, circular veil covering the head was held in place by a small circlet of gold.

Thirteenth century.—When the flowing mantle and long tunic became irksome, men resorted to the close fitting trousers and stockings combined in one garment, the fitted short under-garment, *cotte*, with long, tight sleeves, and the *surcot* which was an adaptation of the covering used by the Crusaders over their armor

FIG. 23. BETROTHAL OF ST. CATHERINE. MEMLING. AN EXAMPLE OF THE SURCOT. Courtesy of the Metropolitan Museum.

as a protection from the glare of the hot Eastern sun on the gleaming metal.

As worn by the gentleman of the thirteenth century, the *surcot* was close fitting at the top with a full, plaited skirt reaching to the hip or below according to the fancy of the wearer. A belt of cloth or of leather was drawn closely at the waist line while the full, open sleeves retained the dagged edges so fashionable in the preceding period. Across the shoulders was a large collar, and in some instances a hood, *chaperon*, with long ends which hung to the heel. Other popular forms of head covering affected by the Beau

Brummels of the age were caps and round brimmed hats of velvet, embroidered and studded with jewels.

Fashion's tendency toward garments more intricate in cut and closer fit is seen in the woman's *surcot* of the thirteenth century. This one-piece fitted robe with its straight, broad neckline fell

FIG. 24. MARGUERITE DE BEAUJEU. AN EXAMPLE OF THE USE OF FUR AS A LINING FOR CLOAK AND HOOD. From an old engraving.

from the shoulders in Watteau-like plaits in the back and had as its distinguishing feature the enlarged armscye extending from the shoulders to the hips and showing beneath the fitted, one-piece under dress, *cotte*, with its normal armscye and long sleeves buttoned closely over the arm from wrist to elbow. The material of this under dress usually differed in color from that of the *surcot* which was frequently parti-colored and embroidered with armorial devices. The ladies of noblest rank placed their husbands' coat of arms on the right hand side of the robe, and that of their own family on the left. Challamel remarks that "a gown was made historical by embroidering it with fleurs-de-lis, birds, fishes, and emblems of all sorts, and thus became a portable guide to geneology."[2]

Over the *surcot* was placed a fur- preferably ermine-stole, known as the *garde-corps*, which, on its advent, consisted of a narrow band outlining the neck of the *surcot* in the back, and falling as a panel in the front from neck to hips. When two strips formed the front panel they were joined by buttons of gold or jewels. During the latter part of the thirteenth century and throughout the fourteenth, when the *surcot* attained the height of its popularity, the *garde-corps* became merely narrow bands edging the neck and large armscyes.

Fur bordered, frequently fur lined, was the large, flowing mantle of silk with its chain or clasp of gold and jewels holding it across the chest. A fur lined, pointed hood of velvet was drawn over the head in cold or inclement weather. The cornette and shoulder length veil so fashionable about 1200 were followed soon afterwards by the coiffure *en guimpe* or wimple. This was a soft silk or linen veil so arranged that it enveloped the head and throat and formed an attractive frame for the face. A survival of this coiffure is seen to-day in the head covering of the nuns of various religious orders. Suspended from the girdle hung a small bag, *aumônière*, of material rich and handsome in itself or of heavy embroidery, and from this the noble lady of the castle dispensed alms to the poor. Besides coins for this benevolent purpose the *aumônière* held jewels, milady's writing tablet, keys, and other small necessities.

Materials.—The materials were increasing in richness and splendor, beauty, and variety with the development of commerce that followed the return of the Crusaders. New trade routes with the East gave greater facilities along the Mediterranean, while the establishment of the Hanseatic League, 1241, resulted in the greater interchange of the products of the north and south of Europe. English and Scottish wools woven on the looms of

---

[2] CHALLAMEL, HISTORY OF FASHION IN FRANCE, p. 37. Scribner and Welford.

Flanders found their way south in exchange for the handsome velvets, silks, and brocades of Italy. The city of Lucca was the center of the weaving industry in Italy at this time, with Rheims manufacturing many of the popular silks of France. The arts of weaving and dyeing had made such progress that people of all classes were clothed in material of excellent quality; the peasants of France were accustomed to fine cloth, linen, and some silk, and the bourgeoisie imitated the nobility so closely in matters of dress that the latter felt called upon to embroider armorial ensigns on their garments to distinguish themselves from their imitators. Fur was used in a lavish manner to line or border the garments of the wealthy, and must certainly have been welcome in the high ceil-inged rooms of the stone castles so devoid of comfort and conveniences.

House of Valois—Fourteenth century.—The accession to the French throne of Philippe VI in 1328 marked the end of the Capetian line and the beginning of the reign of the House of Valois, 1328-1589. The rulers of this house held elaborate courts and apparently encouraged the fine art of dress. Well preserved documents such as sumptuary laws, wardrobe accounts, wills, some sculpture, and portions of the works of the few learned writers of the time supply us with information relative to the late *moyen âge* costume.

The styles of the preceding century remained in fashion until about 1340 when a decided change took place in the garments of the men, particularly in the length and closeness of fit. The hip-length *surcot* became exceedingly short, frequently with merely a three or four inch peplum or fitted piece below the snug belt. It retained its large, long sleeves and in many cases its carefully laid plaits. The clergy and men of the older generation, however, clung to the dignity and comfort of the long *surcot*.

The shortening of the *surcot* necessitated a more abbreviated chemise and *cotte*, the latter showing only at the neck when the *surcot* was left unbuttoned at the throat. The long tight *chausses*, (trousers, and stockings combined like the stage tights of to-day), were frequently made with one leg of a different color from that of the other, and the—to us—incongruous effect was heightened by low shoes with extremely pointed toes. This fashion in footgear is said to have originated in Crakow, Poland, hence the names *crakows* and *poulaines* by which these pointed shoes were known in England and France respectively. This fashion was carried to such extremes by all classes that Philippe IV, le Bel, 1285-1314, felt called upon to issue a decree limiting the length of the points of the shoes of common people to one half foot; of rich bourgeoisie to one foot; and of princes and men of rank to two feet. For convenience in walking a chain of gold or silver was attached to the point of the shoe and to the ankle or knee of the wearer.

The head covering of the men was as ungainly and exaggerated as their footwear. The *chaperon* or hood, with its long end, in this century became the draped turban, the idea of this arrangement having been received doubtless, from close intercourse with the turbaned peoples of the East. Hats of beaver, probably made in Flanders, had acquired a variety of straight or upturned brims and crowns of some pretentions.

A most interesting type of wrap was found in the *houppelande* with its long, wide sleeves, frequently dagged or cut in tongue-like designs along its edges. It was made of wool, silk, or velvet with large pattern and either entirely lined with fur or merely bordered with it.

Increasing closeness of fit characterized the *surcot* as worn by the woman of the fourteenth century, as well as the increased use of heraldic devices embroidered on the dresses, due without doubt to the tendency on the part of the wealthy bourgeoisie to imitate the cut, and as far as possible the color and material of the noble woman's garments. Parti-colored dress resulted from this stressing of the coat of arms in costume. Streamers hanging from the elbows of the sleeves were innovations of this period, otherwise the *surcot* remained much the same in cut as it was in the thirteenth century. The neck line, however, became more open, exposing the neck and throat to an extent that aroused the denunciations of critics and conservatives. The *garde-corps* gradually diminished in breadth across the front, becoming in essence merely bands of fur outlining the much enlarged armscyes.

Fifteenth century.—The tapestries of the period furnish us with delightful examples of the eccentric, exaggerated garments of the Burgundian lords and ladies who played such important rôles in the political and social life of France during the fifteenth century. The fabrics employed were exceedingly rich and handsome, the

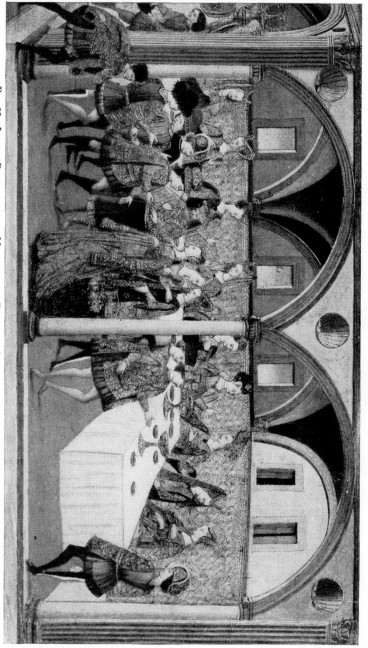

FIG. 25. ITALIAN COSTUMES OF THE MIDDLE OF THE FIFTEENTH CENTURY. Courtesy of the Metropolitan Museum.

red and gold velvets of Italy being used very extensively. The designers of masculine headgear seemed to confine their attention to the crowns giving them considerable height, accenting this feature with an upstanding feather, and all manner of strange contours. The sleeves of the *houppelande* were apparently padded at the top where they stood out, adding breadth to the manly shoulders, but giving a decidedly top heavy effect to the sil-

Fig. 26. Burgundian Tapestry. C. 1435. Houppelandes and Hennins of the Early Fifteenth Century. Courtesy of the Metropolitan Museum.

houette. The legs were incased in tights that were laced at the waist to a close fitting body garment or doublet. The points of the shoes were slender and wisp-like.

The latter part of the fourteenth century saw the introduction of a new style of feminine dress that attained the height of its popularity in the first half of the fifteenth century. The *houppelande* was a two-piece dress with very short, small waist line and

long, sweeping skirt bordered with contrasting material or fur at
the bottom.   Many of the skirts were so long in front that for
comfort in walking the wearer would tuck them up in front or
fasten them to clasps and chains attached to the belt, while the
train became of such length that a "grande dame" of that time
required the services of a page to handle it for her.   Fur was gen-

FIG. 27.   COSTUME OF THE TIME OF CHARLES IV.   From an
old engraving.

erally used on the lapels which outlined the V neckline, a line
which made its first appearance at that period.   The sleeves, in
general, were long and close fitting, very similar to the tailored
sleeve of the twentieth century.   Bell-shaped ones were also in use.

Head-dress.—A variety of hair arrangements and head-dresses
was fashionable during this period.   The hair at times was braided
in two braids and looped over the ears.   Again it was knotted at the

back of the head and concealed by the hood, small veil, or the *gorget*, a species of the *wimple* consisting of a broad band of silk or linen that covered the neck and shoulders. About 1395 appeared the first of the grotesque head-dresses, generally classed as *hennins*, which were worn until 1470 in spite of all the ridicule and denunciations heaped upon their wearers. Isabelle of Bavaria, wife of Charles VI, wore such high head-dresses that the doorways of her castle of Vincennes were raised to accommodate her. The *hennins* varied considerably in form and size: some were heart-shaped, others horn or cone-shaped, the latter type extending as much as three feet above the head of the gracious wearer. Wires and stiffened fabrics were employed in their construction, while sheer gauze formed the floating veils attached to the apex of the cone-shaped head-dress. The hair was entirely concealed.

The Period of transition.—The reigns of Charles VIII (1483–1498) and of Louis XII (1498-1515) covered that period of years at the close of the Middle Ages and the opening decades of the Renaissance in France when there occurred the gradual rejection of all the eccentricities that marked the costume of the late *Moyen Âge* in favor of a simpler and more dignified silhouette and line. Rather wearied with the difficult *hennins* and *poulains*, both men and women eagerly welcomed the novel ideas which Charles VIII and his warriors succumbed to and brought home as a result of that ruler's expedition into Italy for the purpose of restoring Naples to the house of Anjou. Strengthened and increased by subsequent contact and intercourse between the peoples of France and Italy (Louis XII endeavoring to gain the dukedom of Milan), the Italian influences became conspicuous in all French Renaissance costume. Louis XII like his father, was fascinated not only by Italian institutions and culture which were far in advance of everything French at the time, but by the luxuries of dress as well, and soon many of the new ideas found their way into French dress. Men employed the rich, colorful silks or velvets from Venice and Milan in their short doublets with ample skirts to the knees, and in the *houppelandes* or cloaks which lost something of their former length and fullness, and added broad shoulder collars that ended in long revers down each side of the front of the cloaks. The square or V shaped neck of the doublet exposed to view the finely plaited and embroidered but collarless shirt. The former *chausses* became

divided into two garments: the full, short trunks, *haut-de-chausses*:
and the long stockings, *bas-de-chausses*, still frequently parti-
colored; while the grotesque *poulains* were superseded by square-
toed shoes, *pied d'ours*, which, broadly cut and exposing the entire
instep, were held on by a strap near the ankle. *Chaperons* became
as passé as hats were fashionable. The moderate brim of the new
head covering turned up all around, its edges at times slashed,

FIG. 28. MARIE, WIFE OF PORTINARI. MEM-
LING. ILLUSTRATING THE CONE-SHAPED HENNIN
AND THE NECKLINE OF THE WOMAN'S HOUPPE-
LANDE OF THE FIFTEENTH CENTURY.

FIG. 29. A FLEMISH TAPESTRY ILLUS-
TRATING COSTUME OF THE LATE FIFTEENTH
CENTURY.

Courtesy of the Metropolitan Museum.

while the soft crown resembled somewhat the modern tam-
o'shanter. Many portraits of this period show large brimmed hats
worn over close-fitting caps of richly embroidered silk, indicating
possibly, a reluctance on the part of the wearer to discard entirely
the comfortable, close-fitting headgear of an earlier period.

Not to be outdone by the men in adopting the new fashions, the
women hastened to lay aside the pointed *poulains* for *sollerets*,
shoes that were rounded to the shape of the feet: and replaced the

lofty head-dresses with low, close-fitting caps of silk magnificently embroidered, or of net studded with precious stones. Their braided hair was wound about their heads in the mode followed by the ladies of the court of Beatrice d'Este at Milan. At her marriage to Charles VIII, Anne of Brittany introduced into the costume of her fair followers at court the simple, close cap so characteristic of the feminine dress of her native province. This white or black hood-like head-dress, softened by a frill of plaited or embroidered muslin, formed a close frame for the face, practically concealing the hair, and hung down the back in the form of a short veil. Other innovations instituted by this same queen of France were the short skirt, in marked contrast to the training *houppelande* of the fifteenth century; and on the death of Charles VIII, 1515, the wearing of black instead of white for mourning, a custom which persists today in practically all countries of the Occident, while white is still the emblem of mourning in the Orient.

The dress of this period was a modification of the former *houppelande*; the neckline, square and wide, rounded up slightly at the center of the front; the sleeves, wide and fur bordered, rendered visible at the wrist the sleeves of the *cotte*. The skirt of the dress or robe was usually open and spreading in a ∧ shape to the waist line to display the skirt of the rich *cotte* of cloth of gold or silver. About a somewhat lowered waist line was a girdle in the form of a twisted silk rope or heavy chain that hung down the front nearly to the bottom of the skirt, while the necklace, introduced by Isabelle of Bavaria, wife of Charles VI, became gradually heavier and more ornate.

Materials.—The materials, plain as well as patterned, for the sumptuous costumes were imported from Italy, Spain, England, and Holland though the very beautiful and fine cloth manufactured in Bourges was much in demand. In 1480 looms for the weaving of silk were set up at Tours, Louis XI being responsible for these early efforts at silk manufacture in France. His example was follwed by Francis I who in 1520 had looms set up in Lyons thus establishing the foundations for the present day flourishing and influential silk center of the country.

Children's costume.—But little mention, if any, is made in most books dealing with historic dress, of the manner in which children were dressed. This is doubtless but natural when one remembers that before the Italian Renaissance artists usually portrayed children as cherubs, not as human beings. From then on to the late eighteenth century both painter and sculptor have represented the youth of Europe clothed as replicas of their fathers and mothers; the peasant child in the same materials and cut of garments considered suitable for his elders' station in life;

FIG. 30. HUGO VAN DER GOES PAINTING THE PORTRAIT OF MARY OF BURGUNDY. AN INTERESTING EXAMPLE OF CHILDREN'S DRESS OF THE LATE MOYEN ÂGE. Courtesy of the Metropolitan Museum.

the young scion of nobility in the rich silks, laces, embroideries, and feathers affected by his parents. Having but scant attention paid to their own interests of childhood, and expected to assume the responsibilities and duties of adult life while in their very early teens, it was probably natural that children's mode of dress followed that of adult standards. Much of our scant knowledge of children's attire during and immediately after the Renaissance is due to the custom of wealthy patrons of the church of having their entire family portrayed in the background of a painting destined for the enrichment of church or private chapel.

Two bas-reliefs on the church of Notre-Dame and the Trocadero, as well as a stained glass window from Saint-Julien-du-Sault dating from the eleventh, twelfth, and fourteenth centuries respectively, indicate that infants were closely wrapped from neck to toes in bandalettes, narrow strips of cloth embroidered for children of rank, as is still the custom in parts of Italy and central European countries.

REFERENCES

Viollet-le-Duc, Dictionnaire du Mobilier Français, Vols. III, VI.
Quicherat, Histoire du Costume en France.
Racinet, Le Costume Historique, Vols. II, III, IV.
Hottenroth, Le Costume chez les Peuples Anciens et Modernes.
Zur Geschichte der Kostüme, plates 391, 592, 611, 956, 1024, 1214.
Planché, History and Cyclopedia of Costume.
La Croix, Manners, Customs and Dress during the Middle Ages and Renaissance.
Challamel, History of Fashion in France, Chaps. I–VIII.
Jacquemin, Iconographie du Costume.
Piton, Le Costume Civil en France du XIIIᵉ au XIXᵉ Siecle, pp. 7–11.
Giafferri, L'Histoire du Costume Féminin Français.
Enlart, Manuel d'Archéologie Française.
Goddard, Women's Costume.
Pauquet Frères, Modes et Costumes Historiques.
Encyclopædia Britannica.
Fales, Dressmaking, pp. 10–18.
Lester, Historic Costume, Chap. VI.
Sage, A Study of Costume, Chaps. V–VI.
Parsons, Psychology of Dress, Chap. I.
Rodier, The Romance of French Weaving.

CHAPTER V

FRENCH COSTUME OF THE RENAISSANCE

Field of the Cloth of Gold, 1520

Massacre of St. Bartholomew, 1572

Edict of Nantes, 1598

Rabelais, 1490–1553

Clouet, 1500?–1572?

Ronsard, 1524–1585

Montaigne, 1533–1592

DURING the reign of Francis I, 1515-1547, the development of the culture derived from Italy received great encouragement. To his court came the élite of Spanish and Italian society, poets, philosophers, artists, musicians, and men of affairs bringing their contributions to its splendor and brilliancy. The charm and wit of beautiful women added much to its gayety. The material affairs of the country were prosperous so that the examples of extravagance, luxury and display set by the various monarchs were quickly followed by the courtiers. In studying the social life of this period one is impressed with the position of great power and prominence that women had attained, in very marked contrast to the restricted, secluded position they occupied during the Middle Ages. Outstanding feminine personalities in the social and political life of the French Renaissance were Anne of Brittany, the brilliant and able consort of both Charles VIII and Louis XII; Catherine de Medici, the unscrupulous wife of Henri II; her attractive daughter-in-law Marie Stuart; her niece Marie de Medici, second wife of Henry of Navarre; and the famous favorites of the kings, Mme. d'Estampes and Dianne de Poitiers. Each of these women contributed something original to the modes of their day, leaving the imprint of their personalities on matters sartorial as well as literary, artistic, and political.

Francis I, 1515–1547.—As to the costume of the men of the first half of the sixteenth century (Francis I and Henri II), we learn from the paintings of Clouet, the court painter of Francis I, that it was as colorful, decorative and magnificent as that of the women. The full-skirted doublet, *pourpoint*, retained its broad neckline and was cut with a full, knee-length skirt, that was held at the waist by an elaborate sword belt. Its sleeves were roomy and long, and like the body of the doublet, were slashed to permit

47

rich and colored linings to be pulled out between the slashes. Jeweled pins, *fers*, or ties held together at intervals the long slashes and added color and interest to the whole effect. The short, bouffant breeches, *haut-de-chausses*, were similarly slashed,

FIG. 31. PORTRAIT OF FRANCIS I. CLOUET. A STRIKING EXAMPLE OF THE RICHNESS OF DETAIL OF MEN'S DRESS IN THE EARLY PART OF THE SIXTEENTH CENTURY. Archives d'Art et d'Histoire. Louvre.

while the seams of the long cloth or woven silk stockings, *bas-de-chausses*, were joined with embroidery in metallic threads. Even the square-toed shoes of soft leather failed to escape this mania for slashes, introduced about 1520 by the Swiss mercenaries.

This elaborate costume was protected by a knee-length, square-cut mantle with huge open sleeves, and a large rolling collar of fur or of silk. A turban of velvet worn slightly tilted to the left was ornamented with a white feather laid across the front of the soft crown. A square-cut beard was affected by the king and his

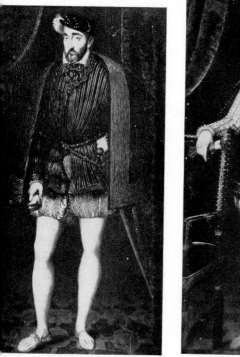

FIG. 32. PORTRAIT OF HENRI II. CLOUET. HIGH COLLAR AND JAUNTY CAPE THAT RE CHARACTERISTIC OF MASCULINE COS- E DURING THE REIGN OF THIS MONARCH. ives d'Art et d'Histoire. Louvre.

FIG. 33. CHARLES IX. CLOUET. C. 1569. THE RUFF WAS MODEST IN SIZE DURING THE EARLY YEARS OF ITS EXISTENCE. Louvre.

ourtiers and the hair worn long until an accident to Francis I ndered it necessary for his hair to be cut short, thus setting the shion for a new mode. A broad, massive chain with pendant oss or reliquary hung from the neck completing the magnificent ostume that changed but slightly during the reign of Henri II.

Henri II, 1547–1558.—The chief innovations during this reign occurred in the doublet. It was generally cut close to the neck with a standing-collar edged with a small ruff, *fraize*, that Henri II adopted about 1540 to conceal a scar, it is said. The sleeves of the doublet reached to the elbow, the elaborate sleeves of the shirt covering the arms to the wrists. The skirt of the doublet became a short peplum. Slashes were still in evidence but gradually became less and less fashionable. A jaunty, waist-length cape lined with brilliant colored silk replaced the large-sleeved coat so necessary for the pretentious sleeves of the earlier doublet. In 1547 from Spain came the first knitted silk stockings. It is said that in 1558, the king, Henri II, wore them for the first time, at the wedding of his sister.

Henri III, 1574–1589.—Throughout the latter part of the century the influence of Spanish fashions was marked in all dress at the French court. Somber and severe, it modified considerably the graciousness and elegance of the dress of the reign of Francis I. Instead of being somewhat square the silhouette became now quite slim, the quilted, padded doublet fitting closely at the waistline received an unnatural outward bend down the front because of the presence underneath of a corset with a long curved steel. It buttoned up the front to the top of the standing collar with its starched ruff of lawn and lace, a neck finish that gradually increased in size until by 1579 "the wearers could scarcely turn their heads, and Henri III declared they looked like the head of John the Baptist in a charger."[1] The peplum, short and fitted like the body of the doublet to which it was attached, was embroidered in strips with gilt and silver threads. The sleeves, while in general somewhat the shape of the leg-o'-mutton, were also found quite short and puffed at the top, and had a wing of stiffened material set into the armscye across the shoulder. The breeches increased in length until they covered the knee, and became closer fitting though still slashed to show the bright lining beneath, and like the doublet, padded to give the desired effect. The mantle most in favor was the short, jaunty Spanish *capa* made without a collar usually because of the large ruff, and worn by young gallants, thrown over one shoulder.

---

[1] PALLISER, MRS. BURY, HISTORY OF LACE. p. 141. Sampson Low Marston and Company, Ltd.

The masculine head-dress consisted of a velvet turban with a high draped crown, and a jeweled and feather decoration in front, or of a short-brimmed hat with a tall, stiff crown that calls to mind the head covering of the Puritans of the following century. With the muffling of the neck in large ruffs the hair was naturally cut short, while the beard became the small, pointed imperial for probably the same reason. Heavy necklaces, jewel-hilted swords, buttons of gold and precious stones and elaborate finger rings as well as ear-rings added their glitter and sparkle to the sumptuous velvets, satins, galloons, and embroideries. Probably the simplest article in the whole costume was the leather shoe that reached to the ankle and was devoid of the elaborate decoration that characterized the shoe of the early Renaissance.

Henri IV, 1589–1610.—Some years after Henri IV, the first of the Bourbon kings, ascended the throne of France there reappeared in masculine dress many features characteristic of the period of Henri II. The short cape so favored by the latter monarch was decidedly fashionable, as was the doublet with its peplum of frill-like dimensions. The ruff soon lost its eccentric width and gradually gave way to a simple, turned-down collar, *rabat.* Gentlemen of fashion had their choice of nether garments— knee breeches or short trunks,—both decidedly padded to the desired shape, while it was customary to have the long hose elaborately gartered below the knees.

Hats and shoes became quite different: the brim of the former was rather wide and rolling and made of beaver; the heels of the latter acquired considerable height while the tops rose to the mid-leg. Russian and Cordovan leathers were greatly favored materials for both shoes and high boots. Gloves of handsome, colorful leather, magnificently stitched with embroidery, were of the gauntlet type.

Women's dress of the early Renaissance.—Many characteristics of the women's dress of the transition period carried over well into the first quarter of the sixteenth century. The gradual shaping of the clothes to fit the body more closely led to the introduction of the steel corset, *basquine,* and, in 1530, of the hoop, *vertugale,* both becoming so extreme in cut that they distorted the human silhouette beyond all semblance of its natural form. The *vertugale* in this, its earliest form, consisted of a wide, funnel-shaped petticoat stiffened with horizontal bands of iron or whale-bone. Over the front of this breadth-giving contrivance, was placed the *cotte*, a strip of velvet, damask, satin, or silver tissue, as taste and season dictated. This was an important part of the costume scheme as the round-length skirt of the robe was open

FIG. 34. QUEEN CLAUDE, FIRST WIFE OF FRANCIS I, WEAR-ING THE ANNE OF BRITTANY CAP. From an old engraving.

from waist to hem, in the front showing the *cotte* as a wedge-shaped panel. The bodice fitted closely and smoothly over the stiff *basquine*, and at the neck, which retained the broad, square shape, showed a bit of the daintily embroidered chemise. The sleeves were close from the shoulder to the elbow where they flared and had their width accented with deep bands of fur, cloth, or velvet.

An inner sleeve of embroidered cambric, or silk was visible at the
lower part of the arm only.

While the hair was simply and becomingly dressed in soft curls
around the face, the head-dresses were of many varieties though
all small and in harmony with the contour of the head. Hood-like

FIG. 35. ELEONORE OF AUSTRIA. MABUSE. PEARLS WERE WORN
IN GREAT ABUNDANCE IN THE SIXTEENTH CENTURY. NOTE THE HEAVY
NECKLACE. Courtesy of the Metropolitan Museum.

coiffes of velvet or satin with short veils hanging down the back,
and bordered with fur, or a net work of precious stones were much
in evidence. Satin shoes, widely open at the instep were frequently slashed to show the lining or the scarlet stockings. As
the century advanced the wearing of jewels became increasingly

lavish, the fair wearers becoming more ingenious in contriving additional ways to employ them. The long chain of gold that encircled the waist fell almost to the feet, ending in a beautiful, jewel-incrusted pendant. The low neck permitted elaborate necklaces and ear-rings, and when slashes became increasingly

FIG. 36. THE INFANTA ISABELLA OF SPAIN. COELLO. THIS SPANISH COSTUME CONTAINS MANY OF THE FEATURES FAMILIAR IN FRENCH DRESS OF THE MID-SIXTEENTH CENTURY. Courtesy of the Metropolitan Museum.

important jeweled buttons and clasps were found necessary to hold the many strips together.

Henri II.—The fashions in neck lines and sleeves were considerably changed during the years that Henri II (1547-1558) and Francis II (1558-1560) reigned. While the square, low neck was retained quite generally, with it was worn the *gorgias*, a high collarette of cambric or silk, much in principle like the net yoke and collar of the twentieth century. At the top of the collar was attached the ruff, *fraize*, which Catherine de Medici is said to have brought from her native Italy. And from Venice came the fine lace that edged the plaited ruff. Some women preferred the bodice cut high to the neck with a simple plaited ruff of linen. The sleeves, now full at the top were usually wrist-length and had many longitudinal slashes held together occasionally with jeweled pins, or caught by crosswise bands into eight or ten puffs. Frequently a false sleeve, *mancheron*, was attached with ribbon or jeweled clasps at the shoulder and fell down the back of the arm. The padded roll or wing found in the armscyes of the men's doublets of this period were also common in feminine fashions.

Hoods continued to be fashionable though velvet caps or toques with small white feathers were considered quite chic. A small cap with a peak at the center of the forehead was styled the "Marie Stuart cap." With the former types of head-covering little of the hair was visible as it was confined in a *cale* or bag of silk at the back of the head.

The large, flowing capes which served as outer wraps retained their former shape, though to some were added standing collars at the back of the neck. The cork-soled pattens, introduced during the reign of Henri II, to protect the thin shoes from the mud of the streets, became exceedingly high, laying their wearers "open to many ill-mannered jests." Masks of black velvet called *loups* or wolves, because at first young children were frightened by them,[2] became exceedingly fashionable among the women of the nobility.

Dress in the late sixteenth century.—Marguerite of Valois was the woman most influential in matters of dress during the latter half of the century. With a decided fondness for dress, as sister of the reigning king, Henri III, and later as wife of Henri IV until his divorce from her in 1601, she was in a position to dictate the frills and foibles of the time. Through her influence and example, the funnel-shaped hoop was replaced by the one then fashionable in Spain, resembling a barrel in form and giving extraordinary width at the hips whose size was accentuated by the addition of a full, plaited ruffle of the same fabric as the dress itself.

[2] CHALLAMEL, HISTORY OF FASHION IN FRANCE, p. 91, Scribner and Welford.

As a result of this changed silhouette of the lower part of the body, the front of the bodice was elongated into a sharp point several inches long, and the *basquine* was worn tighter than ever thus rendering the appearance of the waist line quite wasp-like and out of proportion to shoulders and hips. In order to balance the width of the skirt, which was frequently long and trailing, the

Fig. 37.   Costume Fashionable in 1581 During the Reign of Henri III.   Louvre.

sleeves were increased in size at the top and were finished at the hand with diminutive replicas of the neck ruff.

A more comfortable type of neck finish than the huge millstone ruff was introduced during the period of Henri III. It was a fan-shaped collar that rose from the shoulders, extended across the back of the neck, and was wired to stand away from the head.

Fine cambric with edgings of Milanese and Venetian laces were the delicate fabrics of which it was composed. With such a collar the front of the dress was cut square and low giving excuse again for the wearing of the elaborate necklaces and chains that were almost impossible with the millstone ruff. Such muffling of the neck required simple arrangements of the hair that in general was drawn smoothly over wire rolls at the temples and fastened high on the head, after 1545, with the new wire hair pins imported from England. The velvet caps and toques continued about the same in shape and size.

The accessories of the period became increasingly rich and fine: from the side of the waist hung a small mirror; the black velvet mask was no longer carried in the hand or tied with strings but held before the face by means of a slender wire and button which was placed between the teeth. Fans and richly scented gloves of soft kid and lace-edged handkerchiefs were affected by both sexes.

The fabrics were exceedingly decorative in color and pattern, the designs of fine Italian and Eastern silks being adapted by the French manufacturers though much of the material was imported, both Catherine de Medici and her niece Marie de Medici, the second wife of Henri IV, naturally preferring the Italian weaves. Henri II and his son, Charles IX, endeavored to curb the prevailing extravagance in dress by numerous edicts regulating the colors, fabrics, trimmings, and jewelry which could be worn by the members of the various ranks of society, but means of evading these edicts were found by rich and poor alike. Neither laws nor denunciations by ecclesiastics were able to arrest the extravagances and extremes. Catherine de Medici both as queen and as queen mother, anxious to divert the minds of the courtiers from affairs of state, encouraged their interest in dress and social fêtes, her efforts being willingly seconded by the kings' favorites Dianne de Poitiers and Mme. d'Estampes.

Children's dress in Sixteenth century.—That children of the wealthy shared the discomforts of ruff, corset, hoop, and padded doublet with their parents is indicated in the portraiture of the sixteenth century. Every detail of their costume, the rich fabric, the embroidery of gold and silver, the slashes in doublet and sleeve, reflect the fashions described in the preceding pages. Drawings of the children of Henri II and Catherine de Medici represented at the age of two years, show their little bodies tightly incased in the stiff doublets of adult mode with tiny ruffs at neck and wrist, and toques of velvet with small feathers worn over the more infantile bonnets that tied under the chin with strings.

REFERENCES

Montaille, Costume Féminin.
Quicherat, Histoire du Costume en France.
Pauquet Frères, Modes et Costumes Historiques.
Racinet, Histoire du Costume, Vol. IV.
Planché, History and Cyclopedia of Costume.
Lamesangere, Costumes des Femmes Françaises.
Zur Geschichte der Kostüme, plates 343, 382, 420, 1083.
Piton, Le Costume Civil en France, pp. 112–184.
Giafferri, L'Histoire du Costume Féminin Français.
Challamel, History of Fashion in France, Chaps. IX–XIII.
Lester, Historic Costume, Chap. VII.
Fales, Dressmaking, pp. 18–23.
Sage, A Study of Costume, Chaps. VII–VIII.
MacQuoid, Four Hundred Years of Beautiful Children.
McFall, Beautiful Children.
Boehn, Modes and Manners, Vol. II.
Paintings by Clouet.

CHAPTER VI

FRENCH COSTUME UNDER THE BOURBONS—SEVEN-TEENTH CENTURY

The Thirty Years War, 1618–1648
The Treaty of Westphalia, 1648
The Revocation of the Edict of Nantes, 1685

Richelieu, 1585–1642	Pascal, 1623–1662
Mansard, 1598–1666	Colbert, 1619–1683
La Fontaine, 1621–1695	Mme. de Sévigné, 1626–1696
Molière, 1622–1673	Racine, 1639–1699

The Modes of the Early Bourbons.—Special attention to the details and accessories of dress was paid by the upper classes of France during the seventeenth century. It was preëminently the age of lace, ribbons and buttons. The men, not content to confine the gold, silver and thread laces of Italy and Flanders to their neckwear and cuffs, used it with a lavish hand to edge the broad ribbon garters at the knee; to finish the cambric *bas a botter* or *canons* as they were later called; to offset the instep of the low shoes with large rosettes; or to decorate the handle of the sword which every gentleman carried. The women found varied uses for the fine filaments in their turned-back cuffs and falling collars, their handkerchiefs, caps and Fontanges head-dresses. The edicts passed against the use of foreign lace were evaded by many, while others were obliged to turn to ribbons for the embellishment of their wardrobes. The materials were in general much lighter and daintier than in the sixteenth century, the larger patterned velvets and brocades being replaced by thinner silks with smaller figures that were more suitable for the small areas of a dress or coat. From the middle of the century on, the fabrics of Lyons found increasing favor in the eyes of fashionable France, while Colbert and Louis XIV after their establishment of the first lace factory in France in 1665, did everything possible to encourage the use of French needlepoints known as *point de France, point Colbert,* after the prime minister, *point d'Alençon,* and *point d'Argentan* after the towns in which they were made. Extravagant dress was encouraged by the Grand Monarque who gradually assumed the dictatorship on all matters pertaining to it, and was ably assisted by his mistresses Mlle. de la Vallière and Mme. de Montespan, with Mme. de Maintenon in her turn doing her best to curb the pomp and splendor of court dress and life, both of which were governed by rigid rules of etiquette.

Fig. 38. A Cavalier of the Time of Louis XIII. Meissonier. Wallace Collection.

Louis XIII, 1610–1643.—The dashing cavalier under Louis XIII was a brilliant, striking figure whom the engravers of the period, Callot, and Abraham Bosse have pictured so delightfully and painstakingly. The fondness for Spanish fashions which was naturally increased by the marriage in 1615 of Louis XIII to the Spanish princess Anne of Austria, is shown in many details. The large-brimmed hat, similar to the *sombrero* still worn by the peasants in the south of Spain; the large fur-lined cape wrapped around the shoulders and neck like the Spanish *capa;* and finally the *galilla* of crisp white lawn that stood out beyond the top of the high collar of the doublet, all testify to close intercourse between the courts of the two countries.

The *galilla* was, however, just one type of neck finish in vogue; the soft, falling ruff, *col rabattu,* lace-edged but devoid of starch and underprop of wire, and the flat linen collar, plain or lace-edged as seen in the Dutch paintings of the period, were equally

FIG. 39. A FAMILY GROUP. HALS. A STUDY IN EARLY SEVENTEENTH CENTURY COS-
TUME. The National Gallery.

popular. They were worn with the short-waisted doublet, *pour-point,* which boasted many buttons that frequently were merely for ornament, the doublet being fastened for a few inches at the top, then left open the better to display the linen shirt with its em-broidery in black, blue, or white threads. The sleeves were finished with one lengthwise slash which revealed the shirt sleeve beneath, and at the wrist with turned-back cuffs similar in finish to the collar.

The bouffant trousers of Henri IV's reign continued in fashion

until about 1624 and were accompanied by long silk stockings and
low shoes with a lace decoration in the form of a rosette at the
instep, or in inclement weather by pattens with wooden soles
and heels, and leather toe-pieces. In the second quarter of the
century a longer, closer breeches extending beyond the knee or
slightly lower, was more in evidence and was practically always
secured by a sash-like garter of ribbon and lace. The high, soft

FIG. 40. THE BROTHERS VAN DER VELDE. MEISSONIER.
THE SHORT DOUBLET AND PETTICOAT BREECHES OF THE TIME
OF LOUIS XIV. Courtesy of the Metropolitan Museum.

leather boots that were worn quite generally had flaring tops that
were filled in with *canons*, broad ruffles of linen edged with handsome lace.

The hip-length cape, lined with fur for cold weather, was attached at one shoulder, left hanging, or wrapped around the body.
The large hat with its three waving ostrich plumes, red, white, or
black, was frequently not worn, but carried under the arm or in

the hand, a custom which became more general as the hair was allowed to grow in long curls, or as wigs were adopted. The moustache and pointed beard are familiar to us in the portraits by Van Dyck.

Louis XIV, 1643–1715.—In the early part of the reign of the Grand Monarque a rather fantastic type of breeches, known as the *rhingrave*, or petticoat breeches, was adopted by men of fashionable pretentions. This extremely full, skirt-like garment, reaching to the knees, trimmed with lace and ribbons, was accompanied by a short doublet, resembling the modern bolero, and handsome linen shirt that was much in evidence between the *rhingrave* and the bolero. About 1685 close velvet or satin knee breeches came into popularity. The long silk stockings were brought over the breeches and held by garters of ribbon. The doublet, too, was altered, becoming a rather long, straight garment that showed only when the coat was unbuttoned, its embroidery adding to the general richness of the entire costume. The wide-skirted coat, introduced about 1665, was the true forerunner of the frock coat of to-day. This garment, of handsome texture, extended almost to the knees and had close sleeves that were set into a normal armscye, and were of about three-quarter length to display the muslin and lace cuffs at the wrist. By 1694 there appeared the deep, turned-back cuff with its fastenings to correspond to the buttons and buttonholes that extended from top to bottom of the coat. Pockets with large flaps were other distinguishing features of the coat which at this time was devoid of elaborate neck finish because of the cravat and the periwig with long curls falling over the shoulders.

The broad, lace-edged collar was replaced about 1665 by one of deep folds of heavy lace tied at the throat by elaborate tasseled cords, and in 1692 by the *cravat*, a strip of fine muslin and lace wound around the neck, the ends falling down the front of the coat or tucked into a buttonhole. Landais gives the origin of the name *cravat* as derived from the Croats who are supposed to have originated this particular type of neckcloth. As an example of how new fashions sometimes arise it is interesting to note in Planché the reason for the appearance of the *steinkirk*, that variation of the cravat that was so much in evidence during the latter half of the period of Louis XIV. ''The battle of Steinkerque,

FIG. 41. LOUIS XIV AND HIS FAMILY. LARGILLIÈRE. C. 1710. Wallace Collection.

3rd August, 1692, introduced a new-fashioned cravat, which was adopted not only by men, but by women in France. It was reported that the French officers, dressing themselves in great haste for the battle, twisted their cravats carelessly round their necks; and in commemoration of the victory achieved by the Mareschal de Luxembourg over the Prince of Orange on that day,

Fig. 42. Le Baron de Prangine. Largillière. Costume of the Period of Louis XIV. Courtesy of the Metropolitan Museum.

a similar negligent mode of wearing the cravat obtained for it the name of 'steinkerque.'" [1]

The introduction of the coat relegated the mantle to the position of a garment for protection only, and as a consequence the

---

[1] Planché, J. R., Cyclopædia of Costume, Vol. I, p. 143. Chatto and Windus.

large, circular cape with openings for the arms, was made of heavy and dark colored fabrics.

The wide sash of ribbon worn over the right shoulder and fastened under the left arm; the tall, slender cane with attractive top of gold or silver; and the enormous pillow-shaped muff, suspended from the neck on a long chain, or by a ribbon called *passe-caille*, buckled round the waist, were accompaniments of every gentleman's costume.

Footwear.—The footwear of the late period displayed many innovations, the most striking being the red heel of generous dimensions; the broad, tall tongue held at its base by a metal buckle. The toe was either pointed or cut very square across.

Periwig.—The periwig, which doubtless owed its origin to the naturally long, curled locks of Louis XIV, during the last fifteen years of the century was characterized by the two high peaks into which it was arranged on top of the head. The early years of the next century, 1700–1720, saw it without these exaggerations. In the last decades of the seventeenth century there appeared the *tricorne* hat with its feather decorations that persisted in favor for about one hundred years, a gradual reduction in the width of the brim being practically the only change.

Women's Dress under Louis XIII.—The opening years of the seventeenth century saw but few changes in the women's dress until 1630 when the hoop was discarded, thus modifying considerably the silhouette popular under Marguerite de Valois and Marie de Medici. The dress itself consisted of a sharply pointed bodice with long, puffed, and slashed sleeves with their lace-trimmed, turned-back cuffs, and a straight, full skirt open in the front to show the rich petticoat with its rows of buttons, lace, or braid. Some dresses of the period showed a raised waist line, very small, with a short, slashed peplum falling several inches over the skirt. The overskirt, which was really the skirt of the dress was frequently lifted around the hips in puffs and draperies and held in position by pins or knots of ribbon. Ties of ribbon under the name of *galants*, were much in evidence holding the puffs of sleeves and skirt, and in rows down the front of the bodice. By 1614 the fan-shaped ruff had given place to the broad, turned down collar worn with either the close, round neck, or with the neck line that was cut wide at the shoulders. Other finishes for

Fig. 43. A Galerie du Palais. Note the Elaborate Collars and Boots of the Gentlemen. Bosse. c. 1637.

this décolleté bodice were the fitted strip of heavy lace, or a dainty, draped fichu fastened at the front by a large jeweled brooch.

While little of the satin or velvet shoes and slippers was visible under the long skirts, they were ornamented with lace rosettes at the instep and possessed heels, sometimes red, that gradually reached the uncomfortable height of three inches.

Fig. 44. Mlle. de Gotignees. Van Dyck. The Fan-shaped Ruff So Popular with the Ladies of the Time of Louis XIIIth. Courtesy of the Metropolitan Museum.

Great bunches of curls at each side of the head were the distinguishing features of an otherwise simple, low hair-dressing that permitted the wearing of hoods and small round caps of velvet or muslin.

Pearls were used in great abundance, sewn to the trimming of the dress or in the form of ear-rings, bracelets, and necklaces that fitted closely the base of the neck.

Women's Dress under Louis XIV.—In the early part of the reign of Louis XIV the wide, open neck line with soft lace and muslin finish held full sway, while the close, square-shaped neck line and panel-front bodice prevailed almost exclusively in the latter half. The sleeves came in for their share of attention in the matter of trimming. In general, from 1660–1685 they were short to the elbow, of puffings of self material or sheer lace or muslin, with many elbow ruffles of lace, *engageants*, "concerning the wearing of which in two or three rows there was much etiquette."[2] During the latter part of the period a sleeve of the same material as the bodice was close-fitting to the elbow where it flared forth in wide ruffles and plaitings of silk, lace, and ribbons. With the short sleeves there came into vogue the elbow length glove of white kid. The bodice retained its closeness of fit and its extremely pointed, small waist line, with the skirt of the dress, as the century advanced, becoming more elaborately draped at the back over stiff materials to give the effect of a bustle, and showing more and more of the round length underskirt of contrasting color and texture with its *falbalas*, crosswise flounces and decorations of lace, material, galloon etc. The train was very long for women of the highest ranks of society. By these same devotees of fashion small aprons of fine muslin or of lace were adopted for informal dress.

The wrap for cold weather was an ample cape, and in milder seasons a small shoulder cape of lace or fur called the *palatine* in honor of Charlotte of Bavaria, the daughter of the Elector Palatine.[3]

Hair arrangements were varied, the simply arranged curls about the temples, so popular with Ninon de l'Enclos, being superseded by the elaborate head-dress composed of lace, ribbons, and flowers wired to a great height and sponsored by the king's favorite Mlle. de Fontanges.

It is amusing to compare in the portraits of the period the size of the muffs carried by the two sexes. The pillow-muffs of the men appear extremely large when compared with the tiny, round "dog-muffs" carried by all women of fashion. Scarfs and fans were other important accessories, the latter being al-

---

[2] PALLISER, MRS. BURY, History of Lace, p. 107. Sampson Low, Marston and Company, Ltd.

[3] CHALLAMEL, History of Fashion in France, p. 135. Scribner and Welford.

Fig. 45. Maria Theresa, First Wife of Louis XIV.

Fig. 46. Mme. de Maintenon, Second Wife of Louis XIV. The Black Silk Scarf Worn Over the Fontanges Head-dress.

From old engravings.

most necessities as the corsets compressed the waist line into ever smaller compass. The long-handled fans of silk or parchment were beautifully painted with mythological or pastoral scenes by eminent artists. During this period the folding fan, which had its début in France during the time of Louis XIII, was pre-eminent.

No toilette of the rouged, powdered beauty was considered complete without the presence on the face in a strategic position of a tiny black patch cut in some fanciful design.

Costume of the Children.—When old enough to discard petticoats and wear the doublet and hose of his sex, the young boy living in the time of Louis XIII sallied forth with his play-mates in garments the exact replica, in reduced size, of those of the older generation. Hip-length doublets were finished at the neck with enormous turned-down collars of the period; rich lace was lavished on collar and turned-back cuffs, while ribbon loops formed a fringed edge for the straight breeches that fell over the knee. Slippers with large rosettes or high boots with widely flaring tops shod his feet, and a wide-brimmed beaver hat, some-times plumed, topped the hair that fell in a profusion of curls over his broad collar. That such was the ordinary garb of a very young Frenchman is attested by an interesting old engraving of a schoolmaster and his charges in the first half of the seventeenth century.

The little girls are represented in skirts that reach the floor, equally long aprons, and the feminine bodice or doublet of the day. All these little damsels had long curls escaping from under close fitting bonnets, although it was also customary at that time for the young girls to have their hair coiled at the back of the head and formed into soft ringlets about the face, in imita-tion of the coiffure of their mothers.

The close of the century found juveniles as up-to-date in sartorial matters as their elders, and, as usual, imitating the cut and texture of each and every adult garment.

REFERENCES

RACINET, HISTOIRE DU COSTUME, Vols. IV, V.
PAUQUET FRÈRES, MODES ET COSTUMES HISTORIQUES.
QUICHERAT, HISTOIRE DU COSTUME EN FRANCE.
PITON, LE COSTUME CIVIL EN FRANCE, pp. 185–250.

FIG. 47. LE MAISTRE D'ESCOLE. BOSSE C. 1635. DRESS OF SCHOOL-CHILDREN OF THE PERIOD OF LOUIS XIII.

Giafferri, L'Histoire du Costume Féminin Français.
Challamel, History of Fashion in France, Chaps. XIV–XV.
Planché, History and Cyclopaedia of Costume.
Zur Geschichte der Kostüme, plates 321, 747, 1065, 1205, 1209.
Parsons, The Psychology of Dress, pp. 149–166.
Fales, Dressmaking, pp. 23–28.
Lester, Historic Costume, Chap. VIII.
Sage, A Study of Costume, Chap. IX.
Renan, Le Costume en France.
Boehn, Modes and Manners, Vol. III.
Paintings by Largillière, Mignard, Rigaud, Engravings by Bosse and
    Callot.

CHAPTER VII

FRENCH COSTUME UNDER LOUIS XV AND LOUIS XVI—EIGHTEENTH CENTURY

Regency of the Duke of Orleans, 1715–1723
Seven Years War, 1756–1763
French Revolution, 1789
Bonaparte in Egypt, 1798

Watteau, 1684–1721
Rousseau, 1712–1778
Fragonard, 1732–1806
Mme. de Staël, 1766–1817

WHILE splendid and pompous, court life during the closing years of the long reign of Louis XIV was somewhat irksome to the pleasure loving, thoughtless courtiers who tired of the restraints on their freedom and extravagance instituted by Mme. de Maintenon after her marriage to the king. With the regency of the Duke of Orleans they broke forth into a period of reckless extravagance and luxury that culminated under the leadership of Marie Antoinette, and was stopped only by the Revolution.

Men's Dress under Louis XV, 1715–1774.—Until those trying, reactionary times masculine dress in France during the eighteenth century retained the general characteristics of the costume that prevailed in the late years of the period of Louis XIV, namely the knee breeches, the long coat, the doublet, and the wig. Each of these articles was modified as the century advanced until the charming, courtly costume so familiar to Americans in the painting of the presentation of Franklin at the court of Louis XVI resulted. The skirts of the coat with plaits at the sides became fuller and were held out from the body at the sides and back by the insertion of stiffened materials and whalebones. Although at times buttoned at the waist, the coat was more and more frequently left unbuttoned to display the long-skirted, elaborate waistcoat with its decorative buttons and pockets. Both coat and waistcoat were cut low at the neck revealing the soft, lacy finish of the shirt. The lace ruffles at the wrist of the full shirt sleeves were quite conspicuous below the coat sleeve which retained its three-quarter length and its wide turned-back cuff.

By 1740 the powdered, curled wig had lost much of its original size, and was dressed in a few long curls that fell down the back

74

FIG. 48. THE BREAKFAST. BOUCHER. INFORMAL COSTUME OF THE PERIOD OF LOUIS XV.
NOTE THE COSTUMES OF THE CHILDREN. Archives d'Art et d'Histoire. Louvre.

only. From 1745 to the closing decade of the century a bow of black ribbon at the back of the neck held the long queue, while the correct place for the crosswise curls was in one or two rows above each ear. Finally by 1790 the man of fashion had discontinued the custom of powdering his hair.

Louis XVI, 1774–1789.—As Louis XVI was but little interested in the vagaries of social life, men's dress during his reign under-

went but few and by no means radical changes. The fronts of the coats were cutaway at the bottom; the skirts lost much of their fullness and flare; and the coat sleeve was cut longer and closer at the wrist. Greater closeness of fit also characterized the breeches which were worn over the tops of the stockings, reversing the fashion under Louis XV, and were fastened at the sides of the knees with several buttons or small buckles.

As the size of the tongue of the men's shoe decreased the square buckle of silver or of brilliants grew increasingly larger. The high heels of the earlier years of the century disappeared entirely, though low heels were sometimes found on the tall boots.

FIG. 49. EMPEROR JOSEPH OF AUSTRIA. DROUAIS. COSTUME OF THE PERIOD OF LOUIS XVI. Courtesy of the Metropolitan Museum.

The *tricorne* hat of velvet or felt retained for a time its trimming of white feathers showing as a band edging the upturned brim, but later the *cocarde* of ribbon gradually usurped the place of feathers.

A garment which French costume owed to that of its English neighbors, who were growing more and more influential in the setting of masculine fashions, was the *redingote*. This was a double-breasted coat of heavy cloth with long skirts, long tight sleeves, and several shoulder capes. Large revers and a double row, down the front, of conspicuously large buttons that were sometimes repeated on the sleeves, were striking features of this top coat.

Accessories.—As ribbon bows played an important rôle in the costume of the early Louis XIV period, so tassels seem to have attained a prominent place in that of the period of Louis XVI. In some instances they replaced the buttons on the front of the coat; they hung from the ends of the ribbon bow tied to the handle of the long, slender cane, and from the chains of the two watches

FIG. 50.   A WATCH OF THE EIGHT-   FIG. 51.   A COMFIT BOX OF THE EIGHTEENTH
EENTH CENTURY.   CENTURY WITH A MINIATURE OF LOUIS XV.
Courtesy of the Metropolitan Museum.

which it became the fashion about 1780 for every gentleman to wear in the two front pockets of the breeches. As the waistcoat grew shorter the watches, fobs and seals became increasingly important. The cases of the watches as well as the snuff and bon-bon boxes were exquisite examples of the jeweler's art in gold, silver, rock crystal, enamel, and jewels. Though Louis XVI was averse to the taking of snuff, the courtiers were strongly addicted to the habit. It was quite usual for a gentleman to have several of these lovely boxes filled with snuff about his person.

The Period of the Revolution.—The revolutionary period, 1789–1799, produced sweeping changes in the appearance of both sexes. After 1789 the careful grooming so characteristic of the gentleman became frowned on by the younger men who were apt

Fig. 5°. Portrait of M. Sériziat. David. Note the High Neck-cloth and the Large Revers of the Cloth Coat. 1795. Archives d'Art et d'Histoire. Louvre.

to express their political convictions in a careless, unkempt attire. "No one dared after the Reign of Terror had begun in 1792, to go about clean or carefully dressed for fear of calling down upon themselves the suspicion of the terrorists; many who were found wearing courtly knee breeches instead of the republican trousers paid for what the public considered their treason on the scaffold."[1] Class distinction in matters of dress became impossible, those in power adopting the simple, unpretentious dress of the middle classes as the standard for all.

Fabrics as well as cut were equally changed, cloth and leather being substituted for the former satin and velvet of the nobleman; laces, feathers, and embroidery were likewise taboo.

The English sailor's trousers were the inspiration for the new styles that in 1791 required these garments to reach half way between knee and ankle, and in 1793 to the shoe itself. As the trousers gained in length the waistcoat, then termed the vest, became correspondingly short, barely reaching to the waist line. Like the coat it was cut double-breasted and fastened with a double row of buttons. Above the top of the vest there protruded the extraordinary neckcloth of muslin or silk that was wrapped so high around the neck that the chin was invisible. Adding further thickness to the neck, the turn-over collar of the dark cloth coat stood upright for several inches. The broad swallow-tails acquired length and breadth while the waist line lost in circumference on account of the wearing of the corset, especially by the younger devotees of fashion.

Hats were in general round and narrow as to brim, and had tall crowns, though the two cornered hat, *bicorne*, was much in evidence during the years of the revolution. The natural locks, unpowdered and uncurled, were gathered into a short pigtail or English bagwig at the back.

Short Russian boots seem to have replaced the low shoe, with the very low-cut slipper retained for wear on some occasions.

A short cane of bamboo was substituted for the former tall walking stick.

Women's Dress of the Eighteenth Century—Louis XV and Louis XVI.—The draping and lifting of the skirts worn by women of fashion during the latter part of the reign of Louis XIV resulted in a silhouette that in the eighteenth century was extremely broad and broken. The return of the hoop, *panier*, in 1718 brought

---

[1] Taken by permission from FISCHEL AND BOEHN, MODES AND MANNERS OF THE NINETEENTH CENTURY, Vol. I, p. 142. Published and copyright by E. P. Dutton and Co., Inc., New York.

with it many attendant changes. The draperies of the back of the skirt disappeared leaving a straight, full skirt that billowed over the light *panier* of reeds or wire, and reached just to the floor. The graceful lace-edged round neck line adding at the left shoulder a dainty boutonnière of artificial flowers, the short

FIG. 53. THE MARQUISE DE POMPADOUR. BOUCHER. 1759.
Wallace Collection.

sleeves composed of many ruffles of exquisite lace, and the diminutive, pointed waist line were retained. Latour's portrait of Mme. Pompadour indicates that another type of neck line and sleeves was equally favored. Here we see that the bodice covers the shoulders but is cut in a deep square in front, while down the center front of the bodice are sewn many bows of ribbon. The sleeves of the same material as the dress fit closely from shoulder to elbow where they flare forth in many soft ruffles of silk and lace. The portrait shows also a skirt that is open in the front from hem to waist line, displaying the round-length petticoat of the same figured silk as the dress.

From paintings by Watteau we learn of another type of gown worn by the powdered beauties of the court of Louis XV, a gown which is usually designated by the painter's name. The dress, full, comfortable and loose-fitting, hung from the shoulders with the back fullness caught in a deep box plait from neck to waist (see frontispiece). It, too, had the elbow-length sleeves

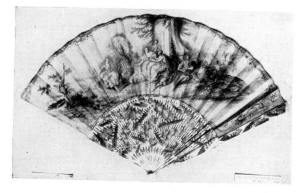

FIG. 54.   A PAINTED FAN OF THE EIGHTEENTH CENTURY.   Courtesy of the Metropolitan Museum.

though the neck varied in shape, being either round or square, with a lacy fichu around the throat. Still another type of dress was the *polonaise*, a one-piece dress with close, tight waist, the usual short sleeves, and a skirt that was draped at the sides into the shape of two broad wings with a third and somewhat longer one at the back. The petticoat worn under this was an elaborately decorated affair that was short enough to reveal to advantage the white silk stockings with their embroidered clocks and satin slippers with high heels and jeweled seams.

Marie Antoinette and her ladies were particularly partial to a very low bodice with fluttering ruffles at the elbow of the sleeves, and long skirts elaborately ruffled or festooned with lace and artificial flowers.

Aigrettes, ostrich plumes, ribbons, gauze, and artificial flowers gave an airy effect to the massive, powdered head-dresses that came into vogue about 1760—in marked contrast to the simple pompadours favored by the ladies of the Louis XV period. So tall were these erections "that their fair wearers were seriously inconvenienced when carried about in their sedan chairs or when attending the theater." Hats were equally elaborate, being heavily laden with flowers, feathers, and lace, and were of a great variety of shapes, caps large and small, or hats with brims as exaggerated as other parts of the ensemble.

The immense *paniers*, some measuring fully six feet from side to side, necessitated wide-skirted mantles, fur-lined for winter, or large capes. The inclination to copy the fashion current in England led in 1787 to the wearing by the French women of long cloth coats with a double row of buttons in front, close sleeves, and shoulder capes. During this same decade the large, eccentric fichu that gave an exaggerated appearance to the chest made its début.

Tall canes, long handled parasols, and large muffs were necessary adjuncts of a costume that was made of light-weight cloth, supple velvet, satin, taffeta, and muslin of delicate values and dainty floral motifs. Printed cambrics were much in demand after 1760 when Phillip Oberkampf established at Jouy, near Versailles, his factory for the making of colored prints. Designs were frequently painted by hand or embroidered on silks that bore such curious names as "stifled sigh," or the "lovely shepherdess" to designate their hue. Silk, lace, fur, gauze, ribbon, and flowers formed the trimmings which were so extensively used on the skirts intended for formal occasions.

For the nine years preceding the revolutionary period unpretentious white lawn or muslin and the fine Jouy cambric quite satisfied the desire for a simpler style of dress than that required at the brilliant court of Louis XVI and Marie Antoinette. Hoops were discarded so that the full skirt hung in straight, long folds about the figure. The open neck was filled in with a fichu of transparent material, and the straight, normal waist line was defined by a wide sash of colored ribbon. The extravagant modes of hair-dressing made some concession to the increasing feeling for simplicity and naturalness by introducing numerous curls all over the head, and transferring the plumes and other numerous decorations to the large, fanciful hats and caps both of which were worn at the same time. Many portraits show ruffled, dainty muslin caps worn under large, heavily decorated hats.

Fig. 55. Mlle. Charlotte du Val d'Ognes. David. Costume of the Directoire Period. Courtesy of the Metropolitan Museum.

The Directory, 1795–1799.—Fashions in France suffered severely through the upheaval of the revolution, and it was not until after 1793 that dress began to crystallize into the definite style which we know as that of the Directoire period. Financially embarrassed, unable to procure the handsome silks and laces, as both industries were seriously affected by the political upheaval, and anxious for something that was in no way reminiscent of the days of the monarchy, the new leaders of fashion—Rose Bertin and other dressmakers to the queen and court ladies having left the country—adopted the so-called classical modes that were prevalent in England and carried them to very great extremes. The corset went the way of the hoop, and the waist line ascended nearly to the armpit. The skirt lost nearly all of its fullness, but gained much in length in the back. The arm covering was extremely scant, just a tiny close sleeve that left the lower arm to be covered by long gloves, while the neck was exceedingly décolleté. This desire for as little clothing as possible affected the undergarments also; silk tights replaced the former full petticoats, and the long silk stockings were plainly visible through the slit sides of the skirt, or when the train was lifted and wound around the arm for convenience in walking and dancing. The Greek and Roman types of footwear were reflected in the heelless, thin slippers of red, white, or black, that were bound to the feet and ankles with cross-windings of ribbon.

Abbreviated, curled locks were the order of the day; when retained, long hair was dressed in the manner portrayed on the Greek and Roman statues in the museums. Ideas for head coverings were obtained from all manner of sources.

Cashmere shawls, delicate scarfs, or simple kerchiefs were the favored wraps, the short close-fitting coat, the *spencer*, with long, plain sleeves not making its entrance into the world of fashion until about 1797. The large, long muff was apparently the only article in the costume that was relied on for warmth.

The simplicity of the Directoire dress permitted the extensive use of jewelry, with cameos, intaglios, corals, and mosaics rather usurping the place of precious stones. For carrying small accessories, keys, kerchief, purse, etc., milady resorted to a commodious bag, *reticule*, decorated with the owner's monogram or figures of classic inclination. Furnished with handle and draw string, the *reticule* was carried in the hand or suspended from the arm.

The Consulate, 1799–1804.—No striking changes in dress took place during the years of the Consulate; the eccentricities and extravagances that followed the reign of terror were discarded and the simple, straight dress which was white by general preference, showing the influence of the Neoclassicists, held the center of the stage. By way of variety some women wore a second dress

Fig. 56a.   Typical Costume of the
Consulate.   1803.   Archives d'Art et
d'Histoire.

Fig. 56b.   The Arrival of the Stagecoach.   Boilly.   Archives
d'Art et d'Histoire.   Louvre.

or tunic of different color and texture from the dress itself and made of lace, satin, muslin, or velvet. The skirt of the dress remained long, and was frequently finished with a delicate embroidery just above the hem; the length of the tunic varied; the

FIG. 57. MARIE ANTOINETTE AND HER CHILDREN. MME. VIGÉE LEBRUN. 1787. THE BEGINNING OF SIMPLICITY IN COSTUME FOR CHILDREN. Versailles.

type that reached almost to the knees and was open in front and at the sides occupies a very prominent place in old prints and portraits of the period.

Children's Dress of the Eighteenth Century.—When observing the fun that children of to-day get from dressing up in their parents' clothes, one cannot but pity the youngsters of olden times for the joy they have missed from this sort of play. Perhaps, however, they had their pleasure in realizing that their full-skirted coat and queue, their Watteau sacque and frilled cap were just exactly like father's and mother's. Not until the second half of the eighteenth century when Rousseau was urging that the interests of childhood be recognized and the child no longer considered as a diminutive man, did there take place a radical change in the manner of dressing French children. Marie Antoinette, it is said, inaugurated the new custom by dressing the young Dauphin in long trousers and a short jacket, double-breasted, that was softened at wrists and neck by plaited ruffles belonging to the cambric shirt. A large sash encircled the waist, and the simple slippers were devoid of the former high heels. Girls, too, benefited by the change of public opinion, although it was not until a few years before the Directory that they were relieved of the heavy, stiff corset. Their gowns gained in simplicity of texture and trimming while retaining more or less the same cut as that of their mothers'.

In the well known picture by Mme. Vigée Lebrun of Marie Antoinette and her children, the infant seated on the mother's lap appears as comfortably and sensibly dressed as is the modern infant of similar age; a contrast indeed to the stiffly caged little body that in the sixteenth century was so tortured in rich, weighty silks, and starched lace ruff, that one wonders what interest he could possibly have taken in the bell and sundry toys that hung from his belt of gold chain.

REFERENCES

RACINET, HISTOIRE DU COSTUME.
PAUQUET FRÈRES, MODES ET COSTUMES HISTORIQUES.
QUICHERAT, HISTOIRE DU COSTUME EN FRANCE.
PITON, LE COSTUME CIVIL EN FRANCE, pp. 251–332.
PARSONS, THE PSYCHOLOGY OF DRESS, pp. 195–220.
CHALLAMEL, HISTORY OF FASHION IN FRANCE, Chaps. XVI–XX.
MODES ET USAGES AU TEMPES DE MARIE ANTOINETTE.
LES MODES DU DIRECTOIRE ET DU CONSULAT.
ZUR GESCHICHTE DER KOSTÜME.
GRAND-CARTERET, ELEGANCES DE LA TOILETTE.
LACROIX, DIRECTOIRE, CONSULAT ET L'EMPIRE.
BOEHN, ROKOKO.
LAUGLADE, ROSE BERTIN.
Paintings, by WATTEAU, LANCRET, BOUCHER, GREUZE, VIGÉE LEBRUN.

CHAPTER VIII

FRENCH COSTUME IN THE NINETEENTH CENTURY

Classical Revival, 1800
Napoleon returned from Elba, 1815
Romantic Period, 1830–1848
Invention of sewing machine, 1841
Franco-Prussian war, 1870

David, 1748–1825
Jacquard, 1752–1834
Ingres, 1781–1867
Daguerre, 1789–1851
Balzac, 1799–1850
Dumas, 1802–1870

FEMININE dress in the nineteenth century presents a decidedly varied panorama and an almost bewildering array of silhouettes and details that owed their rise and fall in popular acceptance to many reasons. Increased facilities for travel, commerce, and for the dissemination of fashion news by means of magazines and books among a constantly widening circle of interested men and women did much to foster a natural desire for change in dress, as did the manufacturers who were desirous primarily in the furthering of their own commercial interests. The monarchs grew less and less influential in sartorial affairs, their former power passing into the hands of rising couturières, popular actresses, and social leaders. The dissemination of wealth and the cheapening of machine-made materials caused the dress of society women to be quickly copied by those of less exalted birth, and naturally led to the desire for constant changes. In marked contrast to the innumerable changes which took place in women's dress at that time is the gradual standardization which came about in men's dress in the first third of that same century. The principles of democracy, simplicity, and uniformity in dress took firm hold on their imaginations and conquered any desire they may have had to return to the picturesque satins, laces, and powdered wigs of other, more romantic days.

The New Era in Men's Costume.—The masculine wardrobe has never recovered from the blow it received at the hands of the Revolutionists; its colorful quality, its assemblage of fine textures, and its luxuries of the goldsmith's art in the form of jeweled buttons, finely wrought shoe buckles, and enameled snuff boxes were completely swept away.

88

The short vest, the pantaloons, and the tail coat continued their general form throughout the nineteenth century with only trifling changes to satisfy the craving for variety. The vest retained its brightness of color and distinction of texture until

Fig. 58. Portrait of M. Philibert Riviere. Ingres. Jewelry—Watches and Rings—Were Prominent in Men's Costume of the Early XIXth Century. Archives d'Art et d'Histoire. Louvre.

about the middle of the century. Velvet, or satin in white, crimson, or yellow, bold check or plaid, gave a touch of brilliancy to the costume which otherwise became more and more somber. In the early thirties it was quite the mode for the dandy to wear two vests, the upper one short enough to show the elaborate under one. The buttons of the vest were likewise colorful and of interesting craftsmanship, while the pin inserted in the large neck scarf was an object of extravagance. The soft, but very high collar attached to the starched shirt was displaced in the second quarter of the century, by the starched, detachable collar and small tie.

The tight pantaloons of the early part of the century were usually of stockinet in the fashionable violet. They were cut long, with straps passing under the shoes and securing them in gaiter fashion. The breeches worn at court functions were completely superseded for general wear by the pantaloons. Dark colored cloths, plain, or with small stripes or checks, were soon adopted by men of good taste who seemed to wish to render their clothes as inconspicuous as possible.

The smallness of men's waists seems extraordinarily pronounced for many decades after 1820 when the corset or basque was introduced. Both the tail coat, of blue or dark green cloth, and the long-skirted cloak with many capes were tight-fitting at the waist. The short jacket of 1850, however, showed a waist line of more comfortable dimensions. The chimney pot hat went through many phases of fashionable cut, while the brim varied from straight to a slight roll, the crown retaining its usual height though with slight changes in its width at base and tip.

Since 1870 men's dress has remained practically unchanged with England still retaining the place it gained in the late eighteenth century as ruler of the realm of masculine clothing.

Feminine Fashions of the Empire, 1804–1814.—With the appearance of a more stabilized government the French were again at liberty to turn their attention to matters of dress. Napoleon, actuated by his fondness for display as well as by a desire to rehabilitate the industries of France which had suffered so severely during and after the Revolution, encouraged the women of his court in the wearing of more luxurious costumes than had been customary during the periods of the Directory and the Consulate. In this he was ably seconded by his extravagant wife Josephine, and later by her successor Marie Louise, as well as by his mother and sisters. As a result richer fabrics, silks, and velvets vied for popularity with the former favorites—mulls, lawns, and batistes.   Decoration in the form of embroidery, fringe, and spangles reflected the influence of the East as a result of the campaigns of Napoleon I, and the trophies which he and his men brought back to France.   The army, too, was responsible for much that was seen in feminine dress; the crowns of the hats imitated the tall ones worn by the soldiers, and the *spencer* and

FIG. 59.   A FASHION PLATE OF 1807.

FIG. 60.   A LADY OF THE COURT OF NAPOLEON.   ISABEY.   Courtesy of the Metropolitan Museum.

the *redingote* were trimmed with braid somewhat after the manner of the military coats.   Fur reappeared as trimming in the form of deep bandings as well as broad collars and cuffs.

While the bodice was as short as ever, the sleeves became a trifle fuller and longer, reaching in some instances to the wrists, and for occasions of ceremony or at court the short ones which we to-day designate as "empire puffs" were much in vogue. The English fashion of wearing a standing ruff of delicate lace, *cherusse*, was introduced about 1801 and continued as one of the character-

Fig. 61. Portrait of Mme. Morel of Tangry and Her Two Daughters in Typical Costumes of the Early Period of the Restoration. Ingres. The Louvre.

istics of Empire costume. The bodice that was separate from the skirt, and had sleeves and a high neck cut much like the shirt of a man, was known as the *canezou*. The short *spencer* had acquired lapels and a round collar.

Other wraps besides the *spencer* were the cashmere shawls whose graceful arrangement was a much practiced art; the scarf-shawl of wool or silk with fringe at the ends; and a long-skirted, long-sleeved *pelisse* with round shoulder collars.

The hair was arranged in flat ringlets about the face or in imitation of the classic modes. Colored wigs were quite à la

Fig. 62. Mme. Leblanc. Ingres. 1823. Costume of the Restoration. Courtesy of the Metropolitan Museum.

mode. Dainty bonnets of organdie, percale, taffeta, and turbans of rich silks were enriched with feathers, ribbons, and flowers though in a restrained manner.

Anxious to surround his court with much of the glamor of the former monarchy, Napoleon encouraged Josephine and her ladies in the matter of handsome and magnificent attire. Jewelry and laces played an increasingly important role in the pageantry of dress at the Tuileries, the former in such profusion that the inevitable revulsion came about in 1810; for several years after that but little jewelry was affected.

FIG. 63. COMTESSE D'HAUSSONVILLE. INGRES. 1845. Copyrighted by the Frick Collection.

FIG. 64. MME. MARIE CROCQ. COURBET. 1867. Courtesy of the Metropolitan Museum.

The Restoration, 1814–1848.—Foreign influences were somewhat marked in the dress of the earlier years of the Restoration following the campaigns of the Napoleonic armies in Europe. The return of the Bourbons caused many to display their political convictions in the color or cut of their gowns, particularly during the year 1815. Then ladies of the Royalist party[1] adopted white gowns with eighteen crosswise tucks in the skirt in honor of Louis

[1] CHALLAMEL, A HISTORY OF FASHION IN FRANCE, p. 196. Scribner and Welford.

XVIII, and white plumes on their chip hats or in their high-dressed hair. During the days of Napoleon's return from Elba the feminine adherents of the Imperial régime wore violets, his favorite flower, on all occasions to indicate their political leanings.

By the end of the first quarter of the century the silhouette of woman's dress was in great contrast to that with which the century opened. The short waist, straight skirt, and small sleeves were obsolete, the return of the corset being in large measure responsible for the new silhouette. By 1822 the waist line was down at its normal position, extremely small, and its presence emphasized by a broad, straight belt. The sleeves, set into lowered armscyes, made up in size for what they had previously lacked in this respect. About 1820 there appeared the leg o' mutton sleeve[2] with its exaggerated fullness at the top held out from the arms by means of boning or padding. With the long sleeves were worn kid gloves of bright hue, the short sleeves for evening being accompanied by white ones with many buttons to secure a trim fit at the wrists.

Louis Philippe, 1830–48.—The long drooping shoulder was a marked feature of the gown, particularly during the years of the Romantic period when Louis Philippe was on the throne. In order to accent the fashionable droop and width of the shoulder, berthas, scarfs, and small shoulder capes were adopted. The low, straight-cut neck line of the evening dresses likewise fostered this broad effect, though for daytime wear the bodice was cut high and a turned-down collar of lace or of allover embroidery, a folded kerchief or cambric ruche served as decorative finish.

In order to preserve some balance in the appearance of the figure the skirts became very wide at the bottom, and the hem several inches from the ground. By 1830, however, they had dropped to conceal all but the points of the high boots of cloth laced at the sides, or of the thin slippers with crossed ribbons at the instep and no heels.

Ruffles, plaitings, flounces, puffings, tucks, all manner of self trimmings were used in profusion as the Romantic period drew to a close. Although the bodice was by no means neglected in the matter of trimming it was the skirt that was rendered con-

[2] CHALLAMEL, A HISTORY OF FASHION IN FRANCE, p. 201. Scribner and Welford.

spicuous by the numerous crosswise decorations that added to its breadth. Light-weight cottons and silks, plain and figured, were adopted by the women of the time of Louis XVIII and Charles X, while velvet, the stiffer silks and brocades were utilized for the Louis Philippe modes. In the descriptions of the fashion plates in "*Petit Courrier des Dames*" for these years, repeated mention is made of such fabrics as gros de Naples, popeline, merino, batiste de laine, organdie, printed mousseline and printed organdie, satin Rachel, rep indien, grenadine, and barège. Laces and ribbons were employed in great profusion; the invention, early in the century, of a machine for the making of net placed this delicate and hitherto very costly fabric within the reach of women of moderate means.

Short shoulder capes, lace and silk scarfs, and long fur boas were about the only wraps which could be worn with the enormous sleeves, though shawls made of lace, of wool from Cashmere, or silk crepe from far off China were draped in dignified manner about the distended figures.

Broad-brimmed hats of straw, *paille d'Italie* and *paille de riz*, and silk heavily laden with flowers and ribbons were demurely tied under the chin with a coquettish bow of ribbon. Dainty caps and hoods of lace, also tied under the chin, and sometimes the large hat seem to have been equally popular, though both styles were destined to be replaced in the late thirties by the bonnet whose shape resembled the humble coal-scuttle.

The hair was tortured into bunches of curls and ringlets at the temples, then brushed smoothly up the back of the head and twisted into incongruous loops and knots that were held by pins and combs and rendered more decorative by the addition of flowers and feathers. The last eight years of Louis Philippe's reign, however, saw a more attractive arrangement; the hair, parted in the center was fastened in a simple knot at the back of the head, and looped braids or soft curls were caught at each temple.

The Second Empire, 1852–1870.—The style of costume that was prevalent during the years 1852–1870, frequently designated in the literature of fashion as the age of crinoline, was in marked contrast to that characteristic of the First Empire. Under the first Napoleonic emperor dress was straight, scant, and simple employing comparatively unpretentious fabrics and decorations;

under Napoleon III and Eugénie the breadth of silhouette, which had been for many years steadily increasing, reached its limit, the number of yards of cloth in each costume, the devices employed to support the crisp and weighty materials were totally different from anything seen in the First Empire, and for that matter, in any previous period.

Fig. 65. Sisley and His Wife. Renoir. 1868. Modes of the Closing Years of the Second Empire. Photo Courtesy of Raymond and Raymond, Inc.

The close fitting bodice with its long sleeves that spread into a bell-shape below the elbow, long shoulder, and neck line that encircled the throat closely, appeared quite insignificant in comparison with the self-asserting ruffles and flounces of the billowy skirts. The two or three ruffles that in 1840 were considered quite sufficient to decorate the bottom of the skirt gradually increased in numbers and spread from hem to waist. Full and starched, the numerous petticoats as well as rolls of horsehair in the lining of the skirt were soon necessary to give the proper support and prominence to the ten yards comprising the skirt's width. In 1854 relief from the burden of sustaining all this weight at the waist was obtained by the invention of a cage-like frame of about twenty light steel wires held together by strips of muslin. This contrivance, swaying from side to side as the wearer walked subjected her to many sermons and as much ridicule as did the *hennins* their wearers in the fifteenth century. Many women preferred to get the desired effect by inserting reeds in the hems of their petticoats. The number of skirts—six or seven being considered quite necessary—seems quite appalling in the light of modern hygiene and simplicity of dress.

A very décolleté neck line finished with a bertha or fichu of lace or other diaphanous fabric was worn in the evening, while the visiting and morning frocks were cut high with a demure turned-down collar of linen or lace, or a plaiting of the material of the dress secured at the throat with a brooch or bow of ribbon. Some cloth bodices were cut without sleeves and very deeply at the neck so that an underblouse of white muslin with a profusion of tiny hand-run tucks and white needlework was extremely prominent. Many of this type are illustrated in *"Le Moniteur de la Mode"* for the years 1864 to 1867. The waist line was small and in its normal position in spite of the tendency which for a while threatened its return to the position it held during the First Empire.

Ruffles were the prominent decoration of the pagoda sleeve that repeated below the elbow the broadening, rounding lines of the skirt. Undersleeves of light material in the form of puffs that extended to the wrist were also quite general from 1850 to 1860.

The bouffant skirts of the Second Empire afforded as much difficulty in the matter of wraps as did those of the eighteenth century. The shawls of silk edged with fringe, or lace, or of wool in summer, gave way to fur, plush, or velvet mantles in winter. Many cloaks were cut *en princesse*, with a defined waist line, touching merely the shoulders and resting on the crinoline from hips to knees.

Trimming was as much used on the bonnets of the period as

on the dresses and cloaks. The velvet, silk, or straw bonnets were cut short in back and in the shape of the coal-scuttle in front. Under the brim were several quiltings and flutings of lace and tulle, while bright flowers, rosettes, and feathers trimmed the crown. To the back of these bonnets were attached small frills of lace or silk that hung over the neck. Broad ribbons tied under the chin held this small but rather heavy headgear in place. The manufacture of artificial flowers had attained a place of great importance as was witnessed by the lavish use of these silk and velvet trimmings for both hat and hair decoration. They were tucked into the curls at the side of the head near the ear where the hair, dyed yellow in imitation of the golden locks of the Empress, swelled into a moderate roll. Large gold combs, velvet bows, and aigrettes were likewise used as hair ornaments, while nets of silk, chenille, or gold-thread mesh incased the coils of hair at the back.

With the ground-length skirt but little of the feet was visible; with the swaying of the crinoline in walking, however, there appeared either a high boot of black kid or patent leather laced at the instep and with high heels, or slippers with bows or buckles.

Considered necessary to complete the costume were handkerchiefs elaborately trimmed with lace and hand embroidery, fans, jet-beaded silk *aumônières*, and dainty parasols of moiré or batiste lined with flattering colours, lace-edged or covered entirely with black or white lace. The straight handles of the sunshades replacing the hinged ones of a previous fashion, were of wood or of ivory with handsome knobs of carnelian, coral, or agate. Muffs entirely of fur, or of velvet combined with fur, were diminutive but important.

Jewelled lockets or crosses suspended from the neck on slender chains or velvet ribbons, necklaces, bracelets, rings, watches, and watch chains, as well as bandeaus of gold for the hair received the painstaking and appreciative attention of both jewelers and women of fashion. Metal buttons with coloured stones were quite modish fastenings for the front of the bodice.

The fabrics in vogue during the Second Empire were rather crude in colour and of a great variety of textures. We read of tarlatan, tulle, taffeta, moiré antique, gros grain, brocatelle, damask, barège, merino, Irish poplin, English alpaca, and jaconet. Plaids, checks, and stripes were more in demand than designs of floral motifs. Fur, fringe, and braid were immensely popular, with Chantilly, Alençon, and blonde laces correct for flounces for skirt and sleeve, berthas, and fichus, as well as bonnet decorations.

In the late years of the sixties, the crinoline had disappeared from the stage of fashion, being superseded by the close-fitting dress whose long skirt was looped up over a tight underskirt that

FIG. 66. HOMAGE TO BEAUTY. TOUL-MOUCHE. AN ILLUSTRATION OF THE USE OF LACE IN 1874.

FIG. 67. PORTRAIT OF CATHERINE L. WOLFE IN COSTUME FASHIONABLE IN 1876. CABANEL.

Courtesy of the Metropolitan Museum.

restricted the free motion of the knees. By 1868 the bustle had quite transformed the entire silhouette, recalling that in existence in the late years of the seventeenth century.

The Modes from 1870 to 1880.—During the Franco-Prussian war 1870-1871, the attention of French women was diverted from matters of dress with the result that in the absence of their inspiration, dress lacked distinction for many years. Both *polo-*

naise—the close fitting gown with elaborately draped-up skirt and the princess dress known as the Gabriel, were worn, the latter being the favorite for evening wear until its disappearance in 1878. Skirts touched the floor in front, swinging off at the sides into long trains that were cumbersome but fashionably correct for all walking costumes.

Décolleté neck lines were seen in strictly formal dress only, the bodices of both street and afternoon dresses being cut with a high neck and finished with flattering ruche and jabot of lace. Buttons of steel or oxydized silver fastened the front of the close, boned bodice. Sleeves were long and close-fitting except for evening wear when the short sleeves of the period of Louis XVI were revived. As many evening gowns were sleeveless, the wearing of long kid gloves became customary. With the formal gown were worn slippers of soft, glacé kid with high heels and narrow, pointed toes; with the walking costume, high boots with cloth tops that matched the colour of the dress.

This was the era of the famous English *chignon*, a heavy, massive erection at the back of the head of natural or false hair the latter obtained in great abundance from the peasant women of northern France. This mode of hair-dressing necessitated a slightly forward tilt to the hat at the back. The hat was very small in size, with every inch of its narrow brim and low crown concealed under masses of feathers, aigrettes, flowers, and plaitings of lace and ribbon. A veil of lace or tulle hung down the back, partially concealing the *chignon*. As this diminutive head covering afforded so little protection from the sun, a small parasol with short handle of ivory achieved a place of great importance in the costumes for walking and driving.

One of the most fashionable wraps was the long mantle of velvet, trimmed in winter with an abundance of fur, and known as the *garrick*. Another popular wrap was the dolman, cut in much the same manner as the *polonaise* but with sleeves that were exceedingly wide and open where they ended about at the wrist.

1880–1890.—The popularity of the *polonaise* continued throughout the eighties with increasing attention paid to the size of the bustle. The cumbersome train disappeared with the advent of the cloth costume for street wear. The close-fitting, cutaway jackets of rather severe cut were worn with plaited skirts and the inevitable bustle. The bodice of the dress fitted the figure more closely than ever; was cut with numerous seams and darts and extended several inches below the normal waistline, with a point in front that was accented by a buckle or a bow of ribbon. Revers, long vests, and jabots broke the severity of the front. A garment that revealed the well-corseted figure of 1881 was the *jersey* of worsted or cashmere introduced from England. It clung very closely to the figure and was worn with a kilted skirt of ground length.

For a very few years the bustle was in evidence.

Sleeves remained close and straight, finished at the wrist with cuffs of the same velvet or passementerie that trimmed other parts

FIG. 68. IN THE HOTHOUSE. MANET. 1879. Photo Courtesy of Raymond and Raymond, Inc.

of the dress, or at the elbow with scant ruffles of the Honiton and Devonshire laces that were then so much used.

A most trying and unbecoming neckline made its début in the late years of this decade. This was the straight, high collar of the fabric of the dress or of velvet, at first unrelieved by any softening ruche.

With the simpler mode of dressing the hair high on the head and in soft ringlets or fringe on the forehead, the hats assumed greater dimensions. In cut and decoration they strove for lofty effects; the crown was high and box-like with flowers, plumes, and wings of birds arranged to give all possible height to the wearer. The brims, though remaining comparatively small, turned up, or down, or extended in front somewhat like the oldtime poke bonnet with broad ribbons tying under the chin.

Parasols became of much greater size as did the folding fans without which no evening costume was complete. The low V-neck permitted the use of necklaces and jewelled lockets.

Fig. 69.   At the Milliners.   Degas. Cir.   1882.   Courtesy of the Metropolitan Museum of Art.

Fig. 70. The Organ Recital. Lerolle. 1885. Courtesy of the Metropolitan Museum

1890–1900.—In 1889 the top of the sleeve began with all modesty and circumspection to show a slight increase in size. Gradually this additional fullness became more conspicuous until by 1896 the huge balloon sleeve with its stiffening and lining dominated the entire costume. From elbow to wrist it fitted the arm closely. Unable to compete with this innovation the bustle disappeared, and by 1894 the skirts were smooth and glove fitting about the hips, spreading at the bottom into wide bells with graceful trains. Numerous gores, godets, and many yards of stiffening

and lining were required to give the desired effect. The petticoats coquettishly displayed by lifting the train in walking were
of bright, rustling silks or lace and embroidery-trimmed muslin.

The waist line was thrown into relief by a highly colored
sash that tied in a bow at the back. Revers of cloth, velvet, or
lace spread from points at the waist
to a width of several inches at the
shoulders, thus repeating the lines of
the hour-glass silhouette. The bodice
was no longer the fitted, boned affair
of the 'eighties, but full and bloused
above the tight belt, its fullness at
times starting from a deep yoke in
front and back. The high collar
was frequently omitted.

The one-piece dress of the 'nineties

Fig. 71. Idle Hours.   J. A. Weir.   Children's
Dress of 1888. Note the Increasing Size of the
Top of the Sleeve in the Woman's Costume.

Fig. 72. Young Woman with
a Muff.   Renoir.   The Silhouette of 1879.

Courtesy of the Metropolitan Museum.

followed closely the lines of the corseted figure. This princess
gown, cut in many gores and seams that extended from shoulders
to hem, was developed in many fabrics and used for formal as well
as informal gowns. As an evening gown its square or round-cut
neck line was softened with lace and tulle, its sleeves taking the
form of short, full puffs.

The tailor-made suit, sponsored as early as 1888 by many English women, became quite fashionable in Paris during the last decade of this century. The coat, fitting snugly at the waist,

FIG. 73. MRS. W. R. BACON. ZORN. AN EVENING GOWN OF 1897. INCREASING BREADTH ACROSS THE SHOULDERS AND TOP OF SLEEVES WAS CHARACTERISTIC OF THE VERY LATE YEARS OF THE 'NINETIES. Courtesy of the Metropolitan Museum.

usually extended to the finger tips. In 1896 its sleeves were but moderately full at the top, indicating the gradual deflation that took place in the late years of the century. The blouse of colored silk or cloth that accompanied the suit, was cut with a high neck line, a jabot or frill adding a feminine touch to an otherwise severe costume.

In order to balance the balloon sleeves and bell skirts, the very tiny hat worn in 1890 was transformed into one that had a broad brim which turned up at the back or the front, and had as its sole trimming two or three upstanding ostrich plumes. The hair was brushed smoothly up the back and secured in a huge loop at the top.

For wraps milady of the early 'Nineties donned a full-length princess-cut *redingote*, one of similar cut that reached only to the knees, or a double-tiered cape of hip-length. Fur was extensively used for shoulder capes, collars, and bandings on all wraps as well as in long boas and small muffs.

High, buttoned boots with tops of kid or cloth were worn on the street; thin slippers with evening gowns.

In the late years of the nineteenth century the former all-important sleeves dwindled in size and returned to the close, modest ones they were in 1887. Skirts, too, followed this seeming desire for straightness of silhouette, though they persisted in retaining their flare at the bottom for several years in the new century that has seen in its first quarter so many and such diversified modes inaugurated by the couturières of Paris.

Simplicity of cut, fabric, and decoration in women's clothes received impetus from the newly introduced sports of golfing and bicycling. These with the older sports of tennis and skating have called for designs more suitable for exercise and have increased the wardrobe demands of all women who make any pretense of keeping abreast of the times. In addition to the costumes suitable for evening, home, visiting, walking, and riding, the well-dressed woman was called upon to acquire those garments and their accessories that were appropriate for the new sports. The bicycle required a short skirt, full bloomers, trim shirt waists and masculine tie, while golf demanded a circular cape. Strange to us now is the fact that both golf and tennis were apparently well played in skirts of the same width and length as those worn on occasions requiring no agility and energy of body. Even the new bathing suits had large sleeves, high collars, and small waist lines, with full, short skirts and bloomers. Ten years later the new pastime of motoring required long dusters of linen or silk and large veils to protect the dress and hat of the open car's fair passenger from the dust of the road.

Such was the beginning of the far reaching influence that woman's entrance into the field of sports soon acquired over her whole mode of dressing. Thirty-five years later the sports frock was no longer an incidental garment, but the all-important one whose ease of fit helped to revolutionize the cut of every other garment in the feminine wardrobe.

Children's Costume in the Nineteenth Century.—The simplification of cut and fabric which took place in the dress of the younger generation shortly after the French Revolution continued in the early years of the new century: materials were light in weight, simple and unpretentious in color and texture; comfort and freedom of motion for active young citizens were important considerations. But it is interesting to note that the general silhouette and details affected by the parents were closely reflected in the dress of their offspring. In the early years of the Restoration when breadth of shoulder and smallness of waist were emphasized in adult modes, those same features were prominent in the dress of children. When grown women loaded their full skirts with crosswise flounces; employed figured and strongly colored fabrics; wore high, cloth top boots of bright hues; coats with full-cut skirts to accommodate broad crinolines; poke bonnets with feather trimmings and ribbon ties—small girls of the household repeated, with slight variations, the same theme in their own costumes.

For approximately over half the century small girls, from their earliest years, wore crisp white pantalettes with decorative tucks, ruffles, and embroidery about the ankles. These pantalettes extended below the straight, slim skirts of the Empire period; below the shorter and fuller skirts of the Restoration period; and continued their position of prominence under the swaying crinolines of the Second Empire. Skirts, in general, throughout the entire century were worn by all young girls several inches below the knee, and were no longer the floor-length, inconvenient ones of earlier centuries that tripped and annoyed the young wearers.

Young boys of the Empire and Restoration periods were, on the whole, miniature citizens with the similarly cut pantaloons, short vests, ruffled white shirts and black ties affected by men of affairs. About the middle of the century, however, the comfortable knickerbockers, loose sacque coat, soft cap, and turned-down collar were recognized as peculiarly appropriate to the needs of growing youth, and with slight modification they have held their position to the present time. The Garibaldi, a red blouse named after the Italian patriot, was an important item in the costume of the boys in the 'sixties.

REFERENCES

LACROIX, DIRECTOIRE, CONSULAT, ET L'EMPIRE.
CHALLAMEL, HISTORY OF FASHION IN FRANCE, Chaps. XX–XXXIV.
PRICE, DAME FASHION.
FISCHEL AND BOEHN, MODES AND MANNERS OF THE NINETEENTH CENTURY.
UZANNE, FASHIONS IN PARIS.
PARSONS, PSYCHOLOGY OF DRESS, Chap. 7.
PITON, COSTUME CIVIL EN FRANCE, pp. 333–380.
BUSZ, DAS KÖSTUM, pp. 130–165.
SAGE, A STUDY OF COSTUME, Chaps. XII–XV.
WORTH, A CENTURY OF FASHION.
GESZLER, DIE MODEN DES XIX JAHRHUNDERT.
ZUR GESCHICHTE DER KOSTÜME, plates 661, 990.
PAUQUET FRÈRES, MODES ET COSTUMES HISTORIQUES.
KÖHLER, A HISTORY OF COSTUME, pp. 374–456.
Paintings by DAVID, INGRES, GERARD, WINTERHALTER, FANTIN-LATOUR, MANET, RENOIR.

CHAPTER IX

COSTUME IN EARLY TWENTIETH CENTURY

THE numerous changes which took place in costume during the early years of the present century are quite startling to the student of dress accustomed though he has become to the bewildering variety of fashions that have sprung up in the last fifty years. The industrial age has had its share in fostering rapid and seasonal changes in practically all types of clothes worn by men and women. The increase in the production of wool, of cotton, of silk, of linen, and particularly since the close of the war, of rayon, has given impetus to the manufacture of ready-made garments, and both manufacturers and retailers have been zealous in conducting campaigns for the sale of their stocks. The wear and tear to which the clothes of women engaged in business or in sport have been subjected have called for more frequent additions to the woman's wardrobe than ever before. The comparative cheapness of clothes in the last few years and the natural desire for change on the part of every woman have been additional factors in the frequent and radical changes to which the clothes of every well-dressed woman have had to submit in the first quarter of the present century.

The Couturière.—One other and very important factor in the rapid whirl of fashion in the past fifty years, grown more powerful in the past twenty-five, is the rise of the commercial designer and dressmaker in Paris. Gone are the old days when an empress or court favorite could start and maintain a fashion of a particular cut or color, and in place of the former leaders of fashion are the men and women of ability in design who coöperate with leaders of society, of the stage, and prominent ready-to-wear manufacturers in the launching of new ideas for gowns, hats, shoes, lingerie, and accessories. Most influential of the pioneers of these designers of the last half of the nineteenth century were Worth, Laferrière, Rodiguez, Doucet, Redfern, Paquin, Chéruit, Premet, Drecoll, and Callot. This small group became augmented in the early years of the present century and received many additions at the close of the World War when many men as well as women of

109

taste and style knowledge turned their efforts in this direction as a means of supporting themselves and rehabilitating their lost fortunes.

Fashions of the Years 1900–1908.—The first years of the new era witnessed a silhouette that in the main retained the same

features as did that of the very late years of the 'nineties—small waist, long, full skirt, and long, close-fitting sleeves. Variations began to be made, however, in 1900: then the straight front corset appeared giving an exaggerated curve to the hips in the back, and defining the bust. The skirt retained the former smoothness of fit

FIG. 74. MRS. THOMAS. S. S. THOMAS. AN EXAMPLE OF THE BELL SKIRT.

FIG. 75. PORTRAIT OF A LADY. HUGO VON HABERMAN. A TYPICAL HAT OF 1904.

Courtesy of the Metropolitan Museum.

about the hips, but from the knees down it flared gently forth into the shape of a large bell with a slight train at the back. The bottom was edged with soft rufflings and plaitings of self material or of delicate, frothy lace and chiffon. The labor involved in the making of one of these skirts was considerable, for many gores—from nine to thirteen—were necessary to obtain the requisite smoothness about the hips and the gradual swelling fullness about the feet.

Sleeves as well as skirts were full. In the year 1902 sleeves were cut with considerable fullness from elbow to wrist in the type known as the bishop sleeve. The armscye remained close, and the top of the sleeve tight until 1904 when additional breadth was given to the shoulders in the form of epaulettes and ruffles as well as a drop shoulder seam. The materials employed in the gowns of those years were soft and pliant, adapting themselves naturally to the new

FIG. 76. THE WYNDHAM SISTERS. J. S. SARGENT. FIG. 77. THE GREEN BODICE. J. A. WEIR. THE POPULAR FEATHER BOA.
Courtesy of the Metropolitan Museum.

silhouette. For daytime use the dresses were cut high in the neck with deep yokes and high collars of lace or net with a soft rippling jabot of lace, lawn, or fine linen at the throat.

The year 1902 saw the pompadour hair arrangement at the height of its career; puffed above the forehead and close at the sides with a large knot of hair at the back of the neck. In a very few years the new marcel wave appeared and the knot at the back was replaced by many soft puffs of hair on the top of the head. Comparatively small hats, flat of crown with many ribbon, uncurled

ostrich, and flower decorations, were perched on top of this elaborate hair arrangement, and given a saucy, jaunty air by means of
a downward tilt to the front of the brim. The last years of the
decade, however, saw the advent of an enormous, wheel-shaped hat,
known in America as the "Merry
widow" hat. Long boas of feathers
and fur, generous-sized muffs, likewise of fur, as well as short coats of
fur were favored articles in the
feminine wardrobe.

**Changes in Fashion from 1908
to 1910.**—A new silhouette com-

FIG. 78. TEA LEAVES. W. M. PAXTON. SMALL   FIG. 79.   LOUISE.   A. JONGERS.   A
WAISTLINES WERE FASHIONABLE IN 1909.   YOUNG GIRL'S COSTUME ABOUT 1910.
Courtesy of the Metropolitan Museum.

manded the attention of women from 1908 to 1910. Its foundation was the new corset, fitting closely over the hips, and cut lower
at the top, with a greater circumference about the waist than
formerly. The resulting lines of the dress itself were straight with
just a slight curve at the hip; the skirts cleared the ground by a few

inches and were moderately full.   Even the waist of the dress partially concealed the natural lines of the body, being cut in a slightly full kimono, with a short sleeve that was an adaptation of the kimono of the Japanese who had centered the attention of the world upon themselves as a result of their war in 1905 with the Russians.   It is interesting to note here that this was the first reappearance of that particular cut of sleeve in French costume since the early Middle Ages.

The coats in those years were semi-fitting, cutaway in front, of hip-length or slightly longer, and frequently with three-quarter length sleeves.   Jabots still ruffled their way down the front of the soft lingerie blouse that was invariably worn with the costume suit.   Gloves were necessarily long, with white kid the favorite color and leather.   Due to the fact that the skirt was worn about four inches from the floor, the footwear received much attention though by no means the amount it has commanded since 1923. Oxfords and high-laced shoes of black or brown leather were considered appropriate for walking and day time wear, with thin, light-weight slippers of satin and kid with large cut steel buckles replacing them for evening wear.

As the width of the skirt decreased in size and prominence, the circumference of the hat increased tremendously.   Large picture hats of velvet or straw with an abundance of flowers, ribbon and plumes as decoration topped the otherwise comparatively straight line silhouette.

The Peg-top Skirts of 1910–1915.—The fashionable skirts of the short period from 1910 to 1913 were extremely narrow causing their wearers considerable difficulty and inconvenience in walking and getting on and off street cars and coaches.   Many women adopted the fashion which received its inspiration from the gowns of the period of the Directoire, of having the skirt slashed from the instep to within a few inches of the knee.   This made for greater convenience of locomotion and afforded an opportunity for the wearing of colorful and elaborate silk petticoats.   Waist lines were slightly above the normal and were accented by broad belts while the kimono blouse with sleeves extending slightly below the elbows was by far the greatest favorite of fashion.   The high net collars disappeared leaving the throat exposed.   Collars were in general of the turned-down variety, rather small and dainty.   In keeping with the demand of the silhouette the materials were sheer and soft, even the wool fabrics employed for the three-quarter length, cutaway coat with its long, tight sleeve were pliable and soft in texture.

It was not for many years that such a restricting type of costume could last, and by 1912 greater fullness was demanded. It appeared in a rather unusual form—puffed from waist to knees like the *paniers* of the eighteenth century, with the rest of the skirt from knees to instep very tight and narrow. This fullness grew to a considerable size about the hips in 1914 and for convenience in walking

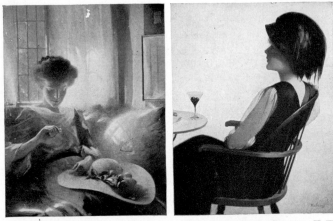

FIG. 80. THE RING. J. W. ALEXANDER. THE BROAD-BRIMMED LEGHORN HAT SO POPULAR IN 1911.

FIG. 81. PASSING OF SUMMER. H. W. WATROUS. TRANSPARENT MATERIAL WAS VERY MUCH USED IN THE SLEEVES OF THE DRESSES IN THE FIRST DECADE OF THE XXTH CENTURY.

Courtesy of the Metropolitan Museum.

the bottom of the skirt, still narrow from the knee down, was open for several inches up the front. This type of skirt was known as the "peg-top."

With this skirt usurping the center of the stage of fashion the size of the hat decreased, becoming quite small with a tiny brim and worn usually with a sheer veil.

1915–1917.—The slashed hem of the "peg-top" skirts accustomed the general public to the sight of women's ankles, so that there was no strenuous opposition to the skirts that measured eight inches from the ground during the years from 1915 to 1919. But shortness was not the only characteristic of the new skirts: they increased greatly in width at the bottom with full tunics, crosswise flounces, ruffles, and bandings of fur all assisting in increasing the width of the silhouette above the ankles. The waist line was at its normal position again, with sleeves generally long and close and neck lines of the *bateau* or boat shape—fairly close to the neck in front and back, but very broad at the sides, in fact very similar to the line so much worn in the tenth and eleventh centuries.

In general the hats were small with heron plumes, aigrettes, and bows of stiffened ribbon attached at the base of the crown in all manner of sharp angles. The hair was dressed close to the head and brushed smoothly back at the sides to expose the ears with their decorative ear-rings. Such jauntiness of outline in coats had not been seen for many years. The outergarments repeated the billowy contour of the dresses and were cut with very decided flares at the hips or a few inches above the bottom of the dress skirt. The usual coat collar was small and buttoned closely about the neck. In 1918 a long, full cape usurped the place of the flared coat in the costume of many fashionable women.

1917–1928.—The general state of affairs existing during the closing years of the World War was profoundly influential in matters of women's dress. The scarcity and costliness of most dress fabrics, the entrance of French, English, and American women into types of work which had never before been open to them, and the demands those positions made for simply cut, comfortable clothes with the absolute minimum of trimming left a marked imprint on costume for several years. The costliness of all fabrics, the many advantages of the short skirt, and the discarding of the corset by practically all women engaged in strenuous home and business duties as well as in the diversified sports militated in favor of a simple one-piece dress that hung from the shoulders in straight, unbroken lines to within ten or twelve inches of the floor. Absolute comfort and simplicity became the keynotes of fashion for several years: skirts were short and scant; neck lines were open and comfortable; sleeves were either long or short as desired by the wearer,—entirely non-existent in some types of dresses for a short period; foot-wear was low in cut with comparatively low heels; hair arrangements were of the simplest variety. In general the hair was cut short, and in the early years of the introduction of bobbed hair, it was worn full and bushy over the ears. Jewelry, bags, scarfs, in fact all accessories, benefited by the era of simplicity and were without elaboration of any kind. As the skirts grew shorter the stockings and shoes received greater attention, the latter forsaking the somber black of other days and appearing almost exclusively in tan and gray.

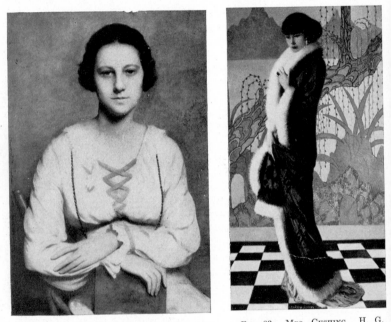

FIG. 82. PORTRAIT OF MISS RYDER. CARTOTTO. HIGH COLLARS WERE RARELY WORN IN THE TWENTIES.

FIG. 83. MRS. CUSHING. H. G. CUSHING. AN EXAMPLE OF A GRACEFUL EVENING WRAP WORN IN 1917.

Courtesy of the Metropolitan Museum.

Hats became diminutive affairs of felt, practically devoid of trimming and fitting very closely to the head with its very short hair which fashion and the followers of the "comfortable creed" declared must be waved and curled with a "permanent."

1929–1937.—The closing years of the third decade saw the slim silhouette change to one decidedly more bouffant with circular insets, flounces and fluttering panels gradually lengthening the skirts that by 1930 were long for evening, ankle-length for informal daytime and quite short for street wear. In that same year the draped neckline, adapted from the Grecian chiton, became fashion's favorite sharing that honor with bows and scarves

FIG. 84. AN EVENING GOWN BY DOEUIL-LET. 1928. Wide World Photos.

FIG. 85. THE COWL NECKLINE AS INTERPRETED BY LANVIN 1936. Dorien Leigh Ltd., from Black Star.

until in 1934 fullness at shoulder and sleeve top called for a new allegiance. The normal waistline, while defined by attractive belts, retained its comfortable size with foundation garments composed largely of elastic, with bones very scarce.

The increasing interest of women in the field of sports had a marked influence on daytime costume. The tailored shirt-waist suit of the early years of the century was revived in 1935 in simple, wash fabrics for wear on the golf course and was soon adopted by women not addicted to active sports. Knitted frocks of wool, silk or synthetic yarns, tailored suits of tweed and evening gowns of Lyons or transparent velvet and lace were in the wardrobe of every well-dressed woman.

The styles of 1937 reflected strong British influence due to the coronations of the British sovereigns King George VI and Queen Elizabeth. Elegance and richness were the keynotes of formal costumes with dull gold embroidery, sequins, rich brocades, royal purple, furs and Scotch plaids paying their respects to one of the most important current events of the year.

In 1930 Paris set its seal of approval on the wearing of the beret, the Basque man's national head covering, while in 1936 hats generally were adaptations of Oriental head-dresses and those of the warriors engaged in the Italo-Ethiopian conflict: chiefly crowns of eccentric shape and size. Fashionable footwear for all occasions during 1936–1937 was built on the lines of the classic Grecian sandal while further reflections of national dress were found in the Dalmatian bolero; in Tyrolean embroidery and dirndl with its short, swinging skirt and tight bodice charmingly interpreted in organdy, lace or taffeta; and Spanish mantillas in black Chantilly lace.

REFERENCES

FISCHEL AND BOEHN, MODES AND MANNERS OF THE NINETEENTH CENTURY.
NYSTROM, ECONOMICS OF FASHION, Chap. XII.
PRICE, DAME FASHION.
GAZETTE DU BON TON. L'ILLUSTRATION.
Paintings by ZORN, TOUCHE, LASZLO, SARGENT, WHISTLER, BOLDINI, DEGAS, MANET, RENOIR.

CHAPTER X

ENGLISH COSTUME DURING THE MIDDLE AGES

Bede, 673–735
Alfred the Great, 849–899
Norman conquest of England, 1066   Richard Coeur de Lion, 1157–1199
Magna Charta, 1215   Roger Bacon, 1214–1294
Battle of Agincourt, 1415   Edward III, 1312–1377
War of the Roses, 1455–1485   Wycliffe, 1324–1384
Chaucer, 1340?–1400
William Caxton, 1422–1491

THE studies of scholars on the customs, manners and social life of the French and English reveal a very great similarity in the dress of the two peoples. Their geographic position, their intermingling after the Norman Conquest, their martial and commercial intercourse, and the numerous intermarriages between the members of the ruling houses were all conducive to the modification and adoption of the sartorial customs of the one by the other. A comparatively detailed description of French dress has already been given in the preceding chapters, and in order to prevent unnecessary repetition, the following outline of English dress has been made as brief as clarity will permit.

The Britons.—The extremely scant material relating to the clothing of the early Britons leads us to picture them in much the same type of garments as were used by the inhabitants of Gaul. We are told that when Cæsar reached Briton in 55 B.C. he found the men simply habited in loose-fitting, belted tunics that extended to the waist; bright-hued, long trousers or *braccae*, which seemed to characterize all Northern peoples in early times, and short cloaks of blue or black homespun. The women were clad in long but sleeveless tunics girdled at the waist, and in long cloaks which answered the requirements of outer clothing. Neither sex was addicted to head covering, the men letting their hair grow in long curls to the shoulders, while the women let nature have her own way. Both adorned their persons with collars, necklaces, and bracelets of twisted wire, the women adding rings and armlets of gold and silver. Crude foot-covering of rawhide reached to the ankles.

119

The Saxons, 460–1066.—The Saxon dressed in somewhat finer garments than did the Briton. The tunic of the former was ordinarily of linen and was completely covered by a longer tunic, the *tunica*, which was distinguished by the length of its sleeves and their crosswise-folds or fullness at the forearm: in cold weather these sleeves were drawn down over the hands. The girdle which encircled the waist was of leather, plain or embroidered. The *tunica* generally covered the short trousers that reached to the mid-thigh, while the legs from ankle to knee were protected by elaborate windings of narrow strips of leather or cloth, (cross gartering).[1] Cloth stockings, long or short, were commonly used with shoes that fastened either at the side or at the front.

A small, pointed cap was fashioned from skins or cloth. The hair was allowed to flow long and unconfined, and the beard was parted in the center of the chin in the style known as "bifid."

The Saxon mantle was interestingly fastened at the right shoulder by a brooch or a large pin, though there are decided evidences that an ingenious method of drawing an end or side of the cloak through a ring of metal existed. In shape the mantle varied, being short and circular, or long and straight. In the latter years of this period both mantle and *tunica* of the men received considerable elaboration in the form of embroidery at the hems and edges.

Skilled with her needle, the Saxon woman embroidered her *tunica* and *gunna*, gown, with threads that harmonized with the textures of those garments as they gradually became richer and more elaborate. The former garment was a long, slightly fitted gown whose long sleeves had the same puckering above the wrist that was found in the *tunica* of the Saxon man. Over this *tunica* was placed the *gunna* with its abbreviated sleeves and skirt that was tucked up on the right side under the belt in order that the colorful *tunica* might be seen to advantage. Embroidery was lavished on this robe as well as on the full, flowing mantle.

Custom apparently decreed that the locks of the fair Saxon woman be entirely concealed, and for this purpose the "headrail" was employed. This strip of colorful silk or linen, measuring two and a half yards by three quarters of a yard, was drawn

---

[1] SHAW, HENRY, DRESSES AND DECORATIONS OF THE MIDDLE AGES. H. G. Bohn, 1858.

over the head from the left to the right shoulder, under the chin, then around the back of the neck to the right shoulder. With it was worn a narrow circlet of gold. Further adornment was found in such jewelry as brooches, rings, and bracelets, containing colorful stones.[2]

The Danes.—The Danes contributed but little to early English dress except sobriety of color. We read that black was much used in their costume, which otherwise resembled that of the Saxons.

The Normans, 1066–1154.—With the appearance of William the Conqueror, England entered into a period of war-like and troublous times that were not conducive to elaboration and extravagance in dress. Consequently during the reigns of William I, 1066–1087, and of William II, 1087–1100, there were but slight changes made in the costume.

The men still wore two knee-length and embroidered tunics as shown in the Bayeaux tapestry, the short sleeves of the outer one displaying the long, wrinkled sleeves of the inner one. The neck lines of both were close and bordered with embroidery. The trousers, however, extended to the ankle; the legs were wound to the knee with strips of cloth or leather. Shoes of black leather and socks of wool completed the protection of the lower extremities. Warm cloth hoods or tight caps of cloth covered the head, while the knee-length cape, rectangular or circular in shape, fastened at the right shoulder, was similar to that of the Saxon, although if anything a trifle larger.

The mode of short hair introduced by the Normans lasted but a brief length of time, the men during the reign of William II letting both hair and beard grow quite long, but spending more time in keeping them well groomed.

The pilgrimages to Palestine and later the Crusades, were doubtless responsible for the reflection of the voluminous features and ornament of Eastern costume in that of all western Europe. As in contemporary French dress both tunics and mantles during the reigns of Henry I, 1100–1135, and Stephen, 1135–1154, were of increased length and width with embroidered borders.

Even the men's shoes succumbed to the craze for ornamenta-

---

[2] *Ibid.*

tion; narrow bands of embroidery were worked along the top and down the instep of the cloth or leather foot-wear that became slightly pointed at the toes for a brief length of time.[3] Under Stephen the tops of the high shoes extended considerably above the ankle and were rolled to show the brilliant lining.

The garments of the Norman women were similar to those of the Saxon women: the chemise of white linen, with long, wrinkled sleeves and long skirt; the robe or gown with loose, elbow-length sleeve, and skirt of three-quarter length. While the *wimple*; corresponding to the earlier Saxon "head-rail," was wound about the head and throat, some women preferred to expose their hair; this was simply coiled at the back and arranged in becoming curls about the face. By the time of Henry I, 1100–1135, all aversion to exposing the hair was lost and the long braids so commonly worn by French women of that century became fashionable. Many Englishwomen intertwined colored ribbons with the braids or bound the ends with strips of silk.

During the first half of the twelfth century slight eccentricities began to appear in the women's dress. The pendulous cuff that began very moderately in the reign of Henry I increased to such a length that the sleeve had to be knotted on itself to prevent its trailing on the ground. In this period, too, appeared the gown that corresponded to the *bliaud* of the French (page 33), with its laced bodice of elastic fabric and full, straight skirt.

The girdle came into great prominence at that time and was generally of two forms: a rather wide strip of cloth profusely enriched with embroidery, or a long rope of silk wound about the waist with tasselled ends falling down the front almost to the hem of the gown.

On the whole, costume during the Norman period was simple for all. Women of wealth purchased imported fabrics from the itinerant merchant and enriched the native English woolens with needlework of their own execution, sometimes adding to it pearls and other precious stones in the current fashion.

The Plantagenets, 1154–1216.—This tendency towards greater luxuriousness in fabrics grew to a marked degree with the Plantagenet rulers. To the sojourns in the East of Richard I, 1189–1199,

---

[3] *Ibid.*

and his Crusaders, were due the increased length and fullness that characterized the loose-sleeved, full-length *dalmatica,* its under tunic of equal length but with close, tight sleeves, and the voluminous mantles, all of fine cloth from Flanders or of rich silks from Italian looms.

In the reign of Henry III, 1216–1272, a garment which appeared first in the time of King John and owed its origin to metal-armoured warriors, attained a place of great prominence. This was the *surcoat,* a full-length garment with very deep armscyes, which was worn over a tunic that had either tight sleeves or loose, flowing ones. The belt which held these garments was of leather with a buckle and long tongue. Warm fur linings, marten, beaver, badger, squirrel or sable, distinguished the capacious circular cloak of silk or cloth. At this period, too, the *capuchon,* or hood, made its appearance in the realm of English costume. It was attached to a short cape that fitted well down over the chest, arms, and back. The pointed-toed shoes that had existed for such a brief time in the twelfth century were finally accepted by all men of fashion. The tights of the period were close-fitting, and made of cloth or silk carefully shaped to the leg.

The use of heraldic devices in civilian costume grew apace, the

Fig. 86. Edward II. Monumental Brass Showing the Flowing Robes of the Period. The National Portrait Gallery.

surcoats worn under Edward I, 1272–1307, being frequently entirely covered with those distinguishing marks of nobility. This idea probably led to the custom of clothing one half of the body in a different color from the other half, a fashion which was very marked at this time on the Continent, and which was more fully developed in England in the time of Edward III, 1327–1337.

FIG. 87. CHAUCER. A FACSIMILE OF AN ILLUSTRATION IN THE BRITISH MUSEUM. The Bettmann Archive.

From the monumental brasses of the fourteenth century are derived most authentic representations of the costume of the time. These frequently depict the *cote-hardie*, a close, coat-like garment that extended about to the knees, was held at the waist by a belt, and buttoned down the front. The close sleeves ended at the elbow in a long hanging strip that fell down the back. This garment was always accompanied by long tights of cloth or silk with one leg of a different colour from the other.[4]

The rather fantastic effect given by these two garments was considerably heightened by the shoes and the hood. The former, of dark leather, were buttoned up the front and had decided points at the toes; the latter had a very long strip of cloth, *liripipe*, that replaced the former peak of the attached hood. The bottom edge of the hood or *capuchon*, was frequently cut in scallops or points. To increase still further the ludicrous effect, a hat of beaver with upturned brim, tall crown, and upstanding feather was perched on top of the hood.

The long circular mantles were the only articles of the flowing, draped costume of the early Plantagenet days that had not suc-

---

[4] COTMAN, J. S., ENGRAVINGS OF SEPULCHRAL BRASSES IN NORFOLK AND SUFFOLK, 1839, H. G. Bohn.

cumbed to the abbreviated styles. One type that persisted was circular in cut with edges dagged or slashed, and was fastened on the shoulders by buttons. A hood was attached.[5]

Under Richard II, 1377–1399, the king who had a passion for fine clothes, and led his courtiers in all matters of dress, a new garment was launched. This was the *peliçon*, or *houppelande*, as it was termed in France. The extremely high, bell-shaped collar and the long, full sleeves with dagged edges were the noteworthy features of the full-length robe. It was buttoned its entire length from collar to hem, or for a few inches only down from the collar, slashed from hem to knee at one side, and at times lined with fur. At the waist it was girt by a narrow belt of leather that had one long end falling down the front.[6] The head covering that accompanied this costume was a turban with a cloth crown whose dagged ends that hung slightly over the edge clearly betrayed its descent from the cloth *capuchon* of other days.

The points of the shoes, *crakowes*, increased to a length of six inches, and were stuffed or wired into the desired shape. Clogs of wood, with long, pointed toes were worn in inclement weather to protect the fine material of the shoes.

From a ribbon or chain at the waist or neck hung a finely tempered steel dagger. The dandies of the age sallied forth with huge rings on their fingers and massive gold chains about their necks. Their hair was worn long.

Feminine dress of the Plantagenet Period.—On the whole the women's dress of this entire period, was marked by extreme simplicity of cut, though with steadily growing richness of material. The loose, comfortably fitting gown with which the reign of Henry II opened, had bands of rich embroidery about the neck and the hem of the long skirt and a belt of silk or leather with a handsome buckle and long tongue in imitation of those encircling the waists of the men. The sleeves fitted closely from the elbow down, extended well below the wrists, and were fastened by a row of buttons. From 1350 to 1380 all women of fashion were to be seen with *tippets* at their elbows. These were long strips of cloth or fur

---

[5] MARTIN, CHARLES, CIVIL COSTUME OF ENGLAND, plate 17. 1842, H. G. Bohn.

[6] *Ibid.*, plate 19.

fastened to the sleeves just above the elbow. They hung down to below the wearer's knee.

During the last quarter of the thirteenth century another dress with wide, short sleeves and long train was frequently worn over the first one, and when, during the reign of Edward II, 1307–1327, the men adopted the *surcoat*, the women followed suit and in winter placed over their gowns the sleeveless *surcoat* with its fur trimmings and elaborate buttons down its narrow front.

From the time of Henry III, 1216–1272, the *aumônière*, a bag of cloth or silk, hung at the left hand side of the belt.

Throughout the entire period of the Plantagenet kings the woman's mantle was a simple affair, a long cloak left quite open in front and secured across the chest with silken cords attached to rich metal fasteners. In the fourteenth century additional warmth was obtained by having the cloaks lined throughout with fur; the *houppelande*, adopted in the time of Richard II, was very similar to that which prevailed among the men.

Soft leather was employed for the shoes, cut to fit the feet closely, and with points that were not quite so exaggerated as those found on the shoes of the men. A variety of fastenings, lacings, buckles, and buttons were then in use.

More changes took place in this period in hair-dressing and head-dresses than in any other part of the costume. During the latter part of the twelfth century and well into the reign of Edward I, all women followed the custom of concealing the hair under a *wimple*. Two bands of white linen were folded lengthwise; one was place over the forehead and pinned at the back of the head; one placed under the chin and pinned together on top. Over all another piece of linen was arranged to fall gracefully over the sides and back of the head.[7] Under Henry III the women parted the hair gathering it at the sides of the head "into an embroidered cloth, and sometimes covering that with a silk net having jewels at the intersections of the meshes. Over this is frequently found a veil . . . called the *couvre chef*." [8] The succeeding reign saw the advent of the *gorget*, a strip of fine linen wound several times about the throat and the ends fastened to the hair above the ears. Some-

---

[7] COTMAN, J. S., ENGRAVINGS OF SEPULCHRAL BRASSES IN NORFOLK AND SUFFOLK, Vol. I, p. XXV. 1839, H. G. BOHN.

[8] *Ibid.*, p. XXIV.

what later the fillet was added to this hair covering, which in turn was superseded by the *nebule* head-dress consisting of stiff wire cages, one on each side of the head joined together by a decorative band that crossed the forehead and in which the parted and braided hair was confined. For out-of door wear this arrangement was covered by the *capuchon*. Handsome gloves and massive rings were as much favored by the women as by the men.

The Costumes of the House of Lancaster, 1399–1461.—On the whole but slight changes were made in English dress for many years. The Lancastrian rulers, Henry IV, Henry V, and Henry VI, and their gentlemen, were too fully occupied with their wars both at home and in France to do more than carry the dress of their fathers to a higher degree of exaggeration. The *houppelande* was as long and as ample as formerly but its fullness was carefully laid in regular plaits; its collar grew somewhat higher about the neck. Besides the long and dagged ones a new sleeve appeared and was much worn after the close of the fourteenth century. This was termed the "bag" sleeve, full at the top to below the elbow, gradually narrowing from there down to the wrist where it was gathered into a deep cuff or a plain, simple band. This type of sleeve was found in both the long and the short forms of the *houppelande*.

Parti-colored costume grew in favor, no gentleman appearing with both legs of his tights of the same hue; even the shoes were of unlike color. The colorful cloths, silks, and velvets, from which the clothes were fashioned were covered with geometric designs.

A new development in men's headgear appeared during the time of Henry VI, 1422–1481, in the form of the *roundlet*. This was a small, round hat with a stiffened, rolling brim, a draped crown, and a broad streamer of the same fabric as the rest of the hat falling over the side. Other hats commonly found in these same years were the turban and the sugar loaf hat, both of which appeared in the reign of Henry V, and on certain occasions, the hood. Short hair became the fashion and for many years was cut close to the head. Men of the period wore a curious accessory, the *baldrick*, a long loop of cloth or leather hung with many small bells, that was placed over the left shoulder and fell diagonally across the person, front and back to the right knee. This was later succeeded by a belt hung with bells across the front. The custom of wearing the *baldrick* "was introduced from Germany where it had been prevalent for many years." [9]

Women of the Lancasters.—Although the women under the last ruler of the House of Lancaster, Henry VI, 1422–1461, adopted the new type gown, short-waisted, and long-skirted, so much in vogue among French ladies of the time, they seemed to concentrate their attention and ingenuity on new forms of head-dresses, receiving ideas, doubtless, from the *hennins* that were so popular on the Continent. Events in Turkey and the long-awaited fall of Constantinople in 1453 gave an Oriental tinge to thoughts on head-dress. Wire was bent into all manner of fanciful shapes as the support for horn, turban, and box-like contrivances that extended many inches above the head of the fair wearer, and from the back of which waved veils of fair linen.

Dress under the House of York, 1461–1485.—The two outstanding features that mark the masculine dress of the years between the House of Lancaster and that of Tudor, and bridged the period between the close of the Middle Ages and the opening years of the Renaissance, were the increasing shortness of the tunics or doublets, and the manner in which those garments were cut to display the rich fabric of the garment worn directly beneath. The long *houppelande*, with but little dagging, was retained by the elderly; the young scions of fashion adopting the new doublet that reached scarcely below the waist, had large sleeves caught at the wrist, and a very widely-cut V neck in front. This deep opening was laced but showed to advantage the bright silk waistcoat beneath, above the top of which protruded a small fluted edging of the linen shirt. The sleeves of the doublet had a broad oval cut lengthwise through their center, were banded with fur, and laced across the opening which revealed the sleeves of the undervest. Broad shoulders and small waists were quite the mode.

Under the York régime there was less use of parti-color than formerly, and the points of the shoes were by law less than two inches in length becoming in the late years of the reign of Richard III rather blunt and square. These shoes received the descriptive name of *duckbills*. Tall boots were becoming fashionable. The

---

[9] ASHDOWN, MRS. C. H., BRITISH COSTUME DURING NINETEEN CENTURIES, p. 139. Used by permission of the publishers, Thomas Nelson and Sons.

tights remained close-fitting, being fastened to the doublets by
points, ribbons tipped with metal.

Hats showed a variety of forms: caps of black velvet with rolling
brims; tall, sugar loaf hats; or high-crowned ones with close brims

FIG. 88. RICHARD III. JEWELRY AND FINE FABRICS WERE MUCH
IN EVIDENCE DURING THE REIGN OF THIS MONARCH. The National
Portrait Gallery.

of fur. The hair was permitted to grow to the nape of the neck and
stand out in quite a bushy manner from the head.

Feminine Fashions of the Yorks.—The steeple or cone-shaped
hennin with its pendant veil was the outstanding feature of the
woman's costume. Every hair was concealed under the stiff con-

trivance, only a small circle of black velvet, the frontlet, at its base breaking the broad expanse of the forehead. It was under the York rulers that a "sumptuary law was passed which permitted only the wives and daughters of persons having possessions of the yearly value of £10 to use and wear frontlets of black velvet, or any other cloth or silk of a black color."[10]

In accordance with the seeming distaste for change the gown was in cut like that worn in the preceding period with the slight addition of turned-back cuffs and broad band at the bottom of the long skirt.

REFERENCES

ZUR GESCHICHTE DER KOSTÜME, plates 463, 1119
MEYRICK AND SMITH, COSTUME OF THE ORIGINAL INHABITANTS OF THE BRITISH ISLANDS.
MACKLIN, THE BRASSES OF ENGLAND.
LONSDALE AND TARVER, ILLUSTRATIONS OF MEDIÆVAL COSTUME IN ENGLAND
PLANCHÉ, BRITISH COSTUME.
MARTIN, CIVIL COSTUME OF ENGLAND.
ASHDOWN, BRITISH COSTUME, pp. 1–195.
CALTHROP, ENGLISH COSTUME, pp. 1–213.
CLINCH, ENGLISH COSTUME, pp. 1–68.
FAIRHOLT, COSTUME IN ENGLAND, pp. 1–182.
HILL, HISTORY OF ENGLISH DRESS, Vol. I, pp. 1–157.
CHAUCER, THE CANTERBURY TALES.
SHAW, DRESSES AND DECORATIONS OF THE MIDDLE AGES.
STRUTT, DRESS AND HABITS OF THE PEOPLE OF ENGLAND.
PARSONS, PSYCHOLOGY OF DRESS, pp. 33–46.
ADAMS, CIVILIZATION DURING THE MIDDLE AGES.
BOAS AND HAHN, SOCIAL BACKGROUNDS OF ENGLISH LITERATURE, Chaps. I–V.
ABRAM, ENGLISH LIFE AND MANNERS IN THE LATE MIDDLE AGES.
WRIGHT, DOMESTIC MANNERS AND SENTIMENTS.

---

[10] ASHDOWN, MRS. C. H., BRITISH COSTUME DURING NINETEEN CENTURIES, p. 187. Used by permission of the publishers, Thomas Nelson and Sons.

CHAPTER XI

COSTUME OF TUDOR ENGLAND

Field of the Cloth of Gold, 1520
Fall of Wolsey, 1530
Sir Francis Drake circumnavigates
the globe, 1580
Sir Walter Raleigh in America, 1585
Spanish Armada, 1588

Holbein, 1497–1543
Spenser, 1552–1599
Sidney, 1554–1586
Marlowe, 1565–1593
Shakespeare, 1564–1616
Ben Jonson, 1573–1637

The Tudors, 1485–1603.—Dress under the Tudors, who maintained a magnificent style of living and were imitated by the great and powerful families of the realm, reflected all the elegance of color and texture which we have always associated with the Renaissance costume on the Continent. Rich, plain silks, large figured brocades, velvets, and cloth of gold were imported from Italy and the Orient, and jewelry took on greater brilliancy of coloring and massiveness in general design and effect.

The dandies surrounding the court of the first of the Tudors, Henry VII, 1485–1509, gave greater emphasis to the linen shirt. It was gathered about the neck into fine plaits and enriched with embroideries in black and white threads, showing to marked advantage above the top of the new stomacher. This last mentioned article of dress was a piece of beautifully patterned fabric, the floral design frequently outlined with threads of gold, extending from chest to waist where it was laced or tied to the long tights. It was worn under the close-fitting doublet at the front of which, and through whose sleeves, its beauty was plainly visible. The doublet, though close-fitting, retained the skirt of the old former tunic, of which it was clearly a development, and was held by a narrow sash. Its close sleeves were laced into the armscye, and extended approximately to the elbow depending on the sleeve of the linen shirt to cover the arm from there to the wrist.

The long cloak of the Yorks was retained but considerably changed. Its sleeves became two long cylinders of cloth with lengthwise openings for each arm; the high collar was transformed into a broad square one that extended down the fronts as broad

131

revers of silk or of fur. Many men preferred a shorter version of the long coat, termed *petti-cote*.

The broad velvet hat was found in two main styles: one in which the brim was turned up and pinched into four corners; the other worn over a close cap had a broad brim heavy with backward

FIG. 89. HENRY VIII. COMPARE THE COSTUME OF THIS RULER WITH THAT OF FRANCIS I OF FRANCE (FIG. 31). Courtesy of the Metropolitan Museum.

turning feathers. Men's hair was worn flowing to the shoulders until Francis I of France set the fashion for close-cropped hair.

Velvet and rich leather were fashioned into blunt-toed shoes which showed the beginning of the craze for slashings and puffings that reached so great a height under Henry VIII, 1509–1547.

Broad, and large of stature, bluff king Hal gave a breadth to the silhouette that it had never before possessed. The full, knee-length skirts of the doublet were balanced by its large, bulky sleeves, and those of the jerkin, the latter a long or a short overcoat of rich materials with huge collar and lapels. The breeches, generally hidden by the skirt of the doublet, shared with that garment the puffings and slashings which were so common at the time, and originated, it is said, in Switzerland. The slashes were fanciful in shape. Through them small puffs of lining or the material of the garment were drawn to give what was known as the "blistered effect." The brim of the flat velvet hat was bent to give as square a contour as possible to the head. At times a small white plume was laid across the front in the French manner.

Mary Tudor, 1553–1558.—Queen Mary's marriage in 1554 to Philip of Spain caused the adoption in British costume of a few of the Spanish modes. In general these consisted of a closer fit to the doublet; a small ruff added to the neck of the shirt, a jaunty circular cape that fell to slightly below the waist, and a pointed beard. The hat brought over by the Spaniards and contemporary with the tall, stiff-crowned hat of English origin, was in reality a circle of velvet stiffened and gathered into a narrow brim of the same material. Shoes were cut more like the natural shape of the foot than formerly and covered the instep.

Elizabeth, 1558–1603.—With the accession of Elizabeth came a period familiar to all. Almost every school child knows the type of dress in which Sir Francis Drake sailed the high seas, can describe the jaunty cape that Sir Walter Raleigh cast at the feet of his sovereign, and speaks glibly of jerkin and ruff. The cape of that gay, gallant courtier was doubtless of the Spanish type with high standing collar, while his doublet may have favored the Italian cut of very close body, with small skirt, really a mere peplum below his belted waist. This type of doublet was padded and boned in front to give it the celebrated outward curve or "peascod" shape. Its sleeves were close, long, and slashed, and laced with metal-tipped ties to the armscye which was outlined with a padded roll or overhanging epaulet.

In 1562, one of the laws with which Elizabeth delighted to curb the growing love of her subjects for finery, of domestic as well as foreign manufacture, limited the amount of kersey for each pair of breeches to one and three quarter yards. Later, however, when the Venetian styles were whole-heartedly adopted, these nether garments were very full at the top, close at the knee, and profusely slashed, puffed, and padded. The trunks that vied with the Venetian breeches were very short, extremely full, and padded to stand out from the wearer's body. The stockings accompanying them were of silk, or of wool, gartered elaborately about the knee.

Fig. 90.   Robert Dudley, Earl of Leicester.   Zuccaro.   The "Peascod" Doublet.   The National Portrait Gallery.

The ruff of Elizabethan times was an enormous affair stiffened with yellow starch, though equally popular was the collar of thin white linen that extended over the high collar of the doublet. The hair was in general worn rather long and brushed back from the face, the beard retaining its pointed shape. Round or flat hats with soft crowns, narrow brims, and feathers were the universally accepted headgear, though this reign saw the advent of the tall-crowned and wide-brimmed hat that was so distinctive of the Jacobean period. Then, too, appeared for men of wealth hats of beaver.

Women of the Early Tudors.—Simplicity and dignity of cut distinguished the dress of the early Tudor women who employed the rich silks from Bruges and Italy for their long, fitted princess robes with the neck no longer a deep V shape but a broad square outlined with bands of embroidery. As a rule the sleeves were close-fitting at the top and quite wide at the elbow and hand. The gowns that were cut very long in the skirt were usually lifted to show the costly material of the underdress or the fur with which the gowns were sometimes lined. When belts were worn they were of elaborate workmanship as were the heavy necklaces and rings worn alike by men and women. The cloaks that covered this somewhat voluminous gown were necessarily full and ample in cut, and had very open sleeves.

In the pictures by Holbein, who left so many delightful records of English dress of the early Tudor period, we see the skirt of the gown was later open in front from hem to waist to display the gorgeous petticoat stretched over its bell-shaped hoop, and the bodice was lined and padded to give a severely plain, stiff effect. Above the square neck appeared the dainty, embroidered chemise, and later the elaborate *partlet*, or tucker of fine linen that filled in the very low neck.

Sleeves were commonly extremely wide at the elbow with broad bands of fur or velvet emphasizing their size; below were close undersleeves of handsome fabric elaborately "blistered" with slashings and puffings.

The head-dress, known by the various names, *pyramidal*, *kennel*, *pedimental*, and *angular*, rendered so familiar to us on playing cards, was at first an extremely simple affair growing during the reign of Henry VIII into a stiff, elaborate and bejeweled creation. Over the parted hair was first placed a simple white hood or coif; this was in turn covered with one of black silk, velvet, or embroidered cloth, that hung over the sides and back of the head and was stiffened in front in such a way that it stood out

from the inner coif in the shape of a tent or sloping roof. There
were strings attached to the sides so that the latter could be tied
back from the neck. This last arrangement soon led to a sewing
of the side pieces permanently in place. Of course with such an
arrangement just a bit of the hair was visible in the front.

Under Mary the head-dress lost its stiffness and elaboration
becoming a simple black velvet cap set rather far back on the head

FIG. 91. LADY GUILFORD. HOLBEIN. FEMININE HEAD-
DRESS AND NECK LINE OF THE PERIOD OF HENRY VIII.
Courtesy of the Metropolitan Museum.

to expose more of the puffed and parted hair, and with a downward falling peak over the forehead. A strip of velvet hung from
the back of the cap.

The most marked change that took place in the gown was in
the neck. The bodice was cut high and the collar opened just
below the throat, spreading out in two points at the sides and
across the back like a fan of fair linen.

Under the Virgin Queen dress took on greater elaboration,

stiffness, and formality.   The foundation consisted of a formidable corset of leather and whalebone, and a huge wheel of whalebone, the *farthingale*, or hoop, that encircled the body just below
the normal waistline.   Over this firm foundation were placed

Fig. 92.   Margaret Wyatt, Lady Lee.   Holbein.   The V-shape
Neckline and Small Collar Commonly Worn in the Time of Queen
Mary.   Courtesy of the Metropolitan Museum.

several petticoats, a linen chemise, and two gowns, the outer one
resembling that of somewhat earlier fashions but with the enormous starched ruff with which we have become familiar in the
costumes of the French.   Cambric and lawn, plain or edged with

heavy lace were the materials usually employed for this neck-wear;[1] an underprop of wire being necessary for the support of the ruff of extremely large circumference. Hanging sleeves of the same material as the overdress were laced into the armscye of the dress giving full play to the long sleeves of the underdress.

Fig. 93. Queen Elizabeth. Heere. An Example of the Elaborate Costume Favored by the Virgin Queen. Courtesy of the Metropolitan Museum.

The cap popular in the time of Queen Mary, and known as the Mary Stuart cap, or a shallow-brimmed, stiff hat, was worn by most Elizabethan women. With all, the hair, dyed in imitation of the golden locks of the queen, was frizzed, curled, and dressed high on the head to accommodate the wide-spreading and en-

[1] Strutt, Joseph, Dress and Habits of the People of England, Vol. II, p. 146. Henry G. Bohn.

veloping ruff. Jeweled pins, strings of pearls and chains of gold were used for the elaboration of the coiffure.

Among the possessions of every Elizabethan lady were small looking glasses that hung from her girdle; scented gloves heavy

FIG. 94. HENRY FREDERICK, PRINCE OF WALES. Courtesy of the Metropolitan Museum of Art.

with embroidery; small handkerchiefs of lace or of silk edged with passamenterie; masks which were quite customarily worn on the street or at the theatre; and flag-shaped fans, either carried in the hand or suspended from the girdle.

Although Elizabeth has been popularly accredited with the

wearing of the first silk stockings in England, history records a gift of hand knitted silk ones by Sir Thomas Gresham to Edward VI.[2] In order to protect their dainty velvet and satin slippers from the mud of the streets, English women readily adopted the Italian custom of wearing *chopines.* These were shoes with soles of cork anywhere from two to seven inches thick. Besides affording protection to the perishable footwear, *chopines* had the additional advantage of adding several inches to the stature of the wearer.

FIG. 95. MARY QUEEN OF SCOTS AND HER SON. Courtesy of the Metropolitan Museum.

English Children's Costumes of the Sixteenth Century.—Children of sixteenth century England, like their contemporaries on the Continent, were weighted and encumbered with the heavy, luxurious, and magnificent fabrics and jewels that played such a conspicuous rôle in the pageantry of fashion of that period. Portraits of royal children indicate that they were garbed in the costly materials considered suitable to their exalted station, while those of lesser rank were doubtless provided with the best permitted by the circumstances and position of their parents.

[2] *Ibid.,* p. 149.

The outstanding features of the adult costume of the age were found in the wardrobes of the children; the ruff, lace trimmed and starched; the sleeves, slashed and puffed; the skirt distended by small vertugales; the breeches, short and puffed; diminutive doublets; and chains for neck and waist, heavy and jeweled. This elaborate costume was worn by children of distinguished families whenever occasion required.

REFERENCES

PLANCHÉ, BRITISH COSTUME.
CLINCH, ENGLISH COSTUME, pp. 18–92.
HUGHES, DRESS DESIGN, pp. 109–139.
CALTHROP, ENGLISH COSTUME, pp. 223–325.
HILL, HISTORY OF ENGLISH DRESS, Vol. I, pp. 165–245.
FAIRHOLT, COSTUME IN ENGLAND, pp. 182–234.
PARSONS, PSYCHOLOGY OF DRESS, pp. 125–148.
ASHDOWN, BRITISH COSTUME, pp. 195–265.
STEPHENSEN, THE ELIZABETHAN PEOPLE.
INNES, ENGLAND UNDER THE TUDORS.
BOAS AND HAHN, SOCIAL BACKGROUNDS OF ENGLISH LITERATURE, Chap. V
Paintings by HOLBEIN.

CHAPTER XII

ENGLISH COSTUME UNDER THE STUARTS

East India Company, 1600
Gunpowder Plot, 1605
The Commonwealth Proclaimed, 1649
The Great Plague, 1665
The Great Fire in London, 1666

Milton, 1608–1674
Lely, 1618–1680
Fox, 1624–1691
Dryden, 1631–1700
Pepys, 1633–1703
Pope, 1688–1744

Masculine Jacobean Modes—James I, 1603–1625.—In the pageantry of English fashions we see the Jacobean men in a costume that in a measure may be considered a transition between the slashed, puffed modes of the Renaissance and that elegant, rather careless dress of the time of Charles I. In the dress of the first quarter of the seventeenth century there were fewer slashes and more padding than in that of the average Elizabethan masculine costume. The breeches were loose but covered the knee where they were fastened with buttons or a sash of ribbon. Rosettes of lace or of ribbon soon appeared at the instep of the red-heeled shoe. A stiff beaver hat with one white plume standing saucily up the back of the tall crown topped the hair that fell half way down the neck.

Charles I, 1625–1649.—The many records of the costume of the second quarter of the seventeenth century left by Anthony Van Dyck, the court painter of Charles I, are so well known that only a brief description is necessary here. In his paintings Van Dyck has indicated clearly the color and texture that prevailed in costume; gleaming satin being apparently a favorite fabric for the doublet, breeches and loose wrap of the men, as well as for the handsome gowns of the women.

The longer of the two styles of doublet that were characteristic of this period, reached well over the hips, and was left unbuttoned to show the fine linen shirt. The shorter doublet exposed the shirt about the waist as well as in front. With both types, the falling band, a turned back collar, variously termed Van Dyck or Louis XIII, was the neck finish required by the long curling locks that fell over the shoulders. The usual sleeve

142

was a long, fairly full one, with either a few slashes or one long one from top to wrist showing the full sleeves of the linen shirt. Falling back from the hand were cuffs edged with the same lace that comprised the decoration of the falling band.

Breeches were either the full but unpadded ones fashionable under James I, or the straight, hanging ones unconfined at the knee but finished with a fringe-like decoration of ribbon loops. This latter cut, deprived of the decorations, was customarily worn in the Commonwealth period, 1649–1660.

Boots were of many varied heights and shapes. In general the tops of the flaring ones were lined with silk and filled in with lace and linen. Some had turned-down cuffs of leather or of lace. All, even the square-toed shoe, had generously high heels and large rosettes of ribbon at the instep. Ribbon played as important a rôle in English dress of the seventeenth century as it did in contemporary Continental costume. Bunches of bright ribbons were sewn to sleeves or waists of the doublets, and at the sides and knees of the breeches, the color being the same as the garment, black,

FIG. 96. CHARLES I OF ENGLAND IN 1629. MYTENS. A FALLING RUFF. Courtesy of the Metropolitan Museum.

white or some delicate hue. Ribbon was also used to hold the long lovelocks in their places, at one side or on both sides of the head. Great bunches were tied at the top of the long gold or ivory-headed cane.

Large watches were commonly used under the Stuarts, and a less useful fashion started with Charles I, that of wearing one costly pearl in the left ear. All of the hats were feathered, though some had much narrower brims than others.

The small moustache and the pointed beard were typical, the latter so well known to us as the Van Dyck beard.

The Commonwealth, 1649–1660.—Under the Cromwells dress was stripped of much of its charm: fabrics were somber in color and unpretentious in texture; ribbons, points, and furbelows were thrown aside, while the former curls of the men were shorn close to the head, and those of the women demurely concealed under simple caps or hoods of black silk. Lace was removed from collars which remained wide for a time but later shrunk to half of their former dimensions.

The Restoration— Charles II, 1660–1685.— With the return of the Stuarts to the throne of England, the stage was set for an era of great luxuriousness and extravagance in dress. The men and women who were ruled by the laws of fashion were surfeited with ten years of quiet, sober dressing; the young king, Charles II, reared in exile amid the extravagant surroundings of the brilliant court of Louis XIV, naturally brought with him on his return to England the styles with which he was familiar in France.

FIG. 97. WILLIAM BEDFORD, FIRST DUKE OF BEDFORD. KNELLER. RIBBON AS DECORATION OF THE RHINGRAVES. The National Portrait Gallery.

We may picture, then, the king and his cavaliers clothed in short doublets, much like the modern Eton jackets, displaying generously the fine linen shirt bloused about the waist; in full, be-ribboned *rhingraves* (page 63); in low, square-toed shoes with high red heels, and stiff ends of ribbon at the instep; with long stockings of bright silk and a jeweled ribbon garter about the right knee; and in broad-brimmed stiff hats with a profusion of feathers. Below this becoming hat the Cavalier's periwig fell in carefully arranged curls well over the shoulder. About his throat was the linen cravat with its ends of exquisite lace, and in his gloved hand was held the usual cane.

The year 1666 saw the advent of a new garment which in modified form has persisted in men's costume until the present. This was a straight, collarless coat buttoned from neck to knees where it ended, and girdled by a wide sash with fringed ends. Its short sleeves were close and finished with deep, turned back cuffs below which extended the lace ruffles of the shirt sleeves. This coat was introduced by Charles II who was much impressed by a Persian coat that had been brought to his attention. Accompanying the coat were full breeches that fitted at the knee, and a long waistcoat that showed only when the coat itself was left partly unbuttoned, a fashion that was more marked in the time of William and Mary, 1689–1702.

Variation of detail rather than striking changes in cut took place in the times of James II and of Mary, the wife of William of Orange. The coats became slightly more fitted, the sleeves longer and the cuffs larger, in some instances as wide as eighteen inches and held up by two or three buttons and buttonholes. With the opening and spreading of the coat, the waistcoat with its pockets came more into prominence and the breeches grew correspondingly smaller. The outer wrap was a large, full cloak, called the *roquelaure*. By the last decade of the century, the periwig had grown to such an extent that the cavalier was so unwilling to disturb his scented, powdered locks that he adopted the French custom of carrying his upturned hat under his arm. Under Queen Anne, 1702–1714, the enormous periwig disappeared, its place being taken by a curious wig, the *ramilie*, named in honor of the victory of the Duke of Marlborough on the battlefield of Ramilies, 1706. In this head-dress the powdered hair protruded in a series of puffs at the side of the head, the back hair being gathered into a long braid secured at top and bottom by a large bow of black ribbon.

On the shoes, buckles were substituted for the ribbons which had had their day and were gradually disappearing from the entire costume.

FIG. 98. MARY SIDNEY, COUNTESS OF PEMBROKE. GHEERAEDTS, 1614. RICH LACE AND DECORATIVE TEXTILE. The National Portrait Gallery.

Women's Costume of the Jacobean Period.—Elizabeth, the last of the Tudor rulers, bequeathed to the woman of the early years of the seventeenth century a costume that was eccentric, grotesque, and judging from the portraits of the time, most uncom-

FIG. 99. GEORGE VILLIERS, FIRST DUKE OF BUCKINGHAM, AND FAMILY IN THE COSTUMES FASHIONABLE IN JACOBEAN ENGLAND. THE National Portrait Gallery.

fortable and unhygienic. The new reign, however, saw the last of the huge ruff and the disfiguring farthingale. The former was soon replaced by a flaring collar of wired lace or cambric, dyed in sundry colors, and rising from the neck of the low-cut gown and spreading fan-like about the head. The latter still persisted for a few years with the addition of the great oddity of the period, a box-plaited

ruff of the same fabric of the gown tied about the waist and supported by the flat-topped *farthingale* or hoop. From waist to hem the skirt of the dress was open in front to show the satin petticoat, both skirts being short enough to expose the instep and dainty lace rosette of the shoe. The bodice was of its usual cylindrical shape with the sleeves tight from shoulder to elbow, falling from there in long streamers down the back, the under sleeves finished at the wrist with ruffs or turned back cuffs of cambric or lace.

Jacobean women forsook completely the caps of old and started the fashion of wearing hats. With little ingenuity and lack of experience in this matter they imitated the headgear of the

Fig. 100. Henrietta, Queen of Charles I. Van Dyck? The National Portrait Gallery.

men and set upon their high dressed hair stiff and be-plumed hats.

Rich necklaces and many strings of pearls were suspended about the neck. The new and dainty folding fan replaced the feather fan and the flag-shaped one that had held its place for such a long time in the history of accessories.

Women's Dress of the Time of Charles I.—Henrietta Maria, wife of Charles I and daughter of Henri IV and Marie de Medici of France, exerted a very beneficial influence on English women's dress. Under her leadership the farthingales with all other stiffening devices, except the corset, were discarded. The skirts hung straight to the floor from a raised waist line, or were open in front and looped back very slightly displaying an untrimmed underskirt.

The falling collar was similar to that worn by the men though of larger size. At the elbow a small puff of cambric or a frill of lace met the soft, full sleeve that was devoid of any trace of stiffening, while the waist line of the bodice was encircled with a peplum cut into tabs. The short sleeves of the bodice led naturally to long gloves, and soon there appeared large muffs of fur or velvet and silk combined with fur. Patches became fashionable with the rouged, powdered beauties of the day, and short strings of pearls were worn to enhance their white throats. Fans were carried.

For wraps the Stuart women adopted circular capes, long or short, lined with fur, or loose, round Dutch jackets both lined and edged with fur.

FIG. 101. A DRAWING BY WENCELAUS HOLLAR SHOWING THE DRESS OF AN ENGLISH GENTLEWOMAN IN THE YEAR 1639
From Or..atus Mulieb-i .

Women's Dress after the Restoration.—Katherine of Portugal, the wife of Charles II, failed in her attempts to reintroduce the ruff and hoop still being worn in her homeland, finding the French modes of Henrietta too well entrenched to be dislodged at the time. Until the reign of William and Mary it was a development of the earlier Stuart dress that prevailed at court. Gone, however, were the falling collars, the deep, open neck being entirely unrelieved until well in the reign of James II when a deep collar of some sheer fabric was pinned about the shoulder. The short sleeves of the gown were slit from the shoulder down and their edges tied together with bows of ribbon of contrasting color. An undersleeve of white prevented the bare arm from showing through the slit, and ended in flattering ruffles at the elbow. The skirt was slightly lifted or puffed about the small waist in order to show the beauty of the satin petticoat.

A modification of the hair arrangement made popular by the French favorite, Ninon de L'Enclos, was in vogue in the years when

FIG. 102. THE DUCHESS OF PORTS-MOUTH. LELY. NOTE THE EXTREME POINT OF THE WAISTLINE AND THE SIZE OF THE UNDERSLEEVES.

FIG. 103. THE CHILDREN OF CHARLES I. MINIATURE REPLICAS OF THE ADULT COSTUMES OF THE PERIOD.

Courtesy of the Metropolitan Museum.

Charles II and James II occupied the throne. Reflecting the sentiment of the age, the long locks of hair falling at the sides of the head over the ears were designated "heart-breakers"; the few curls about the forehead, as "favorites."

Feminine head coverings consisted of the same type of stiff, plumed hats as was worn by the men. The women also followed the custom of carrying the hat under the arm so as not to disarrange the curls piled high on the head and the tall erection of ribbon and lace known in England as the *commode*, and in France as the *Fontanges.* Forming part of this head-dress were two strips of Brussels or Mechlin lace about three inches wide that fell down both sides of the head to the shoulders, and were known as lappets.

FIG. 104. JAMES STUART AND HIS SISTER LOUISA. LARGILLIÈRE. CHILDREN'S DRESS OF THE LATE SEVENTEENTH CENTURY. The National Portrait Gallery.

Later in the century the skirts were looped up quite high at the sides over the trailing petticoats, the fronts of which were covered with aprons, *pinners,* of black silk, white linen, or lace. The stomacher of the bodice was usually laced across the front with ribbons.

Under Queen Anne the bodice was cut high at the back but very low in front, and the sleeve was robbed of much of its fullness. The petticoat of flowered silk, quilted or plain, acquired two flounces at the bottom and was distended, from about 1710 on, by an under petticoat of canvas stiffened with crosswise strips, hoops, or whalebone.

Children's Dress under the Stuarts.—In his well known portraits of the children of Charles I, of the Princess Mary Henrietta Stuart, and of Elizabeth and Philadelphia Carey, Anthony Van Dyck has left wonderfully faithful records of children's dress in England during the early part of the seventeenth century. The doublet and knee breeches of the young boys duplicated in cut and texture those same features of adult dress existing at the time the portraits were painted, while the accessories—beribboned shoes, gartered hose, gauntlet gloves, and large hat—had all the dash and color of adult styles. The flaring cuffs and broad shoulder collar of rich lace were exactly the same as those that figured so prominently in men's and women's dress of the period. As for the girls, they delighted in very long dresses with tiny, nipped in waists, and low necks that in larger sizes graced the fair forms of their mothers. The clusters of soft curls at each side of the head formed becoming frames for their infantile features, while the choker necklace of glistening pearls and soft lace collar enhanced the delicate skin of neck and shoulders. Quite a charming matronly touch was found in the full, long, and lace-trimmed apron.

A simple, close-fitting cap enriched with delicate embroidery was worn by very young children and infants. The dress of the latter was extremely long, its wee bodice cut with an open neck, and its sleeves in tiny puffs. Hand work of great beauty was its chief ornament. For the first few years of their lives boys were dressed in the long, full skirts of their sisters.

REFERENCES

RACINET, LE COSTUME HISTORIQUE, Vol. V.
CLINCH, ENGLISH COSTUME, pp. 92–115.
ASHDOWN, BRITISH COSTUME, pp. 265–311
FAIRHOLT, COSTUME IN ENGLAND, pp. 234–279.
HILL, HISTORY OF ENGLISH DRESS, Vol. I., pp. 245–322.
HUGHES, DRESS DESIGN, pp. 142–201.
CALTHROP, ENGLISH COSTUME, pp. 325–405.
PLANCHÉ, HISTORY OF BRITISH COSTUME.

STUBBES, ANATOMY OF ABUSES.
PEPYS, DIARY.
PARSONS, PSYCHOLOGY OF DRESS, pp. 175–192.
TREVELYAN, ENGLAND UNDER THE STUARTS.
BOAS AND HAHN, SOCIAL BACKGROUNDS OF ENGLISH LITERATURE.
GODFREY, SOCIAL LIFE UNDER THE STUARTS.
Paintings by VAN DYCK, LELY, KNELLER, DOBSON: engravings by HOLLAR.

CHAPTER XIII

ENGLISH COSTUME IN THE GEORGIAN PERIOD

Capture of Gibraltar, 1704
Union of England and Scotland, 1707
South Sea Bubble, 1720
Battle of Culloden, 1746
Stamp Act, 1765
Invention of spinning jenny by Hargreaves, 1767
Power loom patented by Cartwright, 1785
Invention of cotton gin by Whitney, 1793

Hogarth,	1697–1764
Johnson,	1709–1784
Walpole,	1717–1797
Goldsmith,	1728–1774
Burke,	1730–1797
Arkwright,	1732–1792
Gibbon,	1737–1794
Scott,	1771–1832
Coleridge,	1772–1834

George I, 1714–1727; George II, 1727–1760.—As the early rulers of the House of Hanover were disinclined to lead in fashion and gave but little encouragement to extravagant courtiers, the

Fig. 105.   The Price Family, by Hogarth. Adults and Children Are Dressed in Very Similar Garments,   Courtesy of the Metropolitan Museum.

latter turned for leadership in matters sartorial to the French who at that time were revelling in the luxuries and frivolities of the court of the Regency in France.   Until about the middle of the century both coat and waistcoat retained their generous length, the former gaining additional width by means of plaits inserted at the side seams.   In 1756 the waistcoat curtailed its extra inches

154

below the hips and added lace and fringe of gold thread to its
already decorative fabric. As both garments were buttoned at the
waist only, though still retaining the long row of buttons and
worked buttonholes from top to bottom, a large amount of the shirt
was displayed. This, as a result, was of the finest linen with ruffles
of the choicest Mechlin lace
down its front and at the
wrists. The velvet breeches
were still covered at the knee
by the top of the long, colored
silk stockings that boasted
clocks of gold. The square-
toed shoe with heel of red, so
fashionable in France under
Louis XV, was especially popular with the young bloods
of Old England.

The periwig was not so
ungainly in size as in the early
days of the century, but
parted, puffed, twisted, and
tied in numerous arrange-
ments that bore a variety of
fanciful names. One very popular mode was that known
as the "bag-wig" in which
the end of the curled and be-
powdered wig was securely
tucked and tied into a small
bag of black silk. The hat
was not to be outdone by the
wig, and while in general its
brim, wide or narrow, was up-

Fig. 106. Ralph Schomberg. Gainsborough. An Example of the Elaborate Arrangement of Curls So Commonly Worn in
the Time of the Early Georgian Rulers.
The National Portrait Gallery.

turned, the exact tilt of the cock varied considerably. The
Kevenhuller hat was very large of brim and turned up at
the left-hand side with a rosette of ribbon. Feathers and gold
lace were the accepted trimmings for nearly all the hats of the
period.

Walking sticks three or more feet in length with weirdly carved heads for tops, and gloves of fine scented leather embellished with embroidery and gold lace, imported from southern Europe, were carried by the beaux of the day, while jewel-hilted swords hung at their sides.

George III, 1760–1820.—Continental modes again left their imprint on English gentlemen's dress when the Macaroni Club was founded in 1772 by young scions of fashion, recent travelers in Italy and France. These dandies affected the abbreviated waist-

Fig. 107. Henry Fane and His Guardians. Reynolds. Elaborately Embroidered Waistcoats Were the Order of the Day. Courtesy of the Metropolitan Museum.

coat, cutaway coat, and exaggerated hair dressing that so generally prevailed until the French Revolution. In its most extreme form the hair of the enormous wig was brushed back from the forehead, arranged in two or three crosswise curls above each ear, and the ends gathered into a huge knot at the back of the neck—the whole freely sprinkled with powder. On top of this edifice was perched a diminutive *tricorne* hat. The shoes were much like the present day dancing pumps with valuable buckles of diamonds or of paste. These were discarded about 1793 for sturdy shoes with strong laces. Top boots that reached half-way up the calf of the leg became

FIG. 108. PORTRAIT OF A LADY. RAEBURN. THE FICHU, COLORED SASH
AND LARGE HAT WERE PROMINENT FEATURES IN WOMEN'S DRESS IN ENG-
LAND IN THE LATE EIGHTEENTH CENTURY. The National Portrait Gallery.

Fig. 109. J. J. Angerstein and His Wife. Lawrence. The Charm of English Costume in 1805 Is Well Exemplified in This Portrait. The Louvre.

customary with the new long breeches that were close fitting their entire length and closed at the side above the boot with a row of small buttons.

The Parisian type of coat was cut away widely at the front falling into two long tails at the back, while the collar with the gradual decrease in the size of the wig mounted higher up the neck and assumed, with the simple cravat, a position of great importance. The end of the century saw the downfall of the cocked hat, and the rise of the round one which, with its tall, stiff crown in modified form persisted throughout the nineteenth century.

Early Nineteenth Century Men's Dress.—Simplicity was the keynote of masculine dress after the eventful closing decade of the eighteenth century. On the neckcloth or cravat it was no longer fashionable to have lace; the plain stocks of either white linen or black silk were tied about the throat with a small bow at the front; a jeweled pin was the only touch of luxury, with the exception of his handsome watch, permitted the man of fashion. The natural hair was cut short at the back and sides with slightly longer locks left at the front.

Decided changes took place in several details of both coat and waistcoat. In the former the fronts were cut straight at the waistline, the tails falling from there in an abrupt slanting line. Lapels appeared frequently on this type of coat that was double-breasted and fastened with modish buttons of cut steel, elaborate silver, gilt, or precious metal studded with gems. The waistcoat, likewise, assumed a double-breasted, lapelled cut, showing just above the top of the coat opening. As the years advanced trousers gained in popularity to such an extent that with the next reign the short breeches became, for most occasions quite out of the mode.

George IV, 1820–1830.—During the late years of the Georgian period men as well as women seemed to have been interested in wearing clothes that distorted the natural lines of the body. Long swallow-tail coats, short, double-breasted waistcoats, the former with large lapels of velvet and roll collar, were cut snugly at the waist while a slight increase in size in the top of the sleeve was apparent. The bottom of the sleeve was finished at the back seam with a few buttons or a very shallow turned-back cuff. The greatcoat with its flat pockets retained its double or triple shoulder capes. Extremely important at this time was the crisp, carefully fluted frill down the center of the glistening white shirt front. It extended below the stock that was tied about a high linen collar whose upstanding points rose above the stock.

Subtle niceties of curve and width of brim and slant of the tall crown of hat occupied the attention of the beaux of the years 1820 to 1830 who combed the hair to the front and wore side whiskers. Their foot covering was of several varieties; low slippers for wear in the evening with satin or velvet breeches, or in the day time with ankle-length trousers; buckled or latched shoes for wear with peg-top trousers that were cut very long, with a strap passing under the shoe; top boots of soft leather with upward curving front, or straight, even top.

Fig. 110.   Wilhelmina Caroline, Queen Consort of George II.   Jervas.   The National Portrait Gallery.

Women's Dress of the Period of George I and George II.—The low-cut bodice, the full skirt over a moderate hoop, the long apron, the tiny hat, the black hood and scarf distinguished the woman of the early Georgian period from her predecessors. But moderation did not prevail for long, as soon satirists were busy ridiculing the size of the hoop and the inconvenience it caused its fair wearer. A decade before the middle of the century there appeared the *sacque*, a loose dress that hung in folds from the back of the neck over the hoop, open in the front of the skirt to show the petticoat. The front of the bodice was close-fitting, low in the neck, and short of sleeve. The full cape and large, loose hood donned over this dress were certainly not conducive to slenderness or grace of silhouette.

In regard to the vagaries of feminine head-dress of the early eighteenth century much can be gleaned from the following passage written at the time.   In a letter to the Spectator dated June

FIG. 111.   MRS. ELLIOTT, BY GAINS-BOROUGH.   IMPOSING POWDERED HEAD-DRESS.   Courtesy of the Metropolitan Museum.

FIG. 112.   MRS. MILNES, BY ROMNEY.   AN EXAMPLE OF THE HEAVILY LADEN HAT OF THE LATE EIGHTEENTH CENTURY.   Copyrighted by the Frick Collection.

22, 1711, Addison wrote "There is not so variable a thing in Nature as a Lady's Head-dress: within my own Memory I have know it rise and fall above thirty Degrees.   About ten years ago it shot up to a very great Height, in so much that the Female part of our Species were much taller than the Men.   The Women were of such an enormous Stature that we appeared as Grasshoppers before them."

Feminine Dress in the Time of George III.—By 1770 the above quoted words of Addison were again most applicable for the head-dress of the women had attained a remarkable height, adding two or three feet to the natural stature by means of padding, feathers, and ribbons. About 1789, when the somewhat simpler form of frizzled hair, devoid of the former padding reached its zenith, the feathers and ribbons were merely transferred to the high muslin caps and straw bonnets, no actual diminishing of height being permitted to fashion's devotees.

French modes were faithfully copied, the loose *sacque* succumbing to the *polonaise* with its puffed, festooned sides, whose place as favorite was later, in 1794, usurped by the high waisted dress of unpretentious white muslin or printed calico. With this latter dress the hoop was never worn, and soon disappeared entirely, except in court costume, until the Victorian era.

Feminine dress in the latter years of the reign of George III, paralleling the Napoleonic period and early days of the Restoration in France, may be studied with most illuminating results in the engravings of the influential fashion magazine that was then circulating in England, "*La Belle Assemblée*." On its pages are depicted the great variety of costumes which the belle of the day must wear to be in the height of fashion. "Full dress," "half-full dress," "morning promenade gown," "private concert dress," "public concert dress" and "court dress," are a few of the descriptive titles that accompany the colored plates so eagerly studied by the women and girls of those years in their desire to keep up with the leaders of fashion. From this authoritative source we learn that short waists, puffed sleeves—long or short—low necks, and straight-cut skirts were equally favored by both English and French women (page 91). In studying these engravings one is strongly impressed with the brightness of color in both the shoes and gloves that accompanied the white or light colored dresses. Frequently both were of the same color: jonquil, bright blue, and green were the favorite hues. The penchant for color extended to such other accessories as the long, tasseled or fringed scarf and tiny parasol with its enormously long and slender handle. Lace, fringe, tassels, or ruching edged the parasol that was found in a wide variety of materials and shapes, the pagoda form being much in evidence.

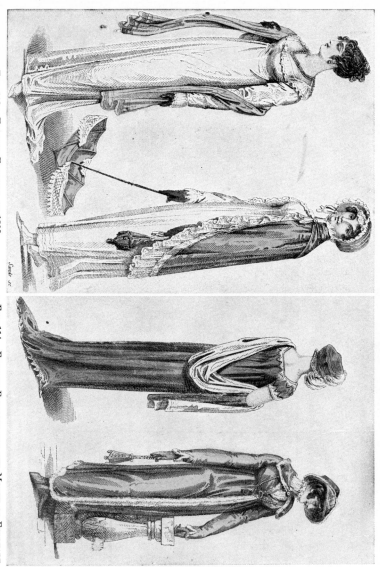

Fig. 113. English Fashions of 1810.

Fig. 114. English Fashions for the Month of February, 1811.

Large, heavy watches were worn, either singly or in pairs in the high-placed belt, while massive ear-rings, necklaces, armlets, and jeweled bands about the head to hold the upstanding plumes above the forehead were requisite for "full dress" and "half-full dress" as well as for other explicitly designated occasions.

Fig. 115. Portrait of a Lady. Beechey. Exemplifying the Simplicity and Charm of Early Nineteenth Century Dress. Courtesy of the Metropolitan Museum.

Ruffs or heavy frills about the neck and shoulders grew into ever greater prominence, while the small bonnet or the one with the poke brim and large feathers and ribbons followed suit. Veils of lace fell from the edge of the brim well down over the face, sometimes extending even to the knees. For wraps the scarf, tiny *spencer*, and long *pelisse* with wrist-length, tight sleeves and broad shoulder collar served according to Milady's choice.

Women's Dress, 1820–1830.—Figured fabrics of increasingly stronger hues began the long period of their popularity during the time of George IV, and with the return of the corset the silhouette began to change. Gone was the classic dress, in its place appearing the one with normal waist line with its defining belt, leg o'mutton sleeve, crosswise flounces, and accompanied by

FIG. 116.   AN ENGLISH WATCH OF THE   FIG. 117.   MISS BARING.   LAWRENCE.
           EIGHTEENTH CENTURY.   ATTRACTIVE RINGLETS AND LOW-CUT NECK-
                                            LINE OF THE LATE GEORGIAN PERIOD.
                   Courtesy of the Metropolitan Museum.

a large brimmed hat with an overgenerous amount of feather, ribbon, and floral trimming. This period marks the beginning of the series of distortions to which the figure and the silhouette of the woman were subjected for approximately the next ninety years.

Children's Dress of the Late Georgian Period.—One must continue to study the portraits of the period for information regarding the costume of children, and from the canvases of the famous English portrait painters of the late eighteenth century one gleans a clear idea of that period's fashions for the younger generation. In general, the dress, at last, considered the needs of childhood to a certain extent: the materials were simpler; the cut such that more freedom was permitted the small limbs; the waists of tiny girls were no longer tortured by the stiff corsets and boned bodices of the earlier, less considerate days. A sash of bright ribbon defined a waist line that was normal and comfortable. The

FIG. 118. LADY SMITH AND HER CHILDREN. REYNOLDS. AN INTERESTING EXAMPLE OF THE SIMPLICITY OF ENGLISH CHILDREN'S COSTUME OF THE LATE EIGHTEENTH CENTURY.

FIG. 119. MRS. GARDNER AND HER CHILDREN. HOPPNER.

Courtesy of the Metropolitan Museum.

thin, white or light colored dresses had skirts that reached just to the ankle and did not interfere with the movements of twinkling young feet. Short sleeves and low-cut bodices offered no impediments to active arms and necks, while the short locks must have saved young heads many hours of anguish under the hands of hair dressers. The following quotation, from a caption under an illustration of a child's costume in *The Gallery of Fashion* for 1797, gives an idea of the materials, colors, and articles in a small girl's costume of the time: "The hair in small curls, plain chignon, cottage cap of fine muslin tied under the chin, trimmed with lace and white satin ribands. Petticoat of muslin richly embroidered at the bottom. Spencer of maroon satin, plain blue cape trimmed with lace. Muslin neckhandkerchief. Fur muff. Red morocco slippers."

In the matter of their clothes young boys were no longer merely miniature men, as the paintings of Gainsborough, Reynolds, Hoppner, Lawrence and Morland show them in very distinctive costume of ankle-length pantaloons, short, double-breasted coat, and broad shoulder collar comfortably open at the throat. Occasionally a broad sash ending in a very large bow was girt about the waist. Although the tall-crowned hat was rather stiff, its brim was wide and shaded the eyes. Light colored hose were customarily worn with buckled slippers—the only part of the costume that bore a slight resemblance to men's dress.

Pantalettes were distinctive of all little girls' costume during the early nineteenth century. Prints from *"La Belle Assemble"* show them with several frills at the ankles, and in colors as well as in white, with dresses of plaid, check, and floral designs in strong colors. When mother was wearing tight, straight belts in 1828 to emphasize the smallness of her waist, small daughter was doing likewise, and encircling her neck and shoulders with a broad frill of white cambric. Crisp white aprons with generously large bibs and two tiny pockets were much in vogue for protecting the wool dresses of young schoolgirls, whose hats for summer were of straw, large of brim, and tied under the chin with narrow ribbons, and whose shoes were of colored leather more frequently than black.

Infants were clothed in white robes with tiny puffed sleeves, low necks, and skirts that were well over a yard in length with panels of grouped or solid tucking, lace, and embroidery of the daintiest design and workmanship. The wee bonnets of similar embroidery possessed crisp frills for framing the tiny features of their infantile wearers.

REFERENCES

RACINET, LE COSTUME HISTORIQUE, Vol. V.
FAIRHOLT, COSTUME IN ENGLAND, pp. 279–309.
HUGHES, DRESS DESIGN, pp. 201–258.
CALTHROP, ENGLISH COSTUME, pp. 406–463.

PRICE, DAME FASHION.

PARSONS, PSYCHOLOGY OF DRESS, pp. 238–264.

BOAS, SOCIAL BACKGROUNDS OF ENGLISH LITERATURE, Chaps. IX, X.

SIDNEY, ENGLAND AND THE ENGLISH IN THE EIGHTEENTH CENTURY.

FISCHEL AND BOEHN, MODES AND MANNERS OF THE NINETEENTH CENTURY.

HOLDEN, ELEGANT MODES IN THE NINETEENTH CENTURY.

LONDON MUSEUM CATALOGUES: COSTUME.

VICTORIA AND ALBERT MUSEUM HANDBOOK: A GUIDE TO THE COLLECTION OF COSTUMES.

Paintings by HOGARTH, REYNOLDS, GAINSBOROUGH, ROMNEY, RAEBURN, LAWRENCE, HOPPNER.

CHAPTER XIV

AMERICAN COSTUME FROM THE SEVENTEENTH CENTURY TO 1950

Settlement of Jamestown, 1607	John Winthrop, 1588–1649
Settlement of Providence, 1636	Roger Williams, 1603?–1683
Discovery of the identity of	William Penn, 1644–1718
lightning by Franklin, 1752	Cotton Mather, 1663–1728
French and Indian War, 1754	Jonathan Edwards, 1703–1758
Boston Tea Party, 1773	George Washington, 1732–1799
Declaration of Independence, 1776	Daniel Boone, 1735–1820
	John Hancock, 1737–1793
	J. S. Copley, 1737–1815
	Gilbert Stuart, 1755–1828
	Noah Webster, 1758–1843

WHEN taking up their new life on the newly discovered continent of North America, the early settlers naturally brought with them the customs of their several native countries, modifying and adapting them to their new conditions of life. They clung with tenacity to the modes of their mother countries sending back as circumstances permitted for a fresh supply of doublets and gowns.

Although the costumes "in Spain, France, England, and the Low Countries were very much alike in the seventeenth century," [1] and that of the Colonials reproduced that of their native land, there was naturally reflected in the various and scattered settlements something of the national character of each. The Spanish settlers of Florida retained, whenever their means permitted, the handsome silks, choice laces, and rich leathers for wear in the new homes across the sea. The English and Dutch colonists before leaving the homelands provided themselves with a supply of garments cut, naturally, in the fashions prevailing at the time of their emigration, while in the French colony of Louisiana the men dressed in heavy overcoats, long doublets or waistcoats, breeches of wool, and leggings of buckskin; the women in short gowns of homespun with bright kerchiefs wound about the head.

---

[1] McCLELLAN, E., HISTORIC DRESS IN AMERICA, Vol. I, p. 27. Macrae Smith and Company.

Dress in the Dutch Colony.—The prosperous Dutch settlers of Manhattan wore a costume more simple in cut than that of many of the other Colonists, in materials both handsome and durable—silk, satins, velvet, lace made in the Netherlands, or sturdy homespun made by thrifty housewives and colored by bright dyes which the Indians had taught them to make. For men, the costume was comprised of the usual seventeenth century waistcoat or doublet, full breeches, long stockings, and broad-brimmed hat. The fastenings of the Dutch gentleman's doublet and coat were of precious stones in settings of gold and silver.

The Goode Vrow was no whit less well dressed than her husband; her short, full petticoats, of which she had and wore an abundance, were especially colorful, being scarlet, or green, striped with black or gray. Another favorite article of dress of the woman was the *samare*, a loose jacket with three-quarter-length sleeves, and edgings of narrow bands of fur. Damask, plain silk, and flowered calico were all used for this jacket. The early housewives of New Amsterdam were well supplied with jewelry brought, of course, from their old homes. Rings, necklaces, and ear-rings of gold were generously incrusted with diamonds. Every Goode Vrow wore suspended from her girdle by ribbons or silver chains, keys, pin-cushion, scissors and other housewifely implements, and aprons were, of course, indispensable. Dainty caps of muslin and lace or of quilted calico covered their simply dressed hair, while fur caps edged with beaver or warm hoods afforded protection on winter days.

Dress of the English Colonists of the South.—Among the English settlers of Virginia, Maryland and the Carolinas were gentlemen whose original wealth brought from England was soon augmented by flourishing plantations. The early settlers kept in close touch with England and from 1625 to 1642 "London fashions were strictly adhered to by the quality, and seem to have been not only the chief amusement of the women, but a matter of great moment to both sexes."[2]

The first of the gentlemen settlers leaving England in the time of James I were attired in padded breeches, brocaded doublet, lace trimmed ruff, and broad hats though they were officially

---

[2] *Ibid.*, Vol. I, p. 51.

advised to provide themselves with two suits each of sturdy frieze and broadcloth.

When the Cromwellians gained control of England after the execution of Charles I, 1649, many cavaliers of the court fled to the colonies bringing with them the luxurious but dignified dress that soon became the frivolous one of the English Restoration (page 144): petticoat breeches, short doublet, and later the long coat buttoned from neck to knee.

The southern colonial women managed to bring with them to their new homes, and later import from the homeland, gowns cut in the London mode, or linens, laces, and silks made by their

FIG. 120. PILGRIMS GOING TO CHURCH. G. H. BOUGHTON. THE PURITANS BROUGHT THE FASHIONS OF THE HOMELAND TO THE NEW COUNTRY. Courtesy of the New York Public Library.

own mantua makers in full size replicas of the clothes of the small dolls, which, before the advent of fashion magazines in the late eighteenth century, were sent with regularity about the Continent as couriers of the latest Parisian fashion. Muffs, long gloves, patches, and fans found as important a place in the toilette of the wealthy Virginia planter's wife as they did in that of the beautiful ladies of the gay court of Charles II.

Costume in the New England Colonies.—The Pilgrims and Puritans who settled in the first quarter of the seventeenth century in Massachusetts, although disapproving of many of the religious and social conditions of their native England, were yet content to retain the English style of clothes, discarding, however, the ribbons, laces, feathers, and costly textures. The Pilgrims, particularly, were determined that the frivolities of dress should be dispensed with in their new conditions of life, and consequently many laws were passed in their settlements concerning what they considered excesses in the use of decorations, cut of boots, sleeves, and hoods, and the amount of income to be spent on the necessities of the wardrobe. The late comers were less averse to fine clothes, passing few restrictions regarding dress and with the years of increasing prosperity and more frequent communication with England became satisfied and valuable customers of the haberdashers and mantua makers of London.

Puritan Dress.—From old records and portraits as well as from laws, we learn that the Puritan fathers were partial to full breeches and doublets of rich browns and russets with equally colorful stockings of wool, turned-back collars—falling bands, with the accompanying turned-back cuffs of white Holland linen entirely free of adornment, and tall-crowned hats of black felt, with small silver buckles fastening the narrow ribbon at the base. Large buckles replaced later in the century the earlier rosettes on the shoes. An innate love of decoration could not be entirely suppressed for the gauntlet gloves were heavily embroidered and fringed.

Until the appearance of the large, powdered wig in 1660 Puritan men wore the hair cut short.

Not many years after Charles II introduced it into English dress, the long coat, accompanied by a waistcoat, took its place in the costume of New England. The linen neckcloth worn with this collarless coat "fastened with silver buckles under the hair at the back."[3]

The Puritan woman's gown consisted of a close bodice and full skirt of camlet, a combination of wool and silk, looped back over a petticoat of homespun, all of green, brown, or dull purple with snowy apron, broad neckerchief, and turned-back cuffs. Her hair, usually parted in the center, was drawn back closely from the face, showing but little under the cap of muslin or net of a variety of shapes. Out-of-doors a hood of dark colored silk or cloth, or broad hat similar to that of the men, was worn. Her wrap was a

---

[3] *Ibid.*, Vol. I, p. 109.

circular cloak of cloth lined with fur. Muffs carried during the early Colonial period were small and round. The shoes were of durable leather with sturdy heels of wood.

Quaker Dress.—When William Penn and his company settled in 1682, in what is now Pennsylvania, they were dressed in the fashion prevailing at the time at the court of Charles II with little to distinguish them from other men of the age but a total absence of feathers and lace, and a certain simplicity and staidness. They employed the materials commonly used then in grayed greens, browns, and purples, with sheer, fine linen at throat and wrist. Although periwigs were occasionally worn, the hair of Quaker men was usually parted in the center, the unpowdered locks falling to the shoulders. The brim of the large hat turned up slightly on both sides but was without adornment of any kind. Both coat and waistcoat were single-breasted fastening with plain buttons and undecorated buttonholes their entire length from collarless neck to knee.

Like the men, Quaker women fancied handsome materials of soft colors for their plain, gathered skirts, and short-sleeved and simple bodices. The dainty under sleeves, shoulder kerchiefs and caps were of spotless white lawn, their long aprons of colored silk. Soft hoods of black silk lined with a bright color were worn out of doors over the ruffled caps. The following century a stiff beaver replaced the hood and was in turn superseded in the nineteenth century by a stiff poke bonnet tied under the chin.

Children of the Colonists.—The children of the Colonials, like those of Europeans, soon after the long dresses of infancy were discarded, romped about in clothes that were the exact reproductions of those of their elders. From two years on tight stays incased the tiny bodies of the girls with their little gowns made of the same Holland linen, linsey woolsey (a coarse cloth of linen and wool), and camlet. Their shoes, masks, fans, gloves, and jewelry copied faithfully those accessories of the Colonial dames.

Exquisite needlework and the finest of embroidery and thread lace distinguished not only the short-sleeved and low-necked shirt of linen, but also the loose sacques drawn up around the neck to form the dress of young Puritan infants.[4]

---

[4] EARLE, A. M., CUSTOMS AND FASHIONS IN OLD NEW ENGLAND, Chap. I. Charles Scribner's Sons.

Colonial Dress in the Eighteenth Century.—With a lessening of the hardships incident to the establishing of homes in the new and undeveloped country, the Colonists were enabled to turn more of their attention to matters pertaining to dress. Philadelphia, New York, and Boston, the chief centers of social life in the Colonies, were the cities to which the new modes from across the sea were sent. An idea of sartorial conditions in the city founded

Fig. 121. Thomas Nelson, Son of Governor Nelson of Virginia. Wissing. The Youth of American Colonists Followed Closely the Fashions of Their Elders. Courtesy of the Metropolitan Museum.

by William Penn is gained from the following: "Probably in no place on the Continent was the love of bright colors and extravagance in dress carried to such an extreme. Large numbers of the Quakers yielded to it, even very strict ones carried gold-headed canes, gold snuff boxes, and wore great silver buttons on their drab

coats and handsome buckles on their shoes."[5] To the stately parties
came the dignified gentleman in his powdered wig, known as the
campaign wig, with its full, long curls, or the *Ramilie,* puffed at the
sides with a long queue at the back. His square-cut coat was
stiffened with buckram and whalebone, standing out from the
figure to show the satin waistcoat with its prominent pockets, and
close knee breeches. His stockings were scarlet, blue, or white with
the elaborately embroidered clocks which gentlemen affected at
the time. Small silver buttons fastened the velvet garters clasped

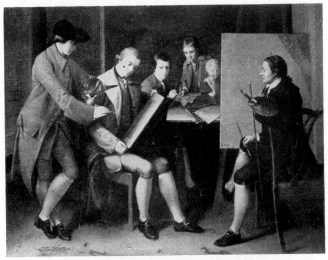

FIG. 122. THE AMERICAN SCHOOL. PRATT. MEN'S COSTUME OF 1765.
Courtesy of the Metropolitan Museum.

just below his knee, larger ones securing the red-heeled shoe. The
front and sleeves of the cambric shirts were finely ruffled, while the
neck-cloth was closely plaited. A heavy cloak *Roquelaure,* of camlet
or of drugget, at times fur trimmed, was thrown over this handsome
costume, with a three cornered hat and a large muff to complete it.

A garment quite commonly worn by men informally at home
was a long gown of damask known as the *banyan,* accompanied by a
small cap. In summer this was of highly patterned calico.

---

[5] FISHER, S. G., MEN, WOMEN, AND MANNERS, Vol. I, p. 368. J. B. Lippincott Company.

With minds free from the fears, anxieties, and hardships that so beset the early women Colonists, those residing in the comparative safety and prosperity of eighteenth-century America were free to indulge their taste for fine raiment. "Stays, or 'a paire of bodices' as they were called in the early part of the seventeenth

Fig. 123. Mrs. Chesbrough, by Blackburn. A Simplified Version of English Fashions. Courtesy of the Metropolitan Museum.

century, were considered a necessary article of woman's dress throughout the eighteenth century, and very, very stiff and straight laced were these colonial great grandmothers of our modern corset."[6] To accompany these, there appeared early in the century a full petticoat distended by hoops of whalebone that characterized woman's dress for the rest of the century. Over it

[6] McClellan, E., Historic Dress in America, Vol. II, p. 190. Macrae Smith and Company.

was worn the popular gown consisting of full skirt looped up at the side, tight bodice with pointed waist, low, square neck and short sleeves. Ruffles and lace, plaitings and puffings of the material of the dress itself were used about the edges of neck, sleeves, and skirts.

About 1775 the *sacque*, known in France as the Watteau, supplanted the earlier dress so favored by Colonial women. This, like its French prototype, was looped *panier* fashion at the sides and had a large box plait down the back from shoulder to waist. The under skirt worn commonly with the *sacque* was of satin quilted

Fig. 124. Washington and Lafayette at Mount Vernon, 1776. Rossiter and Mignot. An Excellent Illustration of the Costume of Men, Women, and Children. Courtesy of the Metropolitan Museum.

over its entire surface. Dainty satin slippers with dangerously high heels peeped out beneath the skirt.

During the first half of the century Colonial hair dressing was extremely simple, but after 1750 it attained enormous proportions, the hair being drawn back from the face over a large cushion of hair and profusely powdered. In order to protect this head-dress a gigantic hood of silk shirred over a framework of whalebone known as the *calash* was adopted. Owing to its construction the *calash* could be thrown back from the head at will like the top of the *calèche*, a carriage very popular on the Continent at that time.

The Revolutionary Period.—Shortly before the opening years of our Revolutionary period men's dress had changed and crystallized into the type rendered so familiar to us in the portraits of Washington and the early founders of the new republic. The skirts of the coats lost their stiffness; the fronts were cut away and rounded, the forerunner of the modern cutaway coat. The waistcoats no longer reached to the knees but were cut to extend slightly below the waist. The wig was entirely out of fashion, the natural hair being powdered, puffed at the sides, and tied at the back of the neck with a bow of black ribbon.

Throughout the years of the war, the women residing in the larger cities, particularly those of large Tory population, were able to keep in touch with the latest fashions from abroad. Eccentric arrangements of the hair were but little in evidence. Powder was still used. Crisp caps of sheer white with ruffles of delicate lace and ribbons made a very flattering frame for the face. An equally dainty gauze fichu was arranged over the shoulder, and fastened with a large pin at the breast. Chintz and striped or checked linen, were the materials used for morning and house dresses, with silk and fine cloth reserved for evening, visiting, and Sabbath day gowns. The petticoats worn with the looped-back dresses were still quilted in elaborate designs.

Costume in the United States.—In the latter years of the eighteenth century the two new republics, France and the United States, had much in common. Intercourse between the two nations increased steadily with the result that French ideas of dress were immediately and whole-heartedly adopted by the citizens of the American republic. The costumes of the French Empire, Restoration and the Second Empire as well as of the closing decades of the nineteenth and the early years of the twentieth centuries were faithfully reflected in dress on this continent. (See chapters VIII and IX.)

With the outbreak of the second World War (1939-1945) the members of the French couture were unable to carry on their work to any great extent and German submarines prevented the shipment of goods overseas. The few really creative American designers turned to native sources of design for inspiration. The Brooklyn, the Metropolitan Museums of Art and the Museum of Costume Art in New York City placed their treasures at the

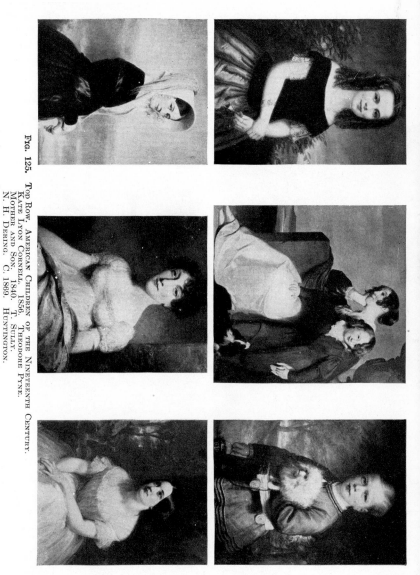

Fig. 125. Top Row. American Children of the Nineteenth Century.
Kate Lyon Cornell. 1856. Theodore Pyne.
Mother and Son. 1840. T. Sully.
N. H. Dering. C. 1869. Huntington.

Fig. 126. Bottom Row. Costumes of American Women of the Nineteenth Century.
Mrs. J. C. Cruger. 1842. Healy.

FIG. 127. THE SILHOUETTE OF PRE-CIVIL-WAR DAYS. 1859. *Godey's Magazine.*

Fig. 128. A Family Group. Johnson, 1871. The Costumes of Youth and Old Age are Carefully Recorded in This Painting. Courtesy of the Metropolitan Museum.

disposal of designers of clothing and textiles for study with the result that from the late 1930's American women were well dressed by their own talented designers. Los Angeles and New York City became two of the leading centers of dress and textile design.

Textile manufacturers are also active though naturally hampered in the production of new fibers and finishes which research promised before the outbreak of war. The two man-made fibers, rayon and nylon, replaced linen and silk and some of the cotton that was necessary for war purposes and proved to be great favorites after natural fibers were again available.

American Dress from 1939 to 1945.—The full and very short-skirted costume which appeared on the fashion scene in 1938 remained popular through the early years of the war, the gathered dirndl and the full skirt with a Victorian type petticoat showing below the hem, the circular, tiered and plumb-line skirts being variations. In all instances they extended just below the knee. In 1942, however, scarcity of fabrics and government regulations caused a curtailment of extravagant width in the silhouette: slim skirts barely escaping the curve of the calf of the leg appeared, with bodices and blouses of deep or open neckline. Shirtwaist and knitted dresses, the two-piece dress with its accompanying jacket became almost uniforms for women busy with some form of war work. Culotte skirts, coveralls and slacks were especially designed for women engaged in war industries.

FIG. 129.   *Left:* PREPARING FOR THE BALL. 1874. A. STEVENS. *Right:* MRS. WILLIAM ASTOR. 1890. CAROLUS DURAND. Courtesy of the Metropolitan Museum of Art.

Many of the capes and box or fitted coats of that day had attached hoods which the sleekly coiffured woman could draw up over her short, curled hair that soon replaced the high-piled hair arrangement of 1938. In 1942 snoods, long strips of soft textured fabric, kerchiefs, and hats like the overseas cap of the aviator took the place of the high-crowned and pill-box hats as well as the one with tilted brim, held on by an elastic or ribbon strap passing under the hair at the back. Many of the young women went entirely hatless winter and summer much to the distress of the millinery trade and the delight of the hairdressers. In 1944 the Breton sailor, Basque beret, and tall, Russian-type hats of mink or other fur reflected the influence of world events.

Characteristic of dresses, suits and coats was the square, broad, and padded shoulder line that did much to give women the appearance of having very small, pulled-in waists. This shoulder emphasis lasted throughout the decade gradually becoming smaller, practically disappearing in 1949.

Fitted coats or double-breasted replicas of officers' great

FIG. 130. PORTRAITS WHICH SHOW THE COSTUME OF AMERICAN MEN OF THE
EARLY TWENTIETH CENTURY.
PORTRAIT OF G. A. HEARN BY I. R. WILES. 1914.
THE THINKER BY T. EAKINS. 1900.
PORTRAIT OF W. CHASE BY J. S. SARGENT. 1902.
Courtesy of the Metropolitan Museum of Art.

coats, sometimes lined with fur, kept milady warm during the periods of coal shortages when coats with removable linings made their first bow to fashion. Silver fox skins formed short, bulky jackets for wear with the narrow-skirted dress or suit of 1943 while mink and mouton furs were favored for long coats.

Footwear was naturally important at the time. Shoes varied in cut from the sensible oxfords, moccasins, and Mexican sandals to wedges, platform-soled and open-toed shoes. Uniform, however, for all women were the beige stockings of rayon or cotton while silk and nylon hose were unobtainable, the younger set taking to socks or using leg film to substitute for hosiery.

1945-1950.—Within a few months after the lifting of government restrictions on the yardage of fabric in clothing the feminine silhouette underwent a decided change. Skirts immediately became very full and much longer reaching to the ankle in 1947 but gradually shortening again until street and sport dresses measured from twelve to fourteen inches from the floor while the skirt which touched the ankle was popular for gowns worn after dark. The bouffant effect, obtained by means of circular cuts, pleats, flares and uneven hemlines, characterized the fashions of 1946, floating panels and full circular or accordion pleated skirts those of 1949.

Fig. 131.   Emma and Her Children.   G. Bellows.   1923.
Courtesy of the Museum of Fine Arts, Boston.

Bodices of daytime dresses had wide, scooped-out necklines, the
Victorian off-the-shoulder line being especially fashionable for
formal gowns.   Many evening dresses had entirely strapless necklines that were cleverly cut and worn over wired brassieres to insure
the comfort of the wearer.   The closing years of the decade favored
for daytime wear a neckline, whether on dress or blouse, that
was a V that plunged deeply in front, or a close round line that
formed a foil for a pearl or metal necklace, always accompanied
by intriguing earrings, and sometimes pairs of decorative pins
on the lapel of coats and jackets.   In 1948 both dresses and coats
possessed forward jutting collars and outsize revers with sharp
points.   This same neckline was found in the dress of 1949 which
had asymmetric balance as its keynote.

An especially striking feature entered the fashion picture in
1947, probably a strong reaction to the shortages of the war years.
This was the coat that fell free from the shoulders, its back
swinging out, sometimes below a yoke, in the form of a huge triangle.   A close rival was the short coat, at times almost a bolero,
whose back flared out saucily about the wearer's small waist and
full-hipped dress.

Fig. 132. The Built-Up Shoulder and Short Skirt of 1941. An Example of Mother and Daughter Fashions of 1946. Courtesy of the New York Dress Institute.

Accessories were important adjuncts of costume. Many-strapped slippers either with a high or no heel were seen at all times of day or night; bright colored gloves of fabric, leather or string added gaiety to the favorite basic black costume; long rectangular stoles of cloth or fur gave grace as well as warmth to a costume. Millions of dollars were spent each year on costume jewelry that was massive and frequently patterned on Hindu ornaments, or on pearls which were worn on practically all occasions.

Although scant in size and number the lingerie worn by women in the 1930's and 1940's was most attractive as well as comfortable and practical. Rayon and nylon in both woven and knitted fabrics in the forties replaced very generally the earlier muslin and silk in nightgowns, pajamas, panties and slips. Soft but firm girdles with panels and insets of elastic took the place of heavily boned corsets while brief brassieres of satin or lace, both wired and strapless for evening wear, gave support as well as freedom to the active American woman.

FIG. 133. A WOOL DRESS WITH THE DOLMAN SLEEVE OF 1949. Courtesy of the New York Times.
A SUMMER EVENING DRESS OF EYELET EMBROIDERY. 1947.
Courtesy of the New York Dress Institute.

Fabrics were varied in texture design and color. Printed cottons and rayons, Swiss embroidered organdies and soft-hued chambrays were approved for summer wear, plain rayons and wools in heavy or sheer crepe, wool or rayon knitted jersey for practical costumes while velvet, satin, tulle or crisp taffeta added charm to bouffant cocktail and evening gowns and wraps. Tweed, gabardine and men's wear worsteds were found in the ever popular suits and light-weight coats. Rain capes and coats, with attached hoods, of plastic film or bright colored fabrics treated with water repellent finish, together with vivid umbrellas furnished notes of cheer to stormy days.

Because sports form such an important part in American life, clothes for such events were found in nearly every wardrobe. Slacks for winter sports as well as for lounging at home, shorts for tennis, and long pants for skiing followed closely the cut of men's nether garments. Brief one-piece bathing suits, form-fitting

FIG. 134.   TYPICAL STREET COSTUMES WORN IN 1948.
Courtesy of the New York Dress Institute.

because of their rayon covered rubber yarn, and short frocks with low-cut backs were worn by devotees of the sun.

Colors ranged from the always chic black to navy and soft blue in addition to rich dark and emerald green. Taupe, beige and gray were fashionable from 1941 through 1949, two tones of the latter color being frequently combined in ensembles. California set the stage for pastel shades of rose, green and blue for sport as well as street wear. Dark or vivid reds appeared in top coats of wool velour, suede cloth or fleece during the winter of 1949. Many colors were found in printed fabrics ranging from small allover designs to the large, bold motifs seen in evening gowns of chiffon and taffeta. Non-tarnishing aluminum and copper threads introduced sparkle to fabrics used for blouses, sweaters, footwear and handbags.

Children's Clothes.—American children of the present century have been freed from the unattractive costumes of the nineteenth. The Fauntleroy and Norfolk suits and striped stockings worn by the small boy from 1870 to 1900 were displaced by shorts, or by knickerbockers caught below the knee by a band of fabric and metal buckle. Cotton shirts or blouses had either standing collars and neckties or Eton collars and flowing Buster Brown ties. Jackets were cut like father's short coat.

Young sister of the same era wore sailor blouses, short pleated skirts of serge or other sturdy material and muslin dresses that were gathered and hung free from shoulder yokes until 1941. Then, reflecting somewhat the style trend in adult clothes, the frock's waistline descended to the young hip line, the short frilly skirt billowing below a gay ribbon sash. Princess-cut dresses appeared next, followed by pinafores of the type worn by Alice in Wonderland and by jumper dresses—dark, sleeveless dresses over white blouses. In 1940 came the urge for mother and daughter to be dressed in garments identical in cut, color and fabric.

Infants and small children have been comfortably and sensibly clothed since the beginning of the century when the baby of four months cast off his long dress and coat and donned either a short cotton frock, a pair of rompers or diminutive sun suit which gave complete freedom to young limbs. Today's wee tot glories in as few garments as possible, in cold weather being "zippered" into long-legged and long-sleeved snow suits with snugly fitting hood or bonnet. Older brothers and sisters don long cloth leggings and simply fashioned coats with turned-down collars. Surely Rousseau, the French philosopher and social reformer of Marie Antoinette's reign, who was the first to inveigh against the absurd and fettering dress of children, would approve of the simple, non-restricting garments of the present youngest generation.

REFERENCES

EARLE, HOME LIFE IN COLONIAL DAYS, Chap. XII.
EARLE, CUSTOMS AND FASHIONS IN OLD NEW ENGLAND; TWO CENTURIES OF DRESS IN AMERICA; COSTUME OF COLONIAL TIMES.
GUMMERE, THE QUAKER.
MCCLELLAN, HISTORIC DRESS IN AMERICA.
SINGLETON, SOCIAL NEW YORK UNDER THE GEORGES, pp. 171–256; STORY OF THE WHITE HOUSE.
WHARTON, SOCIAL LIFE IN THE EARLY REPUBLIC.
PARSONS, THE PSYCHOLOGY OF DRESS, pp. 264–283.

PART II

NATIONAL COSTUME IN EUROPE, NORTHERN
AFRICA, ASIA, AND THE AMERICAS

CHAPTER XV

NATIONAL COSTUME IN SPAIN, FRANCE, ITALY, SWITZERLAND, AND TYROL

PROFOUND changes are taking place to-day in the color, material, cut, and decoration of the clothes which the people of the more remote districts of practically all countries in Europe have, until comparatively recent times, kept the same for generations. Many of these changes are undoubtedly due to the enterprise of the manufacturing and business interests of the western world as well as to factors resulting from the upheaval in Europe after the World War. The products of modern power-driven looms are fast replacing the cloths woven by skillful fingers in modest cottages and small factories; machine-made laces and embroideries are now within the reach of the inhabitants of practically the most remote mountain hamlets, where formerly designs and patterns for these decorations had been cherished in families or parishes for untold years.

Modern aniline dyes have entirely displaced the native dyestuffs formerly gathered and prepared by family industry. As an example of the effect of the war upon some peasant dress is the fact that present-day high taxes in France on felt and silk are largely responsible for the disappearance of many of the picturesque costumes in Brittany. Furthermore, the art and persuasive powers of modern advertising and salesmanship may be responsible in large measure for the growing disuse of peasant dress.

Democracy in Dress.—These are not, however, the only influences at work in creating the tendency for all peoples to dress alike. The barriers making for class distinction in dress are gradually breaking down. Democracy in dress as in other phases of national life is coming to the fore. The peasant girl strives now to look as much as possible like her cousin who lives in town, and who patterns her wardrobe to the best of her ability and financial resources, after that of the woman of fashion, who in turn feels

191

that her frock and accessories must in some manner bear the stamp of Parisian approval. But rarely now does one display one's religious affiliations or designate one's native province by means of the color of gown or type of head covering. Modern newspapers and magazines have done much to spread the idea of democracy in dress, far and wide and just now these forces are being ably assisted by the radio and movie.

Influence of Peasant Dress.—Especially interesting is it, however, to remind ourselves that the influence of this so-called peasant dress of Europe is very evident in the supposedly new fashions which emanate from Paris. In their efforts to produce something different, French, and in fact all designers, turn to the wealth of suggestions for cut, color, and decoration that these traditional types of dress afford. The rich head-dresses of Russia, the dainty caps of Normandy and Brittany furnish ideas for head-dresses for ball and wedding; the short jackets of the Balkans for the new semi-tailored suits; the embroidery stitches and motifs of Roumania, Bohemia, Italy or Sweden, for the elaboration of coats, dresses, and accessories for women and children; and the shawl of Spain plays an important part in the modern evening costume.

It is to be regretted that so many of these bright, picturesque costumes which are usually so well suited to the various types of peoples and their manner of life, are so generally disappearing. Private collectors and museums are now endeavoring to preserve some of the costumes that reveal so much of the character of the people who wore them. To the student and designer they afford a treasure trove of interesting and valuable material. For excellent and abundant drawings and photographs of the details of peasant costume both student and designer are urged to refer to the books listed in the bibliography under the headings of the various countries as only a brief outline sketch of the numerous costumes is possible in the limited space of this book.

Spain.—One of the countries of Europe which has been more successful than some of the others in the preservation of its native costumes is Spain. The characteristic austerity and sobriety of sixteenth-century Spanish dress that had such a marked influence on contemporary French and English dress are still to be found in nearly all varieties of masculine dress throughout the peninsula.

The only really brilliant accents in an otherwise dark blue, green, or black costume are present in the broad silk sash, *faja*, that is still worn in practically all provinces, and the soft silk kerchiefs that are wound around the heads of the men of Valencia and Leon.

In the first of the above mentioned provinces the typical dress of the men consists of a white shirt the large, full sleeves of which are freely exposed to view by the sleeveless jacket; knee-length loose drawers of white linen; a broad, bright sash; hempen sandals,

FIG. 135. TYPICAL COSTUMES WORN IN THE PROVINCE OF CASTILE. SOROLLA Y BASTIDA. Courtesy of the Hispanic Society of America.

alpargatas, that are mainly soles with slight counters and toe pieces, tied just above the ankles; occasionally stockings that are guiltless of feet; a length of striped material thrown over the shoulder to do duty as a cloak when needed for warmth; and a brilliant silk kerchief tied around the head.

The Valencian woman, on the contrary, displays a love of color and sparkle. Lace is very prominent in the decoration of her close bodice, short, full skirt, and straight, spangle-strewn apron. The short sleeves of the bodice are edged with lace at the elbow, the apron at the sides and bottom, while the skirt has several flounces of lace. Lace or fringe edges the small shawl that is worn over the shoulders, crossed in front and tucked into the belt of the apron. Her hair is dressed in tightly twisted rolls which are fastened with long pins of silver gilt that end in large knobs, and are topped with a generous-sized comb. Heavy circles of the same silver gilt pierce both ears. The short skirts display simple, low foot-wear and white stockings.[1]

The Catalonian replaces the plaid or *manta* of the Valencian with the *gambeto*, a thick, wool top-coat. His jacket is extremely short to accommodate the plush trousers that reach nearly to the arms. The characteristic *gorro* of red or purple wool forms the cap. It is much in shape like the stocking cap worn to-day by children and skaters.

Less picturesque is the feminine Catalonian dress of full, ankle-length skirt, tight bodice that is almost concealed by the decorative crossed shoulder shawl, and a white veil over the head.

In the neighboring province of Aragon black velvet is the fabric most favored for the men's button-trimmed jacket and short, close breeches that are open at the knee and slashed at the side the better to display the white lining beneath. The abbreviated jacket reveals a white shirt with elaborate needlework. *Alpargatas* and long stockings, either black or white, are always worn, while a bright silk *faja* about the waist and kerchief around the head enliven this otherwise somber costume.

To the customary close, front-laced bodice, and bright shawl or fichu of all Spanish peasants, the Aragonese woman has added a short, ample skirt of hues that satisfy her craving for color.

To the Galician, brown is apparently the favorite hue, for the clothing of most of these peasants is of this color. He wears the characteristic knee breeches open at the knee like those of the Aragonese, but of brown corduroy. The short velvet or corduroy jacket is of the same hue as the breeches; as is also the *capa*, a long cape reaching below the knee. The hat is of felt. Long cloth gaiters and wooden *sabots* complete the costume.

On the Galician woman of the remoter inland villages where the old customs have not entirely succumbed to modern fashions

---

[1] ZUR GESCHICHTE DER KOSTÜME. See plate 810.

may be seen a gay red fichu crossed over the breast, a bright kerchief wound and tied around the head in a variety of ways, and a scarlet or orange skirt. The embroideries on the costumes commonly worn in this province resemble strongly those found in such profusion in central Europe.

Fig. 136. Catalans in Their Native Costume. Viladrich Vilá. Courtesy of the Hispanic Society of America.

Greater richness characterises the costume found in Leon.[2] The silver buckles on the low leather shoes, the broad-brimmed felt hat, the bright-hued waistcoat, and the full knee breeches of the men possess an individuality that distinguishes them from such articles worn elsewhere in the country. The white shirt is

---

[2] *Ibid.*, plate 810.

richly embroidered, and the long white stockings are of home manufacture.

In addition to the short, full skirt and diminutive velvet bodice over her blouse, the woman of Leon wraps about her waist and hips a long oblong of dark colored cloth. Probably the most important item in the eyes of the fair wearer is the massive necklace with its suspended cross, although the gracefully worn *mantilla* adds more to her charm and attractiveness. Breastpins, ear-rings, and finger rings as well as fans are much affected by the Spanish beauty.

Coral necklaces are favored by the women of the Asturias who revel in green or yellow bodices with a touch of the same color repeated in their leather footgear. Their hair is worn in long braids down the back in marked contrast to the hair arrangement customary in other parts of Spain.

The upper class Spanish woman of the cities and towns rarely appears on the streets in any color but black with a long, black lace scarf over her head. The *mantilla* of black or white lace arranged over an enormously high comb, with flowers at the side, is reserved for special religious and social occasions, as is the colorfully embroidered *mantón de Manilla*, a large shawl of silk crepe edged with deep fringe, and worn by the Spanish woman with such inimitable grace.

Portugal.—Much similarity exists in the dress of the Portuguese and that of their Spanish neighbors. The color of the Portuguese dress is decidedly dull with enlivening touches present in the red silk sash of the men and the brilliant head shawls of the women. The long trousers, high vest, and short coat of the men are usually of black or brown homespun, their head covering either a large felt hat or a long, bag-like cap. Their *alpargatas* are quite similar to those of the Spaniard.

The short, full skirts of the women are commonly black with a broad stripe of brilliant color above the hem, while the small corsage of velvet or silk barely reaches to the waist, revealing, therefore, much of the blouse. Quite coquettish is the wide-brimmed hat of black velveteen that tops the kerchief-draped head. Like the women of the Basques, those of Portugal almost invariably carry large, bright parasols, *chapeo de sol*. Of the elaborate, heavy jewelry of gold filigree, the large hoop-shaped

ear-rings are the most interesting. The wooden-soled shoes with
embroidered toe pieces and heels are for wear on occasions of
importance.

France.—Probably the best known of the provincial costumes
of France is that of Brittany where on fête days, particularly those
known as "pardons," both
men and women array
themselves in the colorful,
decorative old-time dress
that is still cherished and
worn by these hardy folk
whose mode of life is so
little affected by gay Paris.

The two articles of the
men's apparel that are decidedly characteristic of
the Bretons are the broad-
brimmed felt hat, *toc,* and
the full—in many in-
stances accordion plaited
—breeches, *bragon braz,*
that are reminiscent of
those fashionable in the
sixteenth century. The
hat has a slightly rolling
brim and a low, round
crown, at the base of which
is a colored ribbon that is
caught at the back by a
gleaming metal buckle,

Fig. 137.   The Pardon in Brittany.   Dagnan-
Bouveret.   1886.   Courtesy of the Metropolitan
Museum.

and has streamers falling down below the broad shoulders of its
sturdy wearer.

In certain districts, the full breeches are replaced by some of
scantier size, or by long trousers that are somewhat easy through
the hips and knees. The breeches are practically always accompanied by long gaiters that fasten at the side, and either wooden

sabots, hand carved and decorated, or heavy leather shoes. About the waist is a sash of bright color or a broad leather belt with a huge buckle. The sash or belt is placed over the sleeveless, double-breasted cloth vest whose color is usually the brightest of the whole costume, blue, red, or brown, and which boasts two rows of quaint silver buttons from waist to neck line. Bands of gay em-

FIG. 138. TWO RESIDENTS OF BRITTANY IN NATIVE COSTUME.
Wide World Photos.

*o*roidery, in silk or wool, frequently edge the neck line of the vest as well as the collar and the cuffs of the short cloth jacket which is so cut in front that the decorative vest is extremely conspicuous. In some districts a short, sleeveless coat is preferred. The narrow soft collar of the white shirt is exposed to view above the vest and coat. "Much time and zeal are expended on the embroidery of the costume, the ornamental work being done by the men, the women going to the fields." [3]

The modern Breton cuts his hair short, but his forebears of the nineteenth century permitted theirs to grow to shoulder length.

To the resident of Brittany or one well versed in the customs of the province, the crisp, snow-white *coifs* of the women are indications of the wearer's particular place of residence. As there are said to be between eight hundred and a thousand varieties of these head-dresses a detailed description is not feasible here. In general, white linen or net is the fabric from which the *coifs* are fashioned, the latter being ornamented with designs embroidered or darned in by hand. In some districts the close-fitting *coifs* are surmounted for church going by small, round, ribbon-trimmed hats with strings that tie under the chin.

FIG. 139. A HEAD-DRESS TYPICAL OF ALSACE. Photo by Brown Brothers.

The figured and sometimes fringe-edged fichu and the broad flat, white linen collar are the most characteristic neck finishes of the close-fitting bodice worn by the Breton woman. The waist, which is very small, is accentuated by the extreme fullness of the cloth skirt that extends to the ankles and is covered across its entire front by a generously cut, and many times colorfully embroidered apron. Turned-back cuffs finish the straight sleeves that are usually of wrist length. On special festival days many women add to their dress an embroidered "jacket of the bolero order."[4] About the throat is worn a black velvet ribbon from which hangs a small gold or silver cross, which, with the buckles on her low-cut shoes, is the most important of the Breton woman's jewelry.

---

[3] MOSHER, A. M., THE SPELL OF BRITTANY, Chap. XVIII. Duffield and Company. [4] *Ibid.*

Until the age of five or six the young Breton children of both sexes are dressed exactly the same, in long cloth dresses with generous tucks for future lengthening of skirts, flowered aprons or pinafores, and close bonnets of bright colors.   The bonnets of the boys have a gay tassel to distinguish them from those of the gentler sex. After they have attained the ripe age of seven, the boys are promoted to long trousers, silver-buttoned short coats, and broad-brimmed hats that make them miniature editions of their fathers.

In the neighborhood of Strassburg, the Alsatian women are noted for the large bow of wide, black ribbon with fringed ends that forms their picturesque head-dress. In other districts the enormously broad-brimmed straw hats with ribbon trimmings have disappeared, leaving the field to the close bonnets with their plaitings of sheer white to frame the face and almost conceal the parted, simply dressed hair.

The low-cut, front-laced bodice with embroidered front recalls that worn by Swiss and German peasant women. Being of small dimensions it freely exposes to view the loose-sleeved chemise with its turned-down collar in the form of a plaited frill. The black or dark colored fichu is draped over the shoulders and crossed in front. The cloth skirt, but moderately full, extends to within a few inches of the ankle and is frequently ornamented with bands of colored cloth around the bottom, or is cut short enough to reveal a few inches of an elaborate petticoat. A small bow of bright ribbon is sewed to the front of the simple slipper the heels of which are of a modest height.

In Normandy and Savoy the caps of the women are undoubtedly the most unique articles of their costume. The head-dress so commonly worn in Normandy until very recent years had its origin in the tall *hennins* of fifteenth-century France. Of starched muslin, erected in many cases over cone-shaped foundations, these head-dresses concealed the hair, formed stiff, wing-like projections at either side of the head, or fell in streamers down the back. Height and crispness seem to be typical of the numerous present-day varieties of Norman caps with flutings or ruchings in marked evidence. In some districts the women still cling to the bright kerchief pinned in carefully laid plaits over the shoulder, while in others the short, worsted jacket, red, black, or white, is preferred. The striped or plain woolen skirts, full aprons of comparatively somber colors and wooden *sabots* are common in all localities.

In her book "Costumes, Traditions, and Songs of Savoy" Estella Canziani has most interesting illustrations of the lace caps

FIG. 140. DRESSES AND HEAD-DRESSES TYPICAL OF NORMANDY. THE LATTER BEAR A MARKED RESEMBLANCE TO THE HENNINS OF THE FIFTEENTH CENTURY. Wide World Photos.

of the peasant women of Savoy. They all have upstanding plaited lace frills in front with straps of ribbon that pass under the chin. In order to protect this fragile structure on rainy days, each woman puts over it an extremely large hat of black felt and sallies forth to market under an enormous umbrella of scarlet or blue.[5]

---

[5] CANZIANI, E., COSTUMES, TRADITIONS, AND SONGS OF SAVOY, p. 72. Chatto and Windus.

The skirts are bell-shaped, with many small plaits that are caught in at the waistband. The shoulder kerchief and tight bodice differ but little from those worn in other parts of the country. The belt, however, is quite distinctive, consisting of a long strip, the width differing in various sections, of wool or silk very richly embroidered, wrapped several times about the waist and fastened with small chains and hooks.

The men-folk are picturesquely clad in long trousers and jackets of white homespun with many gilt buttons on the latter.

Italy.—The tunics and togas of olden times have left no imprint on the costume of modern Italians. In modern Italy the men are especially fond of elaborate buttons which fasten waistcoat, double-breasted short coat, and knee breeches. Sash and long stockings are the two very colorful items in their costume, though much of the latter are covered by the high boots or gaiters which are so common in Campania. The Calabrian man's hat is an amusing affair with small, upturned brim, and cone-shaped crown to the top of which are attached six or eight ribbons that hang to the waist.

In comparing the peasant costumes of the various countries of Europe one is impressed by the individuality and originality of the sleeves in the dresses worn by Italian women until recent times. In so many parts of the country a cloth or silk bodice, usually separate from the long, billowy skirts, was worn over a white linen chemise or blouse. The sleeves of the bodice were detachable and worn at pleasure. When worn they were attached to the armscye of the bodice by ribbons or laces, folds or puffings of the white chemise showing between the lacings. Many Italian portraits of the latter part of the fifteenth century show somewhat similar types of sleeves, doubtless the ancestors of the modern peasant ones.

While long aprons, gathered into the waistbands, are found in practically every part of Italy today, there is one type peculiar to so many beautiful peasant costumes that have been handed down from mother to daughter, that differs markedly from the aprons in most other countries. This is a long strip of wool or silk of bright color edged with a border of embroidery; large areas of the two ends are likewise covered with similarly worked decorations. The apron is fastened over a skirt with a ribbon or string, about a foot of the upper end of the apron being turned down at the waist. The flat, unbroken areas of this garment afford most interesting opportunities for designs.

The folded shoulder shawl is less evident in Italian peasant dress than in that of other countries, but is found quite generally in parts of Campania. As a head covering the kerchief is commonly replaced by the turban-like head-dress worn in parts of the

Fig. 141. Picturesque Costumes of the Piedmont Section. Photo by Courtsey of Enit.

Fig. 142. A Costume Worn in the Abruzzi. Photo by Courtesy of Enit.

Abruzzi, or by the *tovaglia* characteristic of Basilicata, some sections of the Abruzzi, as well as of a few other districts of Italy. In "Peasant Art in Italy" the *tovaglia* is described as consisting "of a piece of linen, about a half yard wide and two yards long, the ends of which are trimmed with fringes. It is arranged in such a manner that one half falls down over the shoulder to the waist, the other half is folded lengthwise on the forehead into three folds which fall down at the side of the face and are joined to the back part of the veil at the broadest part of the shoulders. The head and bust of the wearer appear to be in a niche, or frame, of the purest white linen, which gives great refinement to the features and intensifies the beauty of the coloring."[6]

Apron, chemise, and shirt as well as household linens are trimmed with beautiful needle-point and bobbin laces, cutwork, drawnwork, and embroidery in white or colored threads which the peasant woman finds time to make while seated in her doorway after the day's labor. Her jewelry consists of gold filigree incrusted with enamels, pearls, of which the Italians are passionately fond, and other precious and colorful stones. Numerous necklaces and chains of coral or gold beads are worn about the throat, while beautiful pearl ear-rings hang from the ears, jeweled pins and combs hold the hair, and elaborate belts of silver encircle the waist.

Switzerland.—A study of the many types of so-called Swiss costume that until recently were worn by the peasants, reveals many indications of relationship to the French fashions of the eighteenth century. As French styles were adopted and quite generally worn by those of the higher ranks of Swiss society, it is probable that the clothes of the socially superior were imitated more or less by those of lower station; and being made from as handsome materials as means permitted, were worn only on holidays and Sundays, cherished, and handed down to succeeding generations.

The bouffant skirt, close, pointed bodice, large hat and elaborate head-dress with its stiffened lace frills, flowers, and ribbons of the wealthy are echoed in the corresponding features of the Swiss peasant dress but modified and individualized by the residents of the various sections of the country. The ankle-length skirt of the city was doubtless shortened considerably by the women of the hamlets for convenience in their work and in climbing the steep mountain paths; the elbow-length sleeves were retained as convenient for working purposes; the different types of caps and head-dresses became symbols of one's social status, religious faith, and place of residence. The mountainous character of Switzerland has had much to do with the preservation of the old modes, but modern means of communication and travel are rapidly doing their

---

[6] HOLME, CHARLES, PEASANT ART IN ITALY, p. 15. "The Studio" Ltd.

share toward the gradual relinquishment of these picturesque styles by the inhabitants of the various cantons.

There appears always to have been considerable uniformity in the dress of the men. In practically all cantons the ordinary costume consisted of white linen shirt, close breeches of leather or cloth, a scarlet vest or short jacket with lapels of bright color, yellow in Schaffhausen, and a three-quarter-length coat of somber colored wool. Long stockings of white or colored wool were in some places, as in Bâle, held by a garter at the knee. Low shoes with large buckles of silver were the general rule, though in Grisons and Lucerne tall boots and long tight trousers were more favored. In this latter canton a dignified black stock was preferred to the blue neckerchief of Schaffhausen and the yellow one of Bern. Interesting touches were added in the leather belts with large buckles that always accompanied the short jackets worn in the cantons of Uri and Schwitz.

Fig. 143. Yodelers from Appenzell Adorned in Regular Sunday Garb. Courtesy of the Swiss Federal Railroads.

Great variety prevailed in the style of the men's head-wear. Old drawings and photographs show a profusion of forms: large, round brims; small, close ones; or moderate sized ones pinched into the *tricorne* shape, a fashion very prevalent in Bâle, Valais, Schaffhausen, Uri, and Grisons. A bouquet of flowers added a smart touch to the hat of the young gallant from the latter canton.

Common to the costume of women in all cantons was the snowy white chemise. Universal, too, was the heavy cloth skirt of red, brown, blue, or black, that was sewn in fine plaits to the waistband and hung at a convenient length somewhere between the knee and ankle, displaying the long white or red stockings, and low shoes of leather with silver buckles of generous size. The apron, while ordinarily much the same in cut, varied in material and color in the different sections; in Zurich, it was generally gayly striped with

Fig. 144. Bernese Costumes. Photo from Brown Brothers.

ed and jauntily short; in Schaffhausen, yellow and long; in St. Gall, striped red and blue; in Grisons white; while in the canton of Schwitz it combined the colors found in all others.

The bodice so decidedly characteristic of Swiss dress, while practically always alike in cut, being close-fitting at the waist, sleeveless, and cut low at the neck both front and back, with narrow straps at the shoulders, varied decidedly in material and color; it was scarlet in Zurich and St. Gall, blue in Schwitz, and black in Schaffhausen, Engadine, and Appenzell. Bright colored ribbons laced the bodice together across the front where it was further decorated with embroidery in colored silks and metallic threads. In many districts a figured silk or embroidered muslin kerchief was folded across the shoulders and chest, with its ends tucked into the top of the bodice. In Uri the women formerly wore velvet collars that were square in shape, and extended to the end of the shoulders. At the corners of the back were attached silver chains that were brought under the arms and fastened with decorative clasps to the corners of the front.[7]

Ear-rings, finger rings, necklaces, and brooches of gold or silver filigree were much prized by the Swiss woman whose choicest possessions, however, were the long pins of twisted wire with heads of enamel or precious stones which secured the thick braids of hair at the back of the neck.

FIG. 145. A SUNDAY COSTUME FROM THE VALAIS. Photo by M. Kettel, Geneva. Courtesy of the Swiss Federal Railroads.

FIG. 146. PARTICIPANTS OF A NATIONAL COSTUME FESTIVAL AT MONTREUX. Courtesy of the Swiss Federal Railroads.

Hair dressing and head-dresses were likewise subject to regional differences, the unmarried women of Schaffhausen wearing their hair in one long braid, those of Uri in two braids, those of Bâle letting it hang free down the back, while the women of Schwitz drew their hair up on the head in the form of puffs between the two wings of their black lace cap, *rosehube*, and held it in place with a long silver pin called the *rosenadel*. The braided and fancifully

[7] ZUR GESCHICHTE DER KOSTÜME. See plate 513.

knotted hair of the matrons of St. Gall, Bâle, and Freiburg, are but
a few examples of the striking and fanciful arrangements that
existed. In many cantons lace played the stellar rôle in the coif.
Black for young girls and white for matrons, it was plaited,
stiffened, and wired into a number of wing-like shapes which,
adorned with artificial flowers and ribbons, were perched on top or
precariously at the back of the head. The *schlappe*[8] of Appenzell
is an excellent example of one of the most picturesque head-dresses
of this character. It was a small bonnet with a pair of semi-
circular wings at each side of the head that gave much the appearance of a lacy butterfly poised ready for flight. Fig. 146.

Tyrol.—In the neighboring Tyrol masculine dress, in general,
is characterized by the white shirt with its comfortable, turned
down collar and bright cravat, a bright-hued woolen vest, a hip-
length coat of brown or gray; and close cloth or leather breeches
that in most cases cover the knee and the top of the long white
stockings. In some districts, particularly at Meran, the breeches
are merely short trunks that leave the knee quite exposed. Very
distinctive are the broad braces or suspenders of red or green
cloth heavily embroidered in bright colors. On occasions of
festivity these are accompanied by an embroidered belt.

Aprons of generous size, many petticoats, extremely ample
skirts that clear the ankles by several inches, and heavy, bright
stockings are characteristic of women's dress in all parts of the
Tyrol, while the hats, neck finishes and bodices seem to differ considerably in various towns and valleys. In Meran, Alsbach, the
Brixenthal, the Pusterthal, the Grödnerthal, the Lower Innthal,
a sleeveless black velvet bodice, quite similar to that worn by the
neighboring Swiss, is worn over a snowy white chemise with short,
full sleeves that extend to just above the elbows where they are
tied with bright ribbons and end in full, embroidered ruffles. The
sleeves only of the chemise are visible as across the front is a
bright colored strip of cloth which shows plainly under the bright
lacings attaching the two narrow fronts of the velvet or cloth
bodice. The neck finish of the dress worn in the Gröden valley
consists of a narrow neck band, to the base of which is attached a
plaited frill so wide that it reaches to the end of the shoulders.

---

[8] BAUD-BOVY, D., PEASANT ART IN SWITZERLAND, p. 41. "The Studio"
Ltd.

In the valley of the Puster one sees the full, wide collar that resembles so closely the ruffs of the sixteenth century. In other districts a colored silk handkerchief is placed around the neck and crossed in front, its ends either knotted or tucked into the top of the bodice. Another form of bodice, favored particularly in the Zillerthal and Innthal, is cut low and square in the front and rather wide at the shoulders, is buttoned down the center front to the close-fitting, round waist line, and has long sleeves that are loose and full to below the elbow and tight from there to the hand. Some of these bodices have sleeves short enough to permit the ruffle of the chemise to show at the elbow. With such sleeves are worn long mitts of warm wool frequently embroidered in bright colors. The low neck is neatly filled in with a gay silk kerchief. In this section, too, are worn the low-cut, low-heeled slippers that are so generally found in the Tyrol, though high shoes are by no means unfamiliar.[9]

The hair dressing of the women is extremely simple, the hair being brushed back from the face, wound or braided into a knot which is secured by silver pins of intricate workmanship.

Like all countries with peasant dress, the Tyrol has her share of variety in head covering, green or black felt being the usual fabric from which the hats are made. Brims are of different widths from the fairly narrow one of the sailor type of black or green felt with its pendant streamers down the back as affected by the women of Innsbruck, to the enormously broad one with small crown and flower decorations seen in the valley of the Grödner. A unique hat is worn by both sexes in the Zillerthal. It is described by one traveler as "made of black felt, and in shape resembles somewhat the traditional cap worn by Mercury in his statues, though the crown is not so flat. It is enlivened by a cord and two gilt or silver tassels which hang down in front."[10] In the neighborhood of Brixen the hats of both men and women have the tall crown so familiar in the Welsh beaver, but with a broader brim that rolls slightly upward. Feathers of the cock and the eagle are distinctive hat trimmings.

---

[9] ZUR GESCHICHTE DER KOSTÜME. See plates 786, 1217, 1218.
[10] From THE SPELL OF THE TYROL by W. D. McCRACKEN, p. 84. Copyright 1905 by L. C. Page and Company, Boston, Mass.

REFERENCES

ZUR GESCHICHTE DER KOSTÜME, plates 786, 810, 840, 866, 1217, 1218.

GIAFFERRI, FEMININE COSTUME OF THE WORLD.

RACINET, LE COSTUME HISTORIQUE, Vol. VI.

HOLME, PEASANT ART IN ITALY.

BAUD-BOVY, PEASANT ART IN SWITZERLAND.

HEIERLI, DIE SWEIZERTRACHTEN.

HEIERLI, DIE VOLKSTRACHTEN DER SCHWEIZ.

HOLME, PEASANT ART IN AUSTRIA-HUNGARY.

HAUSCHOFER, TIROL.

KÖNIG, LORY, UND ANDEREN, ALTE SCHWEIZER TRACHTEN.

CALDERINI, IL COSTUME POPULARE IN ITALIA.

KEIM, LE COSTUME DU PAYS FRANCE.

VINCENT, COSTUME AND CONDUCT IN THE LAWS OF BASEL, BERN AND ZURICH.

CHAPTER XVI

NATIONAL COSTUME IN GERMANY, THE NETHER-LANDS, IRELAND, SCOTLAND, WALES, NORWAY AND SWEDEN

Germany.—The German peasant dress, while consisting of the same number and form of garments, was varied in color and decoration in different sections of the country: being bright and gay in the southern, and dark and somber in the northern parts. In Bavaria and Hessen were found greater elaboration of short coat, vest, and breeches worn by men than in most other states. This decoration consisted chiefly of braided designs outlining the two lengthwise front pockets of the breeches, and in bright facings and numerous silver buttons on the waist-length coat that was worn by men of all ages. In Hessen this coat was a jaunty, jolly affair with intricate pockets, a profusion of buttons, and a narrow standing collar. The vest, too, had its share of buttons extending from the high neck to the waist in single or double row. In many districts in Hessen these fastenings were accompanied by conspicuously worked or braided buttonholes. In Bavaria, coins of the realm performed the duty of buttons.

Common to all districts was the heavy cloth top-coat that had retained the shape and lines of the early nineteenth-century coat. Its full skirts with plaits from the waist line in the back varied slightly in length from ankles to somewhat below the knees. Characteristic of it were the high standing collar, large revers, and buttons of cloth or silver. In many districts, particularly in the Spreewald, the color of this coat was more frequently white than black.

More common than trousers were the fairly close knee breeches with long white or colored stockings, low shoes and gaiters, or high top-boots. In many parts of Hessen the long stockings were invariably finished at the knee with blue woolen gaiters of much pretension, while in Bavaria they failed to meet the short trunks that substituted for breeches, and, as in Meran in the Tyrol, left the knees exposed.

The soft collar of the white shirt turned over a black silk cravat which tied in the front in a double knot with short ends. This form of neckwear prevailed throughout Germany with but very few exceptions.

FIG. 147. BAVARIAN COSTUMES. Photo from Brown Brothers.

The average German indulged his fancy for head-gear of interesting form with but little restraint. No one type seems to have prevailed in all parts of the country. The men in Schleswig-Holstein[1] wore the white stocking cap; those in Württemberg and

<hr>

[1] ZUR GESCHICHTE DER KOSTÜME. See plate 1137.

Baden a felt hat of much the same shape as the modern European top-hat but with a slightly lower crown; men of the older generation in Hessen were picturesque in their enormous *tricorne* hats, while the younger men preferred the less cumbersome small fur toque with crown of green or other colored velvet. In the Spreewald, Prussia, a simple cloth cap with visor was prevalent, while in Bavaria, particularly Schliersee, both sexes favored green or black felt with small brim but fairly high crown that was a trifle smaller at the top than at the base, and trimmed with gay flowers or feathers.

Bavarian men indulged their love of ornament by wearing pretentious watch fobs and seals that hung from the decorated pockets of their breeches. Every man also had his sturdy walking stick always at hand.

With the exception of the head-dress, women's dress in Germany was practically uniform. It consisted of a full, heavy cloth skirt with many very fine plaits from the waist line half way down to the green or blue silk bordered hem; a spencer jacket worn over a white, short-sleeved bodice or one of dark cloth; a kerchief of gaily figured calico about the shoulders and chest; and bright-hued stockings that were quite elaborate in decoration when worn with a very short skirt. Particularly characteristic were the many ribbons that floated about, attached to caps or tied about the waist and hanging down the front. The material for skirt and spencer seems to have been plain more often than figured, and the absence of colorful embroidery, so generally found in the neighboring Slavic costumes, was most marked.

The Wendish women of the Spreewald wore very short skirts, and over the white chemise, whose sleeves were short, close, and finished with a turned-back cuff, a black velvet corset. Into the front of this corset were tucked the ends of the shoulder kerchief. Their spencer was usually of black cloth and had the long, tight sleeves customary in this type of coat. It was their head-dress that was most individual and interesting. Of printed material measuring slightly over a yard square, it was folded into a triangle and placed on the head so that the center point hung down the back of the neck with the two ends from the side knotted at the back of the head but under the hanging point. The neck on fête days was encircled by an enormous white muslin ruff, its ends fastened under the chin by a large bow of figured ribbon.   In Silesia, as in so many sections where peasant dress is common, the head-dresses were prominent.   Along the Mosel river, tiny white bonnets were perched on the back of the women's heads almost concealing the elaborate braids of hair which were held in loose loops by a long, decorative silver gilt pin.   The small black cap worn in the Rhenish province was secured by broad ribbons passing from the sides over the ears and tying under the chin.   Wider and longer

Fig. 148.   Quaint Head-dresses Worn in the Spreewald.   Wide World Photos.

ribbons hung from the back of the cap.   The chief features of the dress were the sleeves of the white chemise—short, puffs much larger than the Empire ones from which they received their inspiration.

In Thuringia, where the dress itself was not unusual, the head-dress was a bonnet with puffings of ribbon,—sometimes intermingled with feathers and lace,—across the front and many long streamers of wide ribbon falling at the back below the hips.   This head-dress did not interfere with the wearing of long gold ear-rings as did so many of the caps.

In the skirts of the Bavarian women it was customary for the plaits to extend the full length instead of part way down from the waist. The front of the corset was hung with numerous small silver chains, while about the neck were worn close collars of garnets or pearls, with occasionally a pendant locket. Both kerchiefs and hats were used as head coverings, the former arranged in a great variety of ways. The black or green felt hats worn in Schliersee were similar to those worn by the men; the one common to the neighborhood of Jachenau had a high, straight crown draped with green ribbon and enlivened with metallic tassels on the right-hand side.

Württemberg women used ribbons for the lacings of their black velvet corsets, omitting the many crosswise chains employed in Bavaria. Their spencers were cut with long shoulders and sleeves with much fullness at the top. There as in Baden the hair hung in two long braids, from the ends of which fell bright ribbons in a variety of arrangements and lengths.

Most attractive was the head-dress of Württemberg—a very wee bonnet with a large fan of transparent material rising from the very back of the head, and held in place by broad ribbons that tied in a smart bow under the chin. Down the back hung many streamers of still wider ribbon. Quite a contrast to this was the tall, stiff, cylindrically shaped hat which the woman of Prechthal, Baden, tied to her head. In Staffen and Müllheim the very diminutive cap was almost concealed by a large bow of ribbon, much like that still seen in some parts of Alsace, and from which the Alsatian bow probably sprang. In the Gutach valley, in the Black Forest, a dainty bonnet with a frill of black lace about the face, ending at the side in small spreading wings like those of the Volendam cap in the Netherlands, was worn at home. For out-of-door wear this was surmounted by a fair-sized hat of felt whose low, rounding, crown and moderate brim were practically concealed by six large pompons of wool, black for matrons, and red for unmarried women.

The quaintest dress of all prevailed in the villages of Hessen where the skirts with many tiny plaits just covered the knees, below which were bright red tasselled garters holding up the white stockings. On the low shoes were large buckles of silver. The velvet corset was very small in front necessitating a broad lacing and exposing much of the printed shoulder shawl whose ends were tucked into the belt of the full, plain apron. The hair hung in braids down the back, or was tucked up under the black silk head-dress with its top bow of black ribbon. In some districts the head covering took the form of a close-fitting cap with ribbon streamers at the side. These were tied under the chin or hung down over the arms. In

Hessen Nassau, a round, box-like affair, probably three inches in diameter and less in height, was perched on top of the head with streamers falling down the side. Here, too, were used the colorful head shawls. The women of Hessen delighted in ornaments for neck and arms. The bracelet was generally a broad strip of ribbon of bright pattern held on the arm with three bright red buttons. Around the throat they wore bands of velvet ribbons studded with pearls or metal disks, and chains of amber.

The   Netherlands.— Although in general present-day European dress has replaced that of former times, one may see today in a few of the provinces of the Netherlands, notably those of North Holland, Friesland, and Zeeland, the billowy skirts, quaint caps, and baggy trousers which

FIG. 149.   THE HAT WITH POMPON TRIM-MINGS WORN IN GUTACH, THE BLACK FOREST. Photo from Brown Brothers.

are characteristic of Dutch costume and reflect the fashions of the times of Hals and Rembrandt.

On the island of Marken, a fishing settlement in the Zuyder Zee, that was formerly a part of the mainland, the natives cling tenaciously to the type of dress that prevailed in the olden times. The men are attired in dark gray, very full breeches which reach just below the knee, and double-breasted jackets of the same hue fastened with silver buttons. For foot-wear they have wooden sabots, *klompen*. In winter a close fur cap is substituted for the broad-brimmed felt hat of summer time.

The feminine costume consists of wide skirts, and gaily striped or flowered bodices which lace in the back and have straight sleeves that reach midway between the elbow and wrist. The sleeves are frequently of a different material from that of the bodice itself. Gaily colored aprons protect the voluminous brown or blue skirts that are held out at the sides and back by a bustle. Out-of-doors the women's feet are hidden in *klompen* that are rendered decorative by hand carvings. These she slips off at the threshold of the house and sometimes replaces them with leather, square-toed shoes ornamented with buckles. Usually, however, she goes about her household duties in her stocking feet, a tribute, surely, to her immaculate floors. The close-fitting head-dress is comprised of five pieces; first, a layer of muslin edged with lace or embroidery; then a strip of colored cotton to add interest to the lace of the two muslin and lawn caps which follow on top of this; finally a close cap of some printed cotton. At marriage the

FIG. 150. DUTCH BREECHES AND KLOM-PEN. Courtesy of Miss M. L. Hook.

women cut their hair short in the back leaving at either side of the face a long curl and on the forehead straight bangs which are rubbed with soap to give the requisite stiffness. [2]

Just across the Zuyder Zee, in Volendam on the mainland, the trousers of the men are large, full, and very long, and usually of navy blue material. The waist-length, double-breasted jacket is sometimes a brilliant red, while the fur cap is rather tall.

When dressing for ceremonial occasions the matron of Volendam dons from six to fourteen skirts depending on her financial status; a close, short bodice that is cut with a square neck finished with a

---

[2] ZUR GESCHICHTE DER KOSTÜME. See plate 479.

crisp kerchief, or vestee of figured light-weight wool; and a lace-trimmed, embroidered cap which, with its two long points standing out from each side of the face, is quite unlike the other caps worn in the Netherlands.

In the southern section of the Netherlands, in the province of Zeeland, the men are forsaking the picturesque, short, full breeches, and adopting in their stead the modern long trousers, holding them

Fig. 151. A Cap Worn in South Beveland. Photo from Brown Brothers.

up with broad belts fastened by large silver buckles, or by four enormous silver buttons. A double row of silver filigree buttons or coins secures the gaily embroidered waistcoat showing at the front of the short, close-fitting jacket. A red tie and a small cap with a leather visor and an embroidered band add interesting accents.

In this same province the woman's costume is made up of the usual full skirt, tight bodice, and very short sleeves so commonly found elsewhere in the country. The dress of the women of Axel has its unique feature in the immensely high puffs which stand above the shoulders like two tall peaks. They are made of flowered material and meet at the waist line in both back and front. The low cut neck of the dark gown permits the elaborately embroidered chemise to show at the neck and chest. A great number of chains and lockets are attached to the front of the bodice, and strings of coral beads form a collar for the throat. Across the chest is folded a gay kerchief whose ends are tucked into the belt of the skirt. In Walcheren this neckerchief is arranged in such a way that a decorative stomacher of gay colors that fills in the low bodice is plainly visible.

The hair of the Zeeland woman is completely covered with a fine cambric or linen cap fitting tightly to the head. Sometimes a small ruffle falls over the neck at the back. With this type of cap is worn across the forehead a silk or velvet band to which are attached elaborate ornaments, golden balls suspended from spiral, cork-screw-like gold wire. Some women still follow the old custom of wearing around their heads the "head irons" or bands of metal with decorative ends. "These knobs, often of exquisite workmanship, form the two ends of the close-fitting metal bands they wear round the head just above the temples. In Zeeland a Protestant may be recognized by her round knobs; a Roman Catholic's are square. Buttons or conical spiral extensions upon which long ear-rings are hung also serve to finish off the rough edges of the head band."[3]

Out of doors a high straw hat is worn over the cap. The women of Ter Goes wear two caps, the under one fitting so closely to the head that only a very little of the hair shows on the forehead. The second one is of lace plaited to stand up and form a frame for the face. To the inner cap at the temples shining gold plates are fastened by means of massive gold pins.

The Frisian woman's sleeves are a trifle longer, and her skirts are somewhat less billowy than those of her countrywomen in other parts of Holland.[4] Above the rounded neck of the tight bodice protrude the folds of a gaudy kerchief. The heavy *sabots* of

[3] PEACOCK, N., WOMEN OF ALL NATIONS, Vol. II, p. 708. Cassell and Company, Ltd.
[4] ZUR GESCHICHTE DER KOSTÜME. See plate 479.

Marken are replaced by simple slippers with straps at the ankles. The apron, while long, covers only a portion of the front of the dress. Here, too, is found a peculiar type of head-dress. It consists of a daintily embroidered cap worn over a skull cap, *oory-zer*, of pure beaten gold, silver, or copper according to the circumstances of the wearer. Attached to this helmet at each side near the temples are elaborate spiral ornaments from which are suspended long ear-rings.

The youth of the Netherlands were formerly attired in exact reproductions of the costumes of their elders. Interesting examples

of this custom may be seen today in Marken, where boys and girls are dressed alike up to the age of seven in trim, straight bodices, long, full skirts, and the typical caps that are adorned with a button as the distinguishing mark of the boy. Like his sisters the boy wears long curls, *pijpekrullen*, until he attains the age of seven when he discards the feminine curls and cap and adopts the fashion of his father.

Ireland.—Since Elizabethan days the dress of the Irish has had little to distinguish it from that worn in England, but before the time of that queen who, like Henry VIII, made many laws pertaining to the clothing of her subjects, Irishmen wore kilts similar to those

FIG. 152. THE YOUNGER GENERATION OF MARKEN. Courtesy of Miss M. L. Hook.

of the Scotchman, accompanied by "leggings laced on by string tipped with bronze," shoes of brown leather and a plaited linen shirt. Over all was a sleeveless, loose cloak that was long and made of bright colored wool. Some wore a fitted coat much like the present-day frock coat with tight sleeves, no collar, and a broad girdle at the waist.[5] Men took great pride in their long beards, and like the women, wore their hair flowing over the shoul-

[5] JOYCE, P. W., A SOCIAL HISTORY OF IRELAND, Vol. II, p. 207. Longmans, Green and Company.

ders or braided, and wound about the head. A marked characteristic of this hair arrangement was the long lock of hair, *glib*, that was left hanging over the forehead. For head covering, caps were used.

The women wore a linen undergarment and over this long gowns of the same material dyed saffron, or of costly fabric imported from the Continent. Their long capes had hoods attached. For jewelry they wore bracelets, pins, brooches, rings, and torques.

Fig. 153. Scots in Native Garb. Courtesy of Associated British and Irish Railways.

Scotland.—John George Mackay describes the belted plaid made of sixteen yards of tartan, and known as the *breacan-feile*,[7] as "plaited and fastened with a belt around the body, one half of the width hanging from the waist to the knee, the other half being tucked up, which was fastened to the left shoulder by a pin or brooch, and in the wet weather could be drawn over the shoulder like a cloak." Occasionally with this colorful plaid the *trews*,[8] close-fitting breeches with stockings attached, were worn;

[7] Mackay, J. G., The Romantic Story of the Highland Garb and Tartan, p. 98. E. H. Mackay.

[8] *Ibid.*, p. 98.

like the kilt, these were made of tartan whose pattern and color distinguished the various clans one from the other. The belted plaid is today accompanied by stockings that are gartered just below the knee leaving that part of the body exposed to the suns and mists of "bonny Scotland." Over the long waistcoat a short coat of velvet or cloth is worn, while from the left shoulder hangs

a folded plaid concealing beneath its folds the sword belt. The other weapon, the *dirk*, is thrust into the top of the right stocking.

Coarse leather shoes, *brogan*, *tionndaidh*,[9] or sandals of rawhide, *cuaran*, protect the feet, and a blue bonnet similar to the tam-o'shanter, or a cocked bonnet with eagle's feather at the side, covers the head. The indispensable *sporan*, a large purse of skin with silver mountings, hangs below the belt in front.

Over her warm cloth bodice and skirt, the Highland lassie was wont to arrange a fine worsted plaid three yards in length. Placed over her head, one end of this plaid hung down to the bottom of her skirt on the right-hand side, while the short end fell over the left arm. Its folds were caught in front by a large brooch.

Fig. 154. The Tall Beaver Hat of Wales. Courtesy of the Druid Publishing Company.

Wales.—While the men of Wales followed the fashions of dress set by the English in the eighteenth and nineteenth centuries, and appeared in jacket, waistcoat, and breeches of flannel,[10] the women until about 1860, clung to a costume that probably originated in the seventeenth century, since it showed the general lines of the dress worn under the Stuarts.[11] This costume, worn now by a few women during the national competitive song festivals, the *Eisthedd-*

---

[9] *Ibid.*, p. 100.
[10] WARNER, R., A WALK THROUGH WALES, p. 183. London, 1797.
[11] RHYS, J., THE WELSH PEOPLE, p. 667. Ernest Benn and Company.

fodau, consisted of a gown, *pais-a-gwn bach*, with a tight-fitting bodice and skirt that was open in front, its edges turned back and fastened so as to expose a striped petticoat; a full apron; a broad handkerchief about the neck and shoulders; a daintily ruffled cap of muslin with ribbons that tied under the chin; and a tall hat of highly polished silk beaver. The tip of the crown of this hat was slightly narrower than the base, while the brim was both wide and straight. The crown of the man's hat was without this slight tapering at the top. The wrap was of two types: a long, circular cape with attached hood that in rainy weather was pulled up over the tall hat, *hat-fawr;* or a large shawl of checked or plaid wool folded diagonally through the center.

Dark blue and brown were the usual colors of the flannel of home manufacture from which both men's and women's garments were made, the cravats contributing touches of brilliancy to the otherwise somber costume of the former.

Denmark.—The dress of the Danish people resembles that of the Norwegians and Swedes. Although each province has slight peculiarities in the matter of dress, the usual costume of the sturdy Dane consists of short trousers, buttoned at the knee, long stockings, low shoes with silver buckles of no mean proportions, and a short coat fastened with a double row of buttons.

Ankle-length skirts, a closely laced bodice with sleeves reaching to the elbow, an apron with crosswise decorations of embroidery, and a small, fringed shoulder shawl are the garments that the Danish peasant woman has in common with her neighbors to the north. It is her elaborate metal belt and her bright bonnet that mark her nationality. The decoration is concentrated on the back or crown piece of the velvet or silk bonnet with its long steamers. This piece, triangular or oblong in shape, is filled with geometric or semi-conventionalized designs worked in silks and heavy gold threads. The severity of the front is relieved by a lace frill about the face and a broad ribbon bow that ties under the chin.

Norway.—A distinctive national costume has been worn for centuries by the country folk of Norway, but is at present found only in the most remote villages and mountain hamlets. The men of Saetersdalen, about the only Norwegian men who have retained their costume, are quite conspicuous in their dark brown frieze trousers which reach almost to the neck in front and back, being held at the shoulders by narrow strips of cloth. On Sundays and festival days a diminutive cloth jacket is added to this extremely simple attire.

Though differing in the various districts, the woman's dress possesses at least one important feature common to all. That is the pure white blouse with its full sleeves gathered at the wrist into a

FIG. 155. TYPICAL COSTUMES OF OLD DENMARK. Photo from Ewing Galloway, N. Y.

narrow band of embroidery. Similar strips of embroidery finish the front and form a small standing collar which is fastened at the throat by a massive silver brooch, usually an heirloom handed down from mother to daughter through many generations.

In Saetersdalen, where some of the quaintest costumes still survive, the women wear a full, heavy cloth skirt which reaches from just under the arm to below the knee. It is held by embroidered braces or straps over the shoulders in much the same fashion as the pinafore of the young English school girl. The bottom of the skirt is edged with two or three bands of equally thick material of a contrasting color, or with embroidery in colored wools.

The full, black skirt of the matron of the Hardanger district, reaching from the waist to the ankle, is rendered festive for ceremonial occasions by two rows of three-quarter-inch-wide red ribbon. Her sleeveless bodice of red cloth is close-fitting at the waist line and its front edges meet only at the waist, spreading apart from there up to show the stomacher. All edges of the small bodice are bound with braid of a different texture and color, while the stomacher is almost entirely covered with a design worked in colored glass beads and edged at the top with a band of black velvet and gold braid. No Hardanger costume is considered complete without the large, spotless apron with its wide band of needlework above an equally generous hem. The waistband of the apron is concealed by a two-inch belt of black velvet ribbon or of brightly knitted yarn and beads fastened at the front by a silver buckle which with the brooch form practically the only jewelry the Norwegian women affect.

The hair of the married woman is covered by a cap peculiar in design and embroidery to the different districts. The *skaut*, a large square of white linen starched, plaited in the tiniest of plaits, folded and tied on the head in an intricate manner, is the distinctive headdress of the Hardanger matron. The hair of young girls and of unmarried women is allowed to fall free over the shoulders or in two long braids down the back. Their square-shaped bonnets are of bright cloth or velvet closely covered with beads in designs that are also found in the embroidery of the apron, belt, and blouse. The seams are joined with colored braids and from each side fall long ribbon streamers.

The sturdy woolen stockings, not infrequently red or of other bright colors, are hand-knitted and worn with strong oxfords or slippers with one strap.

Sweden.—In the few districts of Sweden where the population still clings to the old time costumes one sees a form of dress that is both picturesque and comfortable. While each parish in Delecarlia, where practically the only national costumes are still to be found, has its own arrangement of colors and patterns of weaving and embroidery, the same general features are found in all. The knee-length or slightly shorter coat of the men is made of homespun in dark blue, black, or white; the knee breeches of leather are natural color or white; the long woolen stockings are dark blue or white.[12]   A vest of cloth or leather is worn by the men of Leksand. The fashion of parting the hair in the middle, and of wearing round felt hats is common to all.

FIG. 156.   COSTUME WORN IN HARDANGER,   FIG. 157.   SWEDISH COSTUME.   Photo by
NORWAY.   Photo by Brown Brothers.   Brown Brothers.

Swedish women vary the colors and decorations of the homespun dresses that expose the snowy long sleeves of their chemise and the all important apron, though usually employing the color and design customary in their own parish.   For example the aprons of the Leksand maids and matrons have many perpendicu-

---

[12] PHILIP, J. B., HOLIDAYS IN SWEDEN, p. 177.   Skeffington and Sons.

lar stripes; those of Rättvik, numerous crosswise stripes; and those of Mora, a few horizontal ones at the very bottom.[13] The head-dress likewise reveals the wearer's place of residence. The matron of Leksand conceals all of her hair in a close, lace-trimmed cap of white linen; her daughter, in one of bright color, usually red. The women of Mora prefer brightly patterned kerchiefs drawn over the head and knotted under the chin.[14] Of equal importance with apron and cap is the small kerchief, flowered and fringed, that is worn over the shoulders.

The skirts of blue or black wool, tightly plaited from top to bottom, sometimes with broad stripes of color at the bottom, are short enough for the red or white stockings to be seen. Formerly many skirts were worn at the same time, the inner one being the longest, the outer one the shortest, so that a series of strips of color edged the bottom of the costume.

The silk corselet worn over the blouse is merely a wide band extending several inches above the waist line with narrower straps over the shoulders, and fastened at the front with metal—frequently pewter—eyelets, and laces of brilliant, hand-woven tape. Reminiscent of the Moyen Âge *aumônière* is the flat, square or oval shaped handkerchief bag which is either pinned to the waistband at the left side, or hung from about the waist by a long, narrow handwoven tape. Some of these bags are a riot of brilliant wools embroidered on a foundation of stout black wool. Particularly distinctive of the costume of women of Delecarlia is the sheepskin jacket which is extremely short, barely reaching to the waist with long, fairly close sleeves.

Lapland.—The Laplander, like the Eskimo, is forced by climatic conditions of the land in which he lives to dress with the idea of warmth uppermost in his mind, and to use the materials at hand in the construction of his garments. The reindeer furnish the skins for the ankle-length trousers, for the winter *kapta* or loose tunic, and for the shoes with their pointed, upturned toes. Two *kaptor* are worn on the most intensely cold days, the inner one with the fur next to the body. To prevent any cold air from reaching the body, the neck line and the wrists of the long sleeves fit closely while mittens of goat or cow's hair or of the indispensable reindeer

[13] *Ibid.*, p. 176.
[14] *Ibid.*, p. 176.

skin fit well over the bottom of the sleeve. In like manner the
trousers fit closely into the tops of the boots that are made large
enough to permit the feet to be clad in heavy woolen stockings and
then bound with the grass that grows in the summer and is so
highly prized and used by the Lapp for so many purposes. Strips

FIG. 158. NATIVES OF LAPLAND. Photo from Ewing Galloway, N. Y.

of bright colored wool, generally red, bind the seams of these cold-
proof shoes and fasten them close to the legs and ankles.[15]

Shirts of wool are worn under both winter and summer dresses
by both men and women, the embroidered finishes showing at the
neck of the blue *kapta* that in summer takes the place of the fur
one.[16] Belts of leather about two or three inches wide, thickly

[15] CHAILLU, PAUL, THE LAND OF THE MIDNIGHT SUN, Vol. II, p. 71.
Harper and Brothers.   [16] *Ibid.*, Vol. I, pp. 127–128.

'udded with silver ornaments and fastened with silver clasps girdle the *kaptor* of both sexes. The same blue cloth and scarlet bindings are fashioned into caps for the women and hats for the men.

Necklaces of large glass beads, finger rings of interesting character together with silver belts form the women's chief jewelry.

REFERENCES

Zur Geschichte der Kostüme, plates 1168, 1198, 466, 484, 1202, 1137, 479, 499.
MacIan, Costumes of the Clans.
Mackay, The Romantic Story of the Highland Garb and Tartan.
Kretschmer, Costumes Nationaux Allemands.
Hammerton, Peoples of All Nations.
Haire, The Folk Costume Book.
Holme, Peasant Art in Sweden, Lapland, and Iceland.
Mann, Peasant Costume in Europe.

CHAPTER XVII

NATIONAL COSTUME IN RUSSIA, CENTRAL EUROPE AND THE BALKANS

For brilliancy of coloring, individuality of decorative motifs and materials, particularly in the use of leather in costume, one must recognize the costumes of Central Europe as especially noteworthy. Arresting, indeed, are the examples of leather appliqué, of embroidery in silk, linen, woolen, and metallic threads, of braiding, the use of buttons and jewels, found in such profusion in the costume of the Slavic and Magyar peoples. They have developed and individualized the suggestions and examples received long years ago from Byzantine and Turkish sources and evolved types of costumes that are distinctly national but possess many features in common with those of close neighbors.

Russia.—The peasant costumes of Russia may be traced directly to the mode of dress existing in Constantinople, the former Byzantium, when in the ninth century the peoples of Russia and the Eastern Roman Empire came into contact with each other. From that time until the introduction of Western European manners and customs by Peter the Great during the seventeenth century, Russian art and life were quite largely dominated by Byzantine culture. The long, full gowns, of richly patterned fabrics and gem-studded embroideries, the elaborately conceived head-dresses of pearls and other precious stones, the ornate earrings and necklaces of former court dress were all inspired by Byzantine modes. In the holiday attire of the peasants of Great Russia, these features have been preserved and handed down to succeeding generations.

When posed beside the feminine members of his household, the Russian peasant man is a subdued figure, his long blouse of white linen or bright cloth being the one article of his wardrobe that challenges interest. This blouse, belted and hanging over the trousers, opens at the left side from neck to waist. This opening, the shallow standing collar, the cuffs of the full, banded sleeves, and

230

the bottom edge of the blouse are colorfully and richly embroidered. Into the tops of the tall leather boots are tucked the loose-fitting trousers of homespun or hand-blocked linen, the fabric that has had such an important place in the household and wardrobe of Old Russia.

The old time long cloth *kaftan* of straight, simple cut is still the overcoat for moderate weather, fur capes and long coats of sheepskin being necessary for the rigorous winters. Tall hats of felt or round ones of fur form the usual head covering. In addition to the tall boots of leather, another type of foot-gear worn by the peasant is the *lapot*.[1] This is made of strips of the inner bark of birch and lime trees laced together in the form of a crude shoe.

Until comparatively recent times the principal article of attire of the women's indoor dress was the *sarafan*, a full, plaited, or gathered skirt of rich brocade usually attached to a short, sleeveless bodice of varied cut in the neck line: high and round, or low and square.[2] The lack of arm covering was atoned for by the sleeves of the underbodice which were of ample proportions at the top and invariably long, in some instances coming well down over the hand. They gradually decreased in size from the elbow where they acquired many crosswise folds. This type of sleeve was cut much longer than the arm thus accounting for the surplus of material about the forearm. As a rule very handsome materials were employed in the sleeves which usually differed in pattern and color from the material in the *sarafan*. When of linen they were usually the long full ones gathered into a band or ruffle at the wrist and known today as the peasant sleeve, with embroidery massed between shoulder and elbow. If the neck of the *sarafan* was square, the round, gathered, and embroidered neck of the bodice was revealed to advantage. Beneath the *sarafan* was worn the long skirt of thick woolen material, known as the *paneva*, while over it many women donned a large, long apron fastened to a low bodice which sometimes boasted of sleeves, and was skillfully embroidered in colored silks. Simple heelless slippers were worn, made of leather, felt, or, for gala occasions, velvet or silk generously worked with threads of gold.

The penetrating cold of Russian winters required the free use of

---

[1] HOLME, CHARLES, PEASANT ART IN RUSSIA, p. 9. "The Studio," Ltd.
[2] *Ibid.*, p.8.

furs in the women's long full capes. Even the short coats of silk for summer were edged with fur which was fashioned also into long circular capes.

The imposing, glittering head-dress, prized above all possessions, was worn until recently at all times, both at home and abroad, except in the case of young girls whose hair hung in long braids over the shoulders. This close-fitting head-dress of many shapes and forms completely covered the hair; when the head-dress proper was set slightly back from the forehead a fringe or network of pearls coming well down to the eyebrows effectually concealed any stray locks. On a foundation of stiffened cloth or wire, covered with cloth of gold, silk, or velvet for a background, these head-dresses show a bewildering variety of forms: the moderate sized tiara, the tall, fez-like bonnet, the demure cap, or the striking affair that spread like a fan above and to the sides of the head. Whatever the shape, but little of the foundation was visible so closely was it covered with embroidery in metallic threads, or strewn with pearls. For out-of-door wear these head-dresses were lightly covered with beautiful veils, *fatas*, of diaphanous silk or cotton embroidered in gold or silver threads and sometimes edged with gold fringe. Head shawls played a somewhat less important part as head covering.

Pearls and gems were not reserved for the head-dress alone but were used in great profusion in long chains of gold and silver gilt for the neck and in swinging pendant ear-rings. Examples of old ear-rings now preserved in private collections have tiny fringes of pearls suspended from small plaques of brilliantly colored enamel. Finger rings and bracelets seem to have been regarded with less interest.

Another important detail of the costume was the *chirinka*, a square of silk or muslin embroidered in metallic threads or edged with gold fringe or tassels. We are told "the *chirinka* was an object for display and one of the indispensable adjuncts of the Russian woman's wardrobe, the most obvious and the favorite article; and it was, moreover, the custom always to hold it in the hand when going to church or on visits, or during all ceremonies."[3]

To the south in Little Russia, the Ukraine, the national cos-

[3] *Ibid.*, p. 8.

tume, considerably different from that of Great Russia, is still in evidence on holidays and evinces less magnificence of fabric and decoration; the simple homespuns and linens are substituted for the heavy brocades, with silk and linen threads replacing those of gold and silver so abundant in the dress of Great Russia. Absent, too, are the pearls and elaborate head-dresses. But the full apron that is gathered into a waistband, and the blouse of the Ukrainian peasant woman receive great attention from her skillful fingers.

FIG. 159. RUSSIAN PEASANT WOMEN. BUTSCHKURY.
Photo Courtesy of Raymond and Raymond, Inc.

The blouse, with its large sleeves that are gathered into close, narrow cuffs at the elbows or at the wrists, is beautifully embroidered. The major part of the embroidery is concentrated on the shoulders and upper sleeves with narrow bands of the same motifs extending down each side of the front, or directly down the shallow opening of the front. The collar into which the blouse is shirred is rarely over one and a half inches in width. Bright colored threads and geometric patterns are characteristic of most Ukrainian embroideries though in the southern part of the country more grayed colors and slightly floral designs prevail.

Until the last few decades the skirt worn by all Ukrainian women was the *plahta*,[4] consisting of two strips of wool or silk material with a woven plaid pattern, wound over the back of the body and lapped in front. The apron was then adjusted and both garments were held at the waist by a girdle the width of which varied with the districts, being narrow in the northern, and wide in the southern districts. A sleeveless, wide-skirted coat of dark cloth completed the costume; a sheepskin coat with the skin side decorated with applied pieces of colored leather on skirts and back, being worn in winter.

The cylindrically shaped cap wrapped with a long veil which hangs nearly to the feet successfully conceals the hair of the matron; while the young girl, wrapping her two long braids about her head and securing them with pins and a wreath of flowers has long ribbons floating down the back to take the place of her mother's veil. A gold or silver crucifix or medallion is invariably found suspended about the neck. Strings of coins, beads of glass, and coral harmonize with the simple costume.

The man of the Ukraine is clothed in practically the same type of costume as is his kinsman of Great Russia.

Poland.—Due to its geographic position and the frequent use of its territory as a passage between Russia and Austria Hungary, Poland in its national dress has adopted several features of those of its neighbors. The dress of Polish men of the eastern districts consists of loose trousers, frequently strong in color, tucked into tall boots, and long, smock-like shirts that are secured at the waist by belts of black leather. All of these articles show some Russian influence. Their long coats of sturdy cloth are fastened with elaborate frogs, buttons, and braid, this last medium of decoration also outlining the pockets and side seams of the long, close trousers that are commonly worn in the southern districts. This type of cut and decoration is particularly characteristic of the dress of the Poles residing in the villages of the Tatras mountains.[5] The short coat of sheepskin, frequently sleeveless, strikingly attractive with

---

[4] *Ibid.*, p. 20.

[5] WILLIAMS, MAYNARD O., STRUGGLING POLAND. *The National Geographic Magazine*, August, 1926.

appliqué of leather like those commonly worn in Hungary, is used
by both sexes in the eastern Carpathian mountain villages, where
one may see, also, wool coats curiously trimmed down the front
with large pompons of brilliant yarn. The seams of these coats
are joined and the edges finished with decorative stitches in the

Fig. 160. A Family from Lowicz, Poland. Photo from Ewing Galloway, N. Y.

same colorful threads. A fantastic pipe with long stem, a simple
walking stick, and a round felt hat with an exceedingly low crown
encircled by a string of white beads, feathers, or flowers are further
adjuncts of the masculine costume.

Extremely bright, crude colors are employed in the women's
head shawls, straight aprons, and short bouffant skirts of heavy
wool, with stripes that are most conspicuous, especially in the

neighborhood of Lowicz, between Posen and Warsaw. The white blouse with sleeves of moderate size, close or loose-fitting at the wrist, has blocks of embroidery near the shoulder with narrow bands of the same at neck and bottom of the sleeve. Endless strings of beads, amber and coral, are hung about the neck which is swathed in the folds of a brilliant kerchief that effectually conceals all hair.

The high boots with stitchery and appliqué around the top and down the front, or without any form of decoration, are the joy and pride of the Polish peasant woman's heart. She prefers to be barefooted and comfortable at home, but always wears the boots to church and town. Tourists in Poland remark on the general custom the peasant women have of swinging along the roads free and unencumbered as to feet with boots slung across the shoulders, and then sitting down by the roadside and drawing on those bugbears of civilization just before entering the town.

Wee tots follow the fashions of their elders, the small girls particularly, looking like animated dolls in full skirts and matronly little head shawls.

Finland.—Shut off for so many months from communication with the rest of Europe, the peoples of Finland and Estonia have evolved national costumes that have many features common to both. The men are clad in the Russian blouse with embroidered cuffs, neck-band and leather belt, and full trousers of long close ones that are bound from ankle to knee with narrow bands of geometrically patterned cloth. Their foot covering is of leather or tree bark shaped to the foot and fastened about the ankle like an Indian moccasin. The heavy cloth coat of the Estonian extends to the knee and has a flat collar of cloth. His head-covering is a cap with a visor; while that of the Finn is of felt with a high crown and narrow brim.

Finnish women concentrate the decoration of their simple costume on the small, short aprons, frequently of black cloth. These they elaborate with embroidery, beads, and fringe, and wear over a full skirt of striped woolen stuff. Only the large sleeves and a small portion of the front of the blouse are visible as the sleeveless but high-necked bodice is buttoned from neck to bust line and fastened at the throat by an enormous round brooch. A simple cap or a kerchief has gradually replaced the former head-dress of linen that bound the forehead and fell over the head and down the back like a veil.

Estonia.—The woman of Estonia wears a costume very similar to that of her Finnish neighbor: a full, striped skirt with bright border, and an embroidered white blouse or long-sleeved cloth bodice; but in addition to a large brooch at the throat, she loads her neck with many coins and ornaments of silver. Her head-dress is a

FIG. 161. ESTONIAN COSTUMES, ARRESTING IN COLOR AND PATTERN. Courtesy of the Consulate General of Estonia.

cap which varies in shape in the different parishes. The cap that is characteristic of the Parish of Püha is horn-shaped with a red and white checked kerchief tied over it; that of the Parish of Nissi, like an inverted cooking pot with streamers hanging down the back; while that of the women of Karja is described as "wheel-shaped," being broad and round at top and sloping to a small circle that just fits the top of the head. In Karja the women prefer bobbed hair to long tresses.

The dark cloth coats of the women extend almost to the bottom of the skirts, have long sleeves that fit closely at the hand, and open down the front or in a diagonal line on the left side. The foot covering ranges from the simply cut low slipper to the moccasin-shaped shoe that is bound to the foot and ankle with narrow ribbons.

Georgia.—Quite isolated in their rugged country, the Georgians of the Caucasus have retained for many years their own individual type of dress. The belted Russian blouse of cotton or linen, tall

FIG. 162. THE HUNGARIAN SZÜR.
Photo Erdelyi from Brown Brothers.

boots into which the trousers are tucked, or leggings and stout shoes are worn by the Georgian man and supplemented in very severe weather with a full length *bourka*, of thick black cloth made from goat or horse hair. Warmer days permit the wearing of a lighter weight wool coat, *tcherkeska*. The moderately tall cap of astrakan, dagger and sword with hilts of beautifully chased silver are distinguishing features of the attire. Their wives have appropriated the full-skirted *tcherkeska* as an important part of their costume, wearing it over a simple gown with close bodice and long, full skirt. Among their ornaments are many chains of silver fastened across the front of the bodice and heavy belts of the same metal with massive buckles. They are particularly proud of the two false curls that are suspended from each side of the head band of pearl-studded velvet that is placed under a veil of white lace with which head and shoulders are draped.

Hungary.—Totally unlike that of the previously mentioned national costumes is the dress of the Hungarian who uses white as the basis of a costume that has about it some most unusual features. Certainly the most striking article of the peasant man's dress is the *gatyák* or trousers of white linen of such generous width that they resemble a divided riding skirt. In some parts of Hungary these are replaced by white woolen pantaloons that extend below the knees and are finished at the bottom with coarse peasant-made lace or fringe. The sleeves of the linen shirts are as unusual as the *gatyák*, reaching as they do, particularly when worn by unmarried men, many inches below the fingertips, and being elaborately embroidered. The heavy leather belt holding trousers and shirt is thickly set with circles of brass for ornament. Most interesting of all, probably, is the *szür*, a long coat of white felt with roomy sleeves that are never utilized by the arms, large lapels, and broad sailor collar. This garment, held in place across the chest by a decorative leather strap and large buttons, is abundantly decorated with cotton or silk embroidery or appliqué of various colored felts or leather in the favorite motifs of carnations, roses, or tulips. A somewhat less richly ornamented and shorter coat is the *ködmen* made of sheepskin, as is the long sleeveless *suba* [6] which has the skin side nearly covered with leather ornamentation that is in evidence only in winter when the wool side is worn next to the body.

No less unusual and interesting than these skin coats are the foot and head covering of the average Hungarian. While the shepherds still wear the heelless leather shoes, *bocskor*, much like the Indian moccasin, the top-boot whose pointed toe testifies to Oriental influence is now more commonly worn. Curious also is the small hat of black felt whose round, small brim is decked with gaily hued blossoms. Perched jauntily on the head it is worn only during the summer months, giving way in winter to the warm lambskin cap. In some districts, particularly in Mezö-kövesd, the young bloods do not disdain to wear the apron so generally considered elsewhere as peculiar to feminine attire. They affect long black sateen aprons with borders and waist belts. Sometimes the apron is worn in back, and then it is square in shape, of bright patterns, and finished at the lower edge with long fringe or lace.

The women in former days wore skirts that reached just below the knee, and were so wide and worn over so many petticoats— anywhere from ten to twenty—that the silhouette was indeed unnatural. Today these have been largely supplanted by the more modern bell-shaped skirt, *höndörgö*, that covers the ankles that are

---

[6] HOLME, CHARLES, PEASANT ART IN AUSTRIA HUNGARY, p. 41. "The Studio," Ltd.

clad in red stockings. Over the white cotton blouse with its full, puffed sleeves is worn either the cloth or silk jacket that is diversified in cut according to the locality in which it is worn, or a many hued fringed shawl. For warmth, the sheepskin *ködmen* with ornamentation of appliqué or stitchery is donned. Dear to the

Fig. 163. Hungarian Couple. Photo from International
Newsreel.

feminine heart, also, is the very decorative apron, *kötény* that is held in readiness for wear on festivals and holidays, a plain one rendering service for ordinary occasions. Though not disdaining to wear many strings of beads around her neck the Hungarian woman is more interested in her tall boots than in jewelry. Cut much like the Wellington boot, of soft, colored leather, very frequently crimson, these tall boots have tops embellished with embroidery as well as leather and cloth appliqué.

FIG. 164. COSTUME OF A YOUTH OF CZECHO-SLOVAKIA.   FIG. 165. A YOUNG WOMAN FROM CZECHOSLOVAKIA.

Courtesy of the Czechoslovakian Consulate.

Hungarian children are amusing small replicas of their elders, the boys in voluminous *gatyák* and extraordinarily long sleeves that seem in no way to hamper their movements; the girls in free swinging *höndörgös* and large-sleeved embroidered blouses.

Czechoslovakia.—The recently established Republic of Czechoslovakia is composed of Moravia, Bohemia, Silesia, and Slovakia, four former provinces of the disrupted Austro-Hungarian Empire, and as each province has several types of costumes it is a bewildering array that is presented for our study. Two noteworthy features of Czech dress are its brilliance of coloring and the dominance of embroidery in its decoration.[7] Neither sex, apparently, has the exclusive privilege of using this type of ornamentation, as stitchery is found in great abundance in the men's as well as in the women's dress. The hand-woven linen shirt of the former displays fine embroidery at the wrist and neck; the white trousers, short and wide, are lace trimmed or fringed at the bottom, with either drawn work or embroidery in bands above the lace or fringe. These nether garments are fashioned of buckskin also. When of linen, they are shirred or smocked at the top. Around the waist is wound a sash of red and black, its ends falling to the ankle. The wide leather belt over it is pierced or embroidered. High boots of polished leather encase feet and legs. The short, sleeveless jacket is so heavily incrusted with brilliant embroidery or appliqué that but little of the foundation material, velvet, silk, cloth, or sheepskin, is visible. Moravian swains are wont to add several jaunty, huge pompons of red wool to the front edges of this jacket—a diminutive but exceedingly important article of masculine attire. A felt hat of minute size has for its trimming an embroidered band, or a smart feather and a bunch of flowers. The Czech's overcoat is of skin with the fur worn toward the body. This skin is elaborately ornamented with the customary stitchery or with an appliqué of finer skins which have been colored in vegetable dyes made by the peasants from native plants. The tulip, pink, and star are the favorite motifs used in designs destined for costume, furniture, and pottery alike.

The feminine silhouette is rendered decidedly bouffant by the full, short sleeves and voluminous, ankle-length skirt which is worn over two or three petticoats, each trimmed with hand-made lace. The skirt itself is composed of a series of aprons, very full and straight, and generally of different materials. The darker one,

---

[7] See the natural color photographs of costumes of Czechoslovakia by HANS HILDENBRAND in the *National Geographic Magazine* for June, 1927.

trimmed with lace, is worn in front. Many rows of shirring attach these straight pieces of wool or linen to the straight belts.

The blouse, of soft, fine, white cotton or linen is either gathered or finely plaited at the neck, thus giving much fulness at the front and back. The neck is finished with an embroidered band or a similarly decorated ruffle three inches in width. The most striking part of the blouse is the sleeve which is very full, and quite conspicuous with an oblong of gay embroidery covering a large portion of its surface. It is gathered at the elbow, terminating in an em-

Fig. 166. Interesting Caps from Czechoslovakia. Courtesy of the Czechoslovakian Consulate.

broidered ruffle, or is caught into a band at the wrist. Little of the blouse except the sleeve and neck finish shows, as over it is placed a short, sleeveless close-fitting jacket of dark material, frequently silk, profusely embroidered in rich colors. In Moravia this jacket has enormous bunches of wool pompons down the front.

The Czech woman like so many of her European sisters, delights in an elaborate apron painstakingly embroidered, lace-trimmed, and of bright-hued cotton or silk. Down the front hang the long ends of the colorful brocaded ribbon which fastens it. This highly prized article of attire is donned for church or visiting.

The high boot is generally black with scallops or some form of decoration at the top, in many instances the decorative motif being repeated on the back just above the heel. Long, hand-knitted stockings of red or white wool accompany this sturdy foot-wear.

But little of the woman's hair shows as the entire head is covered by a cap or a kerchief which is worn over the cap and tied in an intricate knot at the back or simply knotted under the chin. This kerchief is folded in a variety of ways, each of which indicates the village or district from which the wearer comes. Both cap and kerchief are beautifully embroidered and edged with lace, though some of the head shawls are of intense red or yellow cotton similar to the bandanna. The small shoulder shawls are of white embroidered in striking designs in colors or black, with fringe as the edge finish.

The men of the Slovaks residing in the Carpathian mountain districts clothe themselves in tunics and voluminous breeches of native white homespun girdled about the waist by broad belts over a foot in width that hold all sorts of implements necessary for hunting, eating, and smoking. Broad-brimmed hats decked with flowers and gaudy beads form a most extravagant, fantastic looking head covering.

Snugly fitting hoods of red cloth, and striped, ankle-length skirts which do not have the bouffant silhouette of the Czech woman's skirt, are the most colorful of the Slovak woman's garments, though the bodice sparkles with embroidery of several hues.

Roumania.—Most typical of the Roumanian dress is the effect of ease and comfort given by the nearly knee-length tunic of the men, and the long tunic dress of the women. The white of the man's tunic and likewise, of his close-fitting wool or linen trousers, forms a pleasing background for the wealth of color employed in the embroidery of the rich velvet vest that is reserved for holiday occasions, and of the black or red leather belt that is broad in width and the receptacle of necessary implements for fighting and eating. Strong color is also present in the embroidery or leather appliqué of the lambswool jacket, sleeved or sleeveless, that every Roumanian peasant possesses in addition to a heavy white cloth overcoat. His cap is tall and of black lambskin, his hat broad of brim and of black felt. His feet are protected by soft leather *opintschin* or sandals bound about the ankles with leather thongs.

Stitchery in gold, black or red thread is prevalent about the collarless neck, down the front, along the seams, and in large masses on the sleeves of the woman's long white dress, and her linen or soft cotton blouse that accompanies a long skirt of blue or the favorite white cloth. This latter garment also has its share of embroidery about the lower edge, likewise the soft veil, the broad belt, and the jaunty sleeveless jacket of silk, velvet, or lambswool. The designs are chiefly characterized by their geometric form and are worked in cross-stitch with the addition of beads and sequins.

In one of its many varieties the ever present apron is found in the shape of a narrow rectangle with horizontal stripes woven or embroidered, reminiscent of the similarly formed ones seen in Italy. Occasionally two of these rectangles are worn, one in back, the other in front. Another unusual example is that consisting mainly of long fringes hanging from a narrow cloth belt that is woven in stripes and geometric patterns.

FIG. 167. DOWAGER QUEEN MARIE OF ROUMANIA AND HER DAUGHTER WEARING NATIVE COSTUMES. Wide World Photos.

The Dowager Queen Marie has done much to foster the love of modern Roumanians for their picturesque costume, and through many photographs of her attired in this type of dress we have become quite familiar with the particularly graceful head-dress, *marama*, worn by Roumanian matrons. This consists of a long veil of thin white cotton or silk embroidered and studded with sequins, wound snugly about the head with one end falling free at the back. In some districts the silk kerchief tied over the head and entirely concealing the parted and knotted hair is very common. Numerous and heavy strings of beads and coins form the women's chief ornaments, the coins being attached to the hair as well as being hung about the neck.

FIG. 168.   A BULGARIAN PEASANT.
Photo from Ewing Galloway, N. Y.

Bulgaria.—Like their neighbors to the north and west, the Bulgarians use white as the basis for their dress, adding sparkling touches of color in sash, shirt, and jacket. The men's wide breeches, *poturi*, of white serge are strikingly braided in black, while the homespun linen shirt, of which a great deal is visible beneath the black coat, *aba*, that reaches to the waist, is embroidered in colored threads among which red is the most frequently found. This same color is repeated in the gay sash, *poyas:* The black lambskin cap which has practically replaced the formerly much worn *fez*, and rough hide shoes, *opinak*, are similar to those worn by other Balkan peoples, as is the sheepskin coat, *jube*,[8] that is always worn in winter though the Bulgar frequently substitutes for this a large cloth overcoat that is conspicuous for the size of its sleeves.

In some regions of the country the wide breeches find less favor than the close-fitting ones, the fabric and color being the same in both styles. From knees to ankles the legs are wound with narrow strips of cloth instead of being incased in stockings.

[8] HANDBOOK OF BULGARIA, p. 82. Geographic Section of the British Naval Intelligence Division. By permission of the Controller of His Britannic Majesty's Stationery Office.

Handwork of surprising beauty is lavished with prodigal hand on the garments of the women. The seams, sleeves, shoulder, neck line, and the bottom of the ankle-length, narrow chemise of heavy white linen are worked with conventionalized designs in whose color schemes red, yellow, and black play the dominant roles. In order to display this wealth of decoration, the over dress of

dark wool is cut with a deep V or a U shaped neck line, and is several inches shorter than the chemise. It, too, is embroidered at the neck, armscye, and hem, and is confined by a "wide leather or embroidered cloth belt" with a massive silver buckle, *pafti*.[9] Not content with embroidery on chemise and dress, the Bulgarian woman lavishes it also on the coat, particularly in large squares or rectangles on the long, loose sleeves of this three-quarter-length garment. No costume is complete without two narrow, straight aprons, one in front, the other in back, of horizontally striped material, the colors and widths of which vary in the different districts, or the bright kerchief, *shamiya*[10], in white, green, or red, which married women tie under the chin

FIG. 169. THE DECORATIVE APRON AND DRESS OF THE BULGARIAN WOMAN. Courtesy of the Bulgarian Consulate.

and young girls wind around the crown of the head. Many necklaces and strings of coins, *naniz*, hang about the neck. Bright wool stockings and *opinak* cover the feet.

---

[9] HARMUTH, LOUIS, A DICTIONARY OF WOMEN'S WEAR. Fairchild Publishing Company.

[10] HANDBOOK OF BULGARIA, p. 82. Geographic Section of the British Naval Intelligence Division. By permission of the Controller of His Britannic Majesty's Stationery Office.

Albania.—In mountainous Albania are found costumes that are decidedly Turkish in cut and type of decoration as a result of the continued occupation of the country by the Turks from their conquest of it in the fifteenth century until 1913. The picturesque effect of the baggy white or colored woolen trousers of the men is heightened by the rich black silk braiding often intermingled with red, down the sides and across the back. Tight-fitting at the ankles they are held at the waist by a broad belt over which is wound a

FIG. 170. A GROUP OF BULGARIAN COUNTRY WOMEN IN THEIR NATIVE COSTUME. Photo by Brown Brothers.

brilliant red sash or *cummerbund* that serves as a pocket for holding small accessories and the formidable array of pistols with beautifully embossed handles. The white shirt has sleeves that, at the wrist, are baggy and full like the trousers. Reaching to the top of the broad sash is a bolero jacket of black rendered extremely decorative with finely wrought embroidery of gold threads, while fringe edges the short black wool coat whose sleeves display the puffs of the shirt sleeves at the wrist.

A long chain of woven silver strands is worn around the neck, and the *fez*, of white felt for the Albanians, of red for the Turks, covers the closely-cropped head.   The feet are shod in *opingas,*

Fig. 171.   Albanian Women Wearing the Ample Chalwar.   Photo from
Ewing Galloway, N. Y.

leather shoes whose ends turn upward and which are bound to the feet with thongs of leather.

The *chalwar* of the Turkish woman have been adopted by the

native Albanian woman in some parts of the country, but have been increased tremendously in width. Like those of the men the trousers are held at the waist by a broad *cummerbund*. The upper part of the body is clad in a white linen chemise that boasts of no collar,

Fig. 172. Residents of Cettinge, Montenegro, Photo by Ewing Galloway, N. Y.

but a finish of multi-colored embroidery about the round, loose-fitting neck.

By far the most interesting item of the woman's wardrobe is the great coat of black or white wool so heavily weighted with gold embroidery and lace or black braid that one scarcely wonders at its reservation for dress occasions. These wonderful examples of the needle woman's skill fit the shoulders rather closely and flare widely from the raised waist line over the hips. So narrow are they in front that a cross band at the chest is necessary to keep them from falling off the shoulders. The sleeves, long and close, or long and wide, receive much of the abundant decoration. The simply dressed hair is covered with a tiny cap or long, crisp veil; heavy chains of coins and necklaces hang from the neck; heelless slippers with embroidered toes protect the feet. Peasant women knit and wear with their leather sandals, a curious red stocking of red, blue, and white that closely resembles a boot.

Montenegro.—A figure that compels interest and admiring attention is that of the well-built Montenegrin in his national dress that is worn alike by men of all ranks with differences in material only. Baggy, knee-length breeches of blue cloth are accompanied by a white or pale blue tunic, also knee-length and open in the front to display the shirt and gay scarlet vest whose edges are heavily embroidered with gold. Girdling the tunic is a heavy leather belt holding the inevitable revolver and almost concealed by the *cummerbund* so commonly found in the Turkish and Balkan costumes. A long coat of blue, green, or white is thrown over the shoulders, the sleeves swinging jauntily free of the arms. An additional protection against the cold is the shawl that until needed is folded and thrown over the left shoulder. White socks, leather *opanki* and white gaiters or high boots clothe the lower extremities.

Peculiar to the Montenegrins' dress, of men as well as of unmarried women, is the *kapa*, a small round cap banded with black. In the center of the red silk crown are embroidered the initials H. I. "the cipher of Nicholas I, surrounded by five semi-circular rows of gold braid to typify the five centuries of Montenegrin independence."[11] A simple design in gold braid is substituted for the initials on the cap worn by the women, who present a very drab appearance by the side of the brilliantly dressed men. Beneath their long beltless tunics are cotton blouses which are caught at the waist by belts of leather or silver, and full, dark skirts. The long coats are practically the same as those of the men. At marriage

---

[11] MOSES, G. H., GREECE AND MONTENEGRO. *The National Geographic Magazine*, March, 1913.

the Montenegrin woman gives up the wearing of the *kapa*, covering her head with a simply arranged kerchief instead.

Croatia.—In Croatia, once a province of the former Austro-Hungarian Empire, but now, since the end of the World War, together with Serbia, Bosnia, Dalmatia, Slovenia, Montenegro, and

FIG. 173. AN EXAMPLE OF THE HEAD SHAWL WORN BY THE CROATIAN WOMAN.

FIG. 174. COSTUME OF A YOUNG GIRL FROM THE VILLAGE OF SISAK.

THESE COSTUMES ARE MADE OF HEAVY HAND-WOVEN LINEN EMBROIDERED WITH WOOL YARN IN VERY BRIGHT ORANGE WITH TOUCHES OF OTHER BRILLIANT COLORS. THE DYES ARE MADE AT HOME FROM BERRIES AND PLANTS. THE SKIRT IS ACCORDION PLAITED, THE PLAITS PUT IN BY HAND WHEN THE GARMENT WAS DAMP.

Courtesy of Miss Marian Willoughby.

Herzegovina, a province of the new kingdom of Jugo-Slavia, the garments of both sexes are of white wool spun and woven in the homes, or of snowy linen, and embellished with appliqué or embroidery in bright colors.

The man's loose shirt and bloomer-like trousers, of red or blue, are further enlivened by a gay red bolero with fastenings of innumerable small silver buttons, while the long, fleece-lined coat is bordered with bands of red felt and patterned on the skin side with cloth or leather appliqué. His hat is usually of somber black or brown.[12] In his broad belt repose long knives and pistols.

Sparkling cross-stitch embroideries are the attractive features of the long, full blouse, short and billowy skirt, apron, and coquettish cap of the Croatian maiden. Long stockings, white for the maids, blue for the matrons, and sandals, *opanken*, that have a jolly ball of red worsted at the top, or tall leather boots, show to advantage below the swinging skirts. But no costume is complete without the sleeveless, collarless jacket of white or red leather or felt that is cut with a flare over the hips, something like the coat of Albanian women. The Croatian coat, however, meets at the waistline in front, sloping off to the shoulder from that point. On it are applied designs that are traditional in the different villages. Further touches of color are added in the long chains and necklaces of beads and corals, and in rings for fingers and ears.

Bosnia.—Along the waysides, in the villages and towns of Bosnia are to be found evidences of the former Turkish domination in the dress of both men and women. From the top of his dark red, black-tasseled *fez* to the upturned points of his shoes, the Bosnian reflects the garb of the Turk: his trousers, blue or red, are roomy and full to the knee, then close-fitting to the ankles; his white shirt is partially concealed by the sleeveless, resplendently embroidered vest and crimson sash.

The Mohammedan woman of Bosnia remains true to the custom of all women of her faith, in wearing on the street a wrap-like garment which successfully conceals her entire form. There are two types of this garment commonly worn, the first, and probably the older one, is called the *feredeza*. This has been described as "a shapeless loose black mantle with floppy sleeves that envelops the figure from neck to feet."[13] Some women prefer in place of the *feredeza*, the *dorino*, a "check overall . . . that is nothing more or less than a huge bag in which the wearer's head, shoulders, arms, and body are effectually concealed. Round what is supposedly the waist of the imprisoned beauty a string is tightly drawn, and the

---

[12] DeWINDT, HARRY, THROUGH SAVAGE EUROPE, p. 31. Ernest Benn and Company.
[13] Taken by permission from W. F. BAILEY'S SLAVS OF THE WAR ZONE, p. 234. Published and copyright by E. P. Dutton and Company, Inc., N. Y.

lower folds of the sack bunch out and terminate about a foot and a half from the ground, leaving the legs and feet free to fascinate by an ample display of gaudily striped hosiery and scarlet or blue heel-less slippers that flap at every step."[14] In order to complete the disguise a large handkerchief is placed over the head and allowed to fall quite far down the back, while the *yashmak*, a long, narrow strip of the same material with slits for the eyes, is hung before the face.[15] This veil is somewhat similar to the one employed for the same purpose by modern Egyptian women (Fig. 179).

While constrained to obscure her feminine charm from the public gaze when on the street, the woman of Moslem faith indulges her love of finery in her clothing designed for wear at home. Her full Turkish trousers, *dimidje*, of silk of gay hues are accompanied by garments similar to those worn by her sister in Turkey: a short but heavily embroidered shirt of gauze-like fabric; a close-fitting, but sleeveless jacket, *jacerma*, of silk or velvet over which is frequently worn a second short and embroidered jacket, and a long coat of magnificent silk with hanging sleeves. "Embroidered slippers or sandals with heels of considerable height, *manule*,"[16] a *fez*, and an abundance of rich, massive jewelry complete the costume.

Bosnian women of Christian faith, dispensing with the wide trousers, wear a long white linen tunic, a red or blue sleeveless bolero rich with braiding and spangles, an extremely massive belt that frequently attains the width of seven inches, and a simple coat of homespun. If unmarried the woman's black hair is confined in two long braids into which are twisted bright ribbons with coins of gold or silver. The matron's locks are gathered up and wound around a small but heavily ornamented cap and all is then covered with a dark veil.

Serbia.—Like his kinsman the Croat, the Serbian man of the country goes about gaily clad in white frieze trousers and long linen smock beneath a short waistcoat or zouave of red or blue frieze that is weighty and stiff with embroidery. Closely rivalling the zouave in interest is his nine or ten-inch belt of leather

---

[14] *Ibid.*, pp. 234–235.

[15] HARMUTH, LOUIS, DICTIONARY OF WOMEN'S WEAR. The Fairchild Publishing Company.

[16] *Ibid.*

enriched with studdings of brass and silver, and gay with tassels of red wool. A sheepskin or heavy coat of black cloth protects him in winter, while his headgear is comprised of a small cap or the broad brimmed hat of the Croatian, and his footgear of the cowhide

FIG. 175. A NATIVE OF OLD SERBIA. Methodist Prints.   FIG. 176. A GREEK SOLDIER WEARING THE FUS-TANELLA. Photo from Brown Brothers.

opanke sandals, bound to his ankles with strips of cloth or braid in the favorite scarlet over-stockings or bandings of white wool.

No less gaily attired is the Serbian woman in her smock-like tunic of linen, with brilliantly colored velvet or frieze short jacket, with its many buttons down the front, and gaudy leather appliqué. Contributing to this wealth of color is the short jacket of brown frieze nearly covered with multi-colored embroidery wrought at home by patient fingers, and the head shawl of blue, violet, or rose. In some districts of Serbia the smooth and glossy black hair is wound around a diminutive red *fez;* in others, drawn closely back from the face and covered by the kerchief. The Serbian woman, like her neighbors, bedecks herself with string after string of beads and coins as well as bracelets of the same, and about her waist wears a leather belt heavy with silver clasp and decorations.

FIG. 177. A WOMAN IN THE DRESS OF MODERN GREECE. Photo from Brown Brothers.

Greece.—Totally unlike the flowing, graceful robes of classic times is the dress of the present-day occupants of Greece. It partakes something of both Turkish and Albanian costume. In the more northernly sections of the country the men are still arrayed in the *fustanella,* which, we are told, is a very ancient form of dress originating in Albania and until very recently the uniform of the king's guard in Athens. The *fustanella* consists of an enormous, billowy white cloth skirt that just misses covering the knees. The large-sleeved shirt is secured at the waist by a long, brilliantly colored *cummerbund* over which is placed a crimson leather belt from which protrude the handles of dagger and revolver. The scarlet vest above is heavily incrusted with embroidery and gold thread. Long white cloth leggins, shoes, *tsarouchia,* with upturned, tasselled points and a red *fez* with the customary tassel of blue silk, put the finishing touches to this picturesque costume.

In the center and southern sections of the country large, baggy trousers are more commonly worn than the *fustanella,* while comfortable woolen coats provide the protection formerly rendered by the graceful, classic *himation*.

Less attractive and unusual is the dress of the modern Greek woman, which consists of a long, sleeveless coat bound round the lowered waist line with a *cummerbund* and a leather girdle that is fastened with a silver gilt clasp of marked size; a blouse with decorated sleeves; long white or blue skirts gaily banded at the bottom, and apron suitably embroidered to harmonize with the rest of the garments. The various arrangements of the head kerchief are distinctive of different districts, though generally it fails to conceal the long braids of hair. Coins, beads, and chains of great weight and number hang about the neck.

REFERENCES

RACINET, LE HISTOIRE DU COSTUME, Vol. VI.

HOLME, PEASANT ART IN RUSSIA.

HOLME, PEASANT ART IN AUSTRIA-HUNGARY.

MOLONYAI DEZSÖ : A MAGYAR MŰVÉSZETE.

TILKE, PEASANT COSTUMES OF EASTERN EUROPE.

HUBBARD AND PEEK, NATIONAL COSTUMES OF THE SLAVIC PEOPLES.

NORTHRUP AND GREENE, Historic Costume Plates.

National Geographic Magazine.

ZUR GESCHICHTE DER KOSTÜME, plates 900, 1030.

OPRESCU, PEASANT ART IN ROUMANIA.

MANN, PEASANT ART IN EUROPE.

CHAPTER XVIII

NATIONAL COSTUME IN NORTHERN AFRICA AND ASIA— MOROCCO, EGYPT, ARABIA, PALESTINE, TURKEY, AND PERSIA

Unchanging Fashion.—Accustomed as we are to the numerous style changes which our wardrobes undergo, it is with considerable wonderment that we gaze upon the costumes of the Eastern peoples which have retained their same cut and contour for such long periods of time. That national characteristics of dress have been preserved is doubtless due to the satisfactory service each particular form has rendered under the conditions set by climate, availability of native materials from which it is made, and the firm hold which custom and reverence for everything pertaining to the past have upon Asiatics generally. The control over matters of dress exercised by certain religious bodies is another factor that has influenced the longevity of certain types of national dress. This is notably true of the many-centuries old custom that requires women of Mohammedan religion to be closely veiled and their forms muffled when it is necessary for them to appear in public. In India certain colors are never seen in the dress of the Hindu, and pure silk unmixed with cotton is never worn by the Moslem.

One of the strongest factors in maintaining the unchanging styles of women's dress in the East has been the sequestered lives they have been compelled to live; mixing socially only with members of their own sex, and even then in a very restricted circle of relatives and close friends, they have not had to meet the necessity of social competition that is so prevalent in the lives of Western European and American women. In connection with this matter it is interesting to note that the changing political and social life in Turkey today is causing radical changes in the customary dress of the Turkish women. A few of the most advanced and modern women are beginning to be seen at public entertainments with their husbands and to meet the friends of the latter in their own homes. As a result the veil is being gradually discarded except by the more

258

conservative women of the interior of Turkey, and French fashions are being very commonly adopted.

Changes from the West.—Slowly and gradually the influence of the West is being felt and reflected in Eastern dress. Cottons manufactured in Manchester, England, for instance, have so successfully competed with the native woven fabrics which the Javanese have used for their *sarongs* that the Javanese product is now rarely seen. In Burma the European umbrella is gradually supplanting that of native construction. But aside from the foreign innovations that have crept into dress in the East during this first quarter of the twentieth century, it would be erroneous to say changing fashion had no part to play. The height of the collar on Chinese coats, for example, and the width of the sleeves vary from year to year as does the length of the straight-cut sleeves of the Japanese kimono, but the changes are so slight that they rarely affect the silhouette, and to the average Occidental beholder are apparently unnoticeable.

Color and Symbolism.—The pageantry of color and the glint of gleaming textures in the costumes of all of the eastern nations are exceedingly prominent features, and color with them is truly symbolic, and designates class distinction, religious affiliation, and personal achievement on the part of the wearer. The green turban of the Moslem indicates that he has performed the pilgrimage to Mecca; certain colors are particularly favored by the Hindu, and in China under the Emperors the wearing of yellow was the prerogative of the ruler alone. In Japan bright, intense colors and conspicuous textile designs are reserved for youth, and as the woman advances in years somber hues dominate her entire wardrobe.

Additional color and glitter are obtained in the masses of jewelry which are found on the persons of the women of India and the Near East in particular. The decorative quality of the jewels themselves, their elaborate settings, coins, and beads, add much to the picturesqueness of the feminine attire and serve to indicate the relative wealth of the husbands and fathers of the wearers.

The marvelous quality of the embroidery that is used in such profusion is a cause of much admiration on the part of Western women who are doing less and less of such handiwork themselves. But seldom do they realize or appreciate the symbolism that is involved in the painting with colorful threads; the religious and poetic significance which the designs have for the Chinese and Japanese especially. An oriental expresses this as follows: "The eastern artist thinks primarily of the symbolism of the various objects which he weaves into designs of beauty; the western artist

FIG. 178. MOROCCAN WOMEN IN NATIVE DRESS. Photo from Brown Brothers.

is usually concerned above all else with the effect of his production as a work of art and hence uses motifs which will further his purpose irrespective of their super-obvious significance."[1]

---

[1] HAGUE, CAROLYN, COLORFUL EMBROIDERIES FROM CHINA, *Arts and Decoration*, September, 1923.

FIG. 179. WEALTHY EGYPTIAN WOMEN WEARING THE WHITE VEIL. Wide World
Photos.

FIG. 180. MOROCCAN MEN WEARING THE BURNUS. World Wide Photos.

Very marked examples of faithfulness to old customs and traditions may be seen today in the costumes of the various peoples of northern Africa, as well as examples of interesting cut, arrangement of drapery, color and ornament that well repay careful study.

Morocco.—The Moor is a handsome, striking figure, wrapped head and body in a creamy, white wool or cotton *k'sa*[2] that is merely a strip of material about six yards long, draped with skill and grace. When unwound this out-of-door garment displays very loose cotton drawers that scarcely reach to the ankles; the *kumya*, a shirt that fastens down the front with very close-set buttons and loops; and a similarly secured roomy coat, the *farrajîyah*, with extremely wide and long sleeves. Brown, light blue, and green are the favored colors for this garment. In inclement weather a three-quarter length cloak with hood, the *djellaba*,[3] is worn. The *selhám*, or *burnus*, so generally used in the north of Africa as a travelling garment, is a somewhat elliptically-shaped cloak of striped or plain wool or camel's hair cloth that matches in color the rest of the costume. The square-cut hood with heavy tassels at the corners may be drawn over the head, or allowed to fall down the shoulders and back. It is tied at the neck or held by a clasp. Final touches of color are added in loose-fitting slippers of lemon-colored leather and a red *fez, sháshîah*, or a large white turban, *amárah*.[4]

When out of doors the Berber woman is enveloped in a large *haik* so arranged over face and head as to screen the latter from view, true to Moslem custom. Her indoor costume consists of a linen shirt with short and comfortably loose sleeves over which is placed a vest-like garment, the *firmla*,[5] that extends below the hips and upon which embroidery is lavished with a prodigal hand, the usual full, long trousers, *serul*, and silk sash striped in many colors. While the red leather slippers have the toes turned up, they have not the pointed ones so prevalent in the East. Conspicuous bracelets, anklets, and necklaces of silver, as well as enormous ear-rings and strings of coins about the neck, are considered necessary to complete the costume of every woman. Cosmetics are much indulged in.

[2] MEAKIN, B., THE MOORS., p. 52. Allen and Unwin.

[3] *Ibid.*, p. 58.

[4] *Ibid.*, p. 58.

[5] HARMUTH, LOUIS, DICTIONARY OF WOMEN'S WEAR. The Fairchild Publishing Company.

Egypt.—Another type of costume found in northern Africa that has something in common with that worn in Morocco is the simple costume of the modern Egyptian. Today the Sphinx looks over a people clothed in a manner quite foreign to the modes that prevailed in the days of the ancient pharaohs, as the modern Egyptians have adopted the long, full garments of their neighbors to the east and the west.

Moving about in the bright sunshine of the narrow streets or the shaded recesses of the native bazaars, the Egyptian men make brilliant spots of color in their gaily striped *kaftans*, red *fez* with blue tassels, and pointed red shoes. The *kaftan*, quite commonly worn by both higher and middle classes, is a very long, coat-like garment girdled about the waist by a long cloth sash; its sleeves are narrow and very long so that the hands may be readily concealed; it is usually made of cotton or a mixture of silk and cotton, and lined throughout with ramie cloth.[6] Its overlapping fronts reach from side to side at the bottom, narrowing gradually until the edges just meet at the round neck line that is finished with a very narrow standing collar. This fine garment is protected when necessary by a loose outer one, the *joobeh*,[7] which is more complicated in cut than the *kaftan* and of more somber color.

Beneath the *kaftan* are worn cotton trousers, *libas*,[8] of unusually generous width and fullness; some forms cover the knee while others fall to the ankle. These accompany a white or colored shirt and a striped vest with elaborately buttoned front openings and small side pockets. The feet are either unshod or incased in shoes of stiff red leather that have their points curling upward, or more simple slippers of soft, yellow-colored leather.

A soft shirt and ankle-length trousers comprise the indoor dress of the well-to-do upper class woman; out of doors she envelopes her body in a large, dark mantle and conceals her head and face in the Turkish *yashmak*, of soft, thin material. A woman of the lower class fastens over her face just below the eyes, a narrow strip of dark cloth that falls in a slender panel considerably below the knee. This veil is kept from touching the mouth and nose by a slender cylinder of light metal that is secured to the hair at the top of the

---

[6] TILKE, MAX, ORIENTAL COSTUMES, p. 11. Brentano.

[7] *Ibid.*, p. 11.

[8] *Ibid.*, p. 10.

head and rests on the forehead between the eyes. Another strip
of cloth forms the head shawl; in the case of the woman of wealth
this is worn over a close-fitting turban that is studded with jewels
All classes wear an abundance of massive necklaces, bracelets, and
long ear-rings of jewels, beads, or coins.

Arabia.—Modern Egyptian costume reflects strongly the influence of the Arabs whose picturesque clothing is voluminous
enough to protect them effectually from the intense heat of the
torrid climate, yet may be closely wrapped around the body to keep
out the cool of the nights and the sifting sands, as is particularly
necessary for the Bedouin tribes in their travels over the desert.
While much variety of dress is found among the Arabs, the most
general type of masculine array consists of loose, wide trousers, a
cotton shirt, *kamis*, that reaches from neck to ankles and is elaborately embroidered around the neck and across the front with red
or white silk, and girdled about the waist with a wide sash; a *kaftan*
or an *aba*, and a close white cotton skull-cap for indoor wear. The
feet are covered by bright yellow or red leather sl ppers, *papush*,
or thick-soled and heeled sandals with an ornamental nail in the top
of the sole toward the front that is placed between the big and first
toes. While stockings as the Europeans know them have no place
in the Arab wardrobe, many do wear *mizz*, tight fitting slippers of
soft Cordovan leather. These serve as stockings, being worn inside
the slippers. "They are always clean, so they may be retained in
the mosque and on the divan."[9]

The *kaftan* is a long, coat-like garment worn over the *kamis*
and trousers by people of rank as well as by those of the middle
class. Its tight sleeves reach to the wrist, while the close neck line
is finished with a narrow standing collar. Rich satins and brocades
were formerly the materials from which the *kaftans* were usually
made. The white sash, *hizaam*, that confines the *kamis* or the
kaftan holds the silver-hilted dagger, without which the Arab is
rarely seen.

The *aba* is a mantle, square in shape, of silk for the upper classes,
and of camel's hair for travellers. It is made in various colors,
either striped or plain. The seam at the shoulder, the openings for
the arms, and the edges of neck and front are ornamented with em-

---

[9] BURTON, R., A PILGRIMAGE TO MECCA, Vol. I, p. 289. Longmans,
Green and Company.

broidery, while cords of silk ending in tassels are used to tie it in front. Over his long hair—occasionally it is cut close to the head—the Arab places a large square kerchief folded diagonally, and binds it round with an *ogal*, a filet of wool wound with gold or silver threads. The *kúfiȳah*, as this head covering is termed, is generally of cotton background with woven stripes of silk, red and yellow being the colors usually used in combination.[10] From its border hang twisted silk strands that reach about to the waist and terminate in small tassels.

Colorful brocades, satins and velvets fashioned into full trousers, and a loose, ankle-length garment, *gondura*, form the cool weather costume of the Arab woman, thin, simple, calicoes and muslins being preferred in hot seasons. Her wrap, *shale*, is large and loose and generally of black silk embroidered around the edges with gold or silver threads. Over the head and long braids of black hair hangs a loose veil, *haik*, which,

Fig. 181. A Young Arabian Girl in Her Wedding Gown. Wide World Photos.

like the other garments, is embroidered in metallic threads.[11] Shoes and sandals are much like those worn by the men, the yellow leather *papush* for street wear being richly embroidered. About

[10] Burton, R., A Pilgrimage to Mecca, Vol. I, p. 345. Longmans, Green and Company.

[11] Strachey, L., Memoirs of an Arab Princess, Chap. 8, p. 90. Reprinted by permission of Doubleday, Page and Company.

the ankles are clasped heavy, broad anklets with tiny bells and ornaments; bracelets encircle both wrists and forearms, while massive ear-rings hang from the ears. Nails are stained, lips rouged, and eyelashes dyed.

Remembering their isolated mode of life in the desert, one can readily believe the statement that the dress of the Bedouins, the wandering tribes of the Arabs, have retained the same features that characterized it in the tenth century. The man's *tobe*, a close or a loose-sleeved shirt of blue cotton, covers him from neck to ankles, a short opening down the front enabling him to slip it on over the head. A leather belt encircles the waist while an additional belt, worn crosswise over the shoulder holds the firearms. The trousers, the *aba*, of striped camel's hair cloth, and *kúfíyah*, are those typical of Arabian dress.

The Bedouin woman's *tobe*, dark blue like that of the man's or sometimes of black or red, is large and loose. Close white trousers replace the full ones affected by the women of the towns. In her freer life in the open she goes about unveiled, though when in a town she frequently wears the *yashmak*, or veil, over her face; and instead of the one long braid into which the townswoman twists her hair, the nomad dresses hers in many tiny ones.[12] Wound round her body is a long piece of striped cloth, *barracan*, one end covering the head and the other brought up over the left shoulder. The whole is held in place by a long woolen sash, *hezaam*, wrapped round the body with its ends hanging at one side.[13] While the Arab woman wears ear-rings from babyhood on, these articles of personal adornment are rarely seen on the Bedouin woman, though bracelets, necklaces, and rings of brass, copper, and beads are worn in profusion. Open sandals or heelless slippers are the usual foot wear.

Palestine.—The resident of Palestine is quite colorfully clad. Bands or stripes of gay colors, red and yellow combined, or the more striking black or blue and yellow, form the chief patterns or designs of the man's long coat, *dimâyeh*, his silken girdle, and homespun *aba*[14] that serves as cloak and blanket alike. As head covering the Arab *kúfíyah* is prominent.

---

[12] BURTON, R., A PILGRIMAGE TO MECCA, Vol. III, p. 90. Longmans, Green and Company.

[13] FORBES, ROSETTA, THE SECRET OF THE SAHARA, p. 44. George H. Doran Company. Copyright, 1921.

[14] GRANT, E., PEOPLE OF PALESTINE, p. 90. J. B. Lippincott Company.

The woman's dress, *khurkeh*,[15] of linen is exceedingly long and for convenience in walking is bloused up over an interesting belt of figured linen or silk. Its sleeves, close at the top, flare widely at the bottom in the style so common during the Middle Ages in France whence it may have been introduced by the Crusaders. The front

Fig. 182. A Woman of Bethlehem. Photo from the American Colony Stores.

of the blouse is trimmed profusely with embroidery and heavy beads, the design frequently repeated in bands on the sleeves and skirt. The women of Bethlehem add to this gown a close jacket so cut as to reach slightly below the waist with sleeves that cover the elbow, and open down the front. The bright hues of the materials

[15] *Ibid.*, p. 91.

comprising these jackets are intensified by the decoration in the form of embroidery and braiding.   Dark blue and rich red seem to form the bases of the color schemes, generously interspersed with violet, pink, green, and yellow.

The head-dress is especially interesting.   It is in the form of a close, tall cap to the front of which are sewn many gold and silver coins, and is covered with an exceedingly long, large veil, *khalak*. The *tarboosh*, as this tall head-dress is called, is worn by matrons of the Moslem faith, unmarried women wearing the large white veil alone.   After the coins on the head-dress, the most prized piece of jewelry is the *iznak*, a long heavy chain for the neck.   On the fingers are jewelled rings; on the arm many bangles and bracelets.[16]

Boys and girls are dressed in the manner of their parents, the boy of twelve wearing for the first time the *fez* with its blue silk tassel.

Syria.—Among the Druses who dwell in Syria the man wears the usual *fez*, large trousers, colorful broad silk belt, short jacket and coarse woolen cloak, while the most striking part of his wife's attire is her extraordinary head-dress, *tantoor*.   This consists of a silver horn about twenty inches high superimposed on a close-fitting cap and fastened to the upper part of the forehead by "two silk cords which, after surrounding the head, hang nearly to the ground terminating in large tassels."   From the apex of the horn, which is worn at all times of the day and night, hangs a long, fringed veil, another of thinner texture serving as a covering for the face.   Like most women of the Near East, the Druse women hang coins and heavy jewelry about the neck, and are fond of heavy ear-rings and bracelets.

The Syrian man confines his baggy trousers, white shirt, and long, striped cotton or silk robe with a wide belt at the waist.   His feet are incased in tall boots from the front of which at the top swings a gay tassel similar to the one on his red *tarbush* which he wears at times, instead of a large turban.   His cloak is a square of cloth that is used interchangeably as tent, blanket, or body garment.   A warm lambskin jacket protects him on cold days.

Peculiar to the costume of the Syrian woman is the strip of dark cloth which encircles her head in such a manner that the top is left uncovered.   If of Moslem faith, she of course, adds a veil for her

---

[16] *Ibid.*, p. 91.

face. Her out-of-door wrap, the *izar*, is a voluminous cloak of white or black, and her main garment is a long gown that is closed from the girdle-encircled waist to the bottom. Rings for ears and bracelets for wrists and ankles are abundant and costly.

FIG. 183. A TURK IN DECORATIVE RAIMENT.　FIG. 184. A TURKISH WOMAN IN OUTDOOR COSTUME.

Photos by Brown Brothers.

Rich silk with colored stripes forms the full-length robe and long, loose sleeveless cloak of the Armenian woman. A red *fez* and kerchief cover her head, and pointed *babuch* encase her feet.[17] Her black hair is gathered into long, hanging braids.

Turkey.—The Turk is easily recognized, whether at home, in Asia Minor, or in the Balkans, by his characteristic red *fez*, with its long blue tassel reaching to the shoulder, and his wide pantaloons

[17] HARMUTH, LOUIS, THE DICTIONARY OF WOMEN'S WEAR. Fairchild Publishing Company.

or *chalwar*. Over his linen shirt, *camyss*, the older, more conservative Turk first dons a vest, *antery*, which sometimes reaches considerably below the knee, then a long *kaftan* girdled with a Cashmere shawl, and finally a long robe, the *djubbeh*, which is open down the front, and in winter is lined with fur. This garment, of magnificent fabric, has in contrast to the *kaftan* of bright Indian print or damask, very long sleeves which cover the hands in cold weather, but are turned back in the form of generous cuffs on warm days. The red felt *fez* had, until very recently, taken the place of the gorgeous turban of other days with its sparkling jewelled aigrette and many ample folds. Since 1925 by proclamation of the Turkish government, the *fez* has been displaced by the cap of cloth or the Occidental felt hat. Red leather slippers repeated the color note of the head covering.

The emancipation of the Turkish woman from her hitherto very secluded life will doubtless very soon be manifested by the discarding of the enveloping cloak in which for centuries the woman of Turkey has been shrouded when appearing on the street, on her way to the *hamman*, public baths, to perform her ablutions, meet her friends and exchange the gossip of the day. Early in the year 1928 it was decreed that the Mohammedan woman need no longer wear the long veil with which for centuries it has been customary for her to cover her face when appearing out of doors or before men other than members of her own family.

The cloak, known as the *feridgé*, a loose, ankle-length mantle with a large cape of silk or wool, depending on the wealth of the owner, is now rarely seen in the larger cities of Turkey, and is being gradually replaced by the more informal wrap, *tcharchaf*. This garment is "best described as two silken skirts of unequal length open in the front, the upper and shorter one being thrown over the head and secured under the chin. A square piece of dark colored silk or muslin attached to this with pins, hangs over the face."[18] By the women who prefer the old time head-dress, the *yashmak*, or veil, is arranged over a small cap. The *yashmak* is comprised of two squares of semi-transparent fabric, each folded diagonally. The small one is placed over the head with the bias fold well down on the forehead, and pinned at the back; the larger one is similarly

---

[18] GARNETT, LUCY, TURKISH LIFE, p. 103. G. P. Putnam's Sons. Quoted by permission of the publishers.

secured at the back with its fold so adjusted across the lower part of the face that only the eyes and nose are exposed to view. The ends fall down over the chest and shoulders.

At home the Turkish woman wears the *chalwar*, full ankle-length trousers of red silk, a chemise, *berundjuk*, of white silk "worn under a *yelek*, a sort of long coat, tight-fitting above the waist, and buttoned from the bosom to below the girdle, but open on each side from the hip downwards and trailing a few inches on the floor. For full dress another *yelek*, wider and looser is worn, also open at the sides and trailing, the sleeves of both garments being rather tight-fitting, but open for some six inches at the wrist, where they are often shaped *en sabot*. The outer robe is usually of some rich material worked round the borders, or all over, with elaborate trailing pattern in colored silks, or gold and silver threads to which pearls are sometimes added." [19]

Turkish women are very fond of cosmetics, applying kohl to the eyelids and brows, staining the fingers and toe nails with henna, and brushing various scented preparations into the free-hanging or braided glossy black hair.

Richly jeweled bracelets, necklaces, ear-rings, finger rings and girdle clasps ornament the person of the Turkish woman. Diamonds form her chief wealth and are to be found in practically all of her jewelry. For street wear tiny heelless slippers, *babouches*, of Moroccan leather incase the feet, and are usually the only protection they receive, the yellow leather boot being worn occasionally indoors by the woman of fashion.

A simple dress of calico or brocade that opens down the front, and a short, full skirt is the usual costume of the young Turkish girl, who until her early teens is permitted to run about with face and head uncovered.

Persia.—About equally fascinating to the Occidental are the costumes of the Turks and the Persians. Old, jewel-like miniatures and illuminated manuscripts portray dress with but slight differences from that worn by modern Persians, particularly the men in their straight cotton or cloth trousers, and the soft white and embroidered shirt that shows at the neck line and front of the tunic, *kamarchin*, and is fashioned of silk or velvet intricately embroid-

---

[19] GARNETT, LUCY, THE TURKISH PEOPLE, p. 279. Methuen and Company.

ered with gold threads, or of fine Cashmere shawling.[20] The length of the *kamarchin* varies with the rank and class of the wearer, and has at each side a lengthwise pocket hole through which one reaches to the pockets of the collarless, close-fitting chintz *alkalouk* beneath. The camel's hair coat, *kulijah*, either silk or fur-lined,

FIG. 185. PERSIAN WOMEN IN INDOOR DRESS. © Board of
Foreign Mission Presbyterian Church, U. S. A.

differs from most overcoats of the East in its possession of a decidedly rolling collar, lapels, and many full plaits in the back.[21]

Formerly every true follower of Mahomet left one lock of hair on his otherwise shaved head in order that by it he might be drawn up into Paradise. The head is always covered with the *kolah*, a

---

[20] LORY AND SLADEN, QUEER THINGS ABOUT PERSIA, p. 74. Eveleigh Nash and Grayson, Ltd.

[21] HOUTUM-SCHINDLER, SIR A., Article on "Persia," ENCYCLOPÆDIA BRITANNICA, Thirteenth Edition.

rather tall, brimless hat of lambskin or cloth, or with a ten-to twenty-yard strip of fine muslin of various colors wound into a turban, the color and method of winding denoting the wearer's rank, those of royal descent adding their badge of aigrette or heron tuft. Short socks of cotton and slippers, *kafsh*, with the counter folded down under the heel, comprised the most common covering for the feet.[22]

Close-fitting or very loose, baggy trousers, *chalwar*, secured at the ankles formed the customary attire of all Persian women until the return of the ruler Nair-Ne-Din from an eventful trip to Europe in 1890. We are told the Parisian ballet so strongly took his fancy that on his return to Persia he ordered all of the women of his harem to adopt the abbreviated skirts in place of their usual long trousers. So today the indoor dress of the Persian woman has two, sometimes three plaited skirts called *zirjoumeh* barely reaching to the knee. The lowest skirt is stiffly starched to hold out the top one which generally corresponds in material and color to that of the very short, tight-sleeved bodice.[23] During the cold weather many women have adopted straight, long trousers of silk, velvet, or cloth, and white socks. In summer the legs are entirely bare except for the *khalkhal*, heavy anklets of gold and silver. The wide-open, short jacket with its rows of unused tiny buttons reveals the thin muslin, richly embroidered and pearl-studded shirt, *pirahan*, whose long sleeves are caught in at the wrist. The coat worn during the cold weather is, like the *kulijah* of the men, lined and trimmed with fur, and has quite short sleeves.

The hair of matrons rendered red with henna or given a bluish tinge with mesmeh, is parted in the center and allowed to fall straight over the shoulders and in a short fringe over the forehead. Unmarried women dress it in numerous tiny braids which call to mind the braided locks of Topsy. At home the head is enveloped in a three-cornered white, transparent piece of muslin, the *chargat*, which is fastened under the chin with a jeweled pin, otherwise hanging over the shoulders. Another form of headgear for wear in the privacy of the home is a tiny skull-cap ornamented with jewels

---

[22] *Ibid.*
[23] LORY AND SLADEN, QUEER THINGS ABOUT PERSIA, p. 107. Eveleigh Nash and Grayson, Ltd.

or an aigrette.[24]   One traveler gives the following description of the Persian woman when abroad on the streets: "The Persian woman's outdoor costume is a complete disguise, as she is shrouded from head to foot in a shapeless black *chadar*.   Trousers and socks in one, usually of green or purple, are drawn up to her waist, and over her face is a white silk or cotton covering with a small strip of lace-work across the eyes."[25]

The feet, with toes and heels stained with henna, are shod in dainty, high-heeled slippers, *pah-poosh*, of velvet embroidered with metallic threads and studded with precious stones.   Those worn out-of-doors are of red leather with small heels of iron.[26]

Children's clothes in Persia duplicate the cut and material of their elders, the small boys playing about in hip-length and girdled shirts, over long, full trousers with sugar loaf hats perched on their restless, small heads.   The girls wear enormously full velvet trousers, girdled silk or cotton tunics and small jackets.   Their tiny slippers are soled with durable wood and at a very early age their small persons are decked with a surprising amount of jewelry, even their hanging hair being intertwined with precious jewels.

Turkestan.—In Turkestan, Central Asia, dwell the Turkomen, a people of Mongolian origin with as strong a love for color as any people in the Orient.   And it is the men who are decked in the gayest of striped orange, green, and red *tchapans*, long, loose gowns of silk or cotton, padded and quilted, that rival the bright dresses of the women.   Both sexes wear, baggy, white cotton trousers to which the men add a long shirt whose sleeves show plainly under the extremely large ones of the *tchapan*; a skull-cap richly embroidered; a turban, or a round cap of lamb's or sheep's wool; and shoes with high heels and the pointed toe so customary in the East. A brilliant scarf is wound several times around the waist.   For warmth in winter many *tchapans* are donned, one over the other, with one lined with fur when means permit.[27]

Like all Moslem women, those of Turkestan are completely

---

[24] *Ibid.*, p. 106.

[25] Sykes, Ella C., Persia and Its People, p. 199.   Methuen and Company, London, 1910.

[26] Lory and Sladen, Queer Things About Persia, pp. 108–109.   Eveleigh Nash and Grayson, Ltd.

[27] Schuyler, Eugene, Turkestan, Vol. I, p. 124.   Scribner, Armstrong Company, 1876.

swathed, when appearing on the street, in long, dark colored wraps, *khalats*, "the sleeves of which, tied together at the ends, dangle behind."[28] A black veil of horsehair conceals the features of every woman. Massive and abundant is the silver jewelry that hangs from throat, ears, and head-dress and encircles wrists, fingers, and ankles.

Afghanistan.—Persia and Turkey have left the imprint of their costumes on that of the natives of Afghanistan, who are clad in garments made of plain cotton, calico, quilted silk, and velvet with a generous quota of embroidery in gold and silver threads. Both men and women wear cotton trousers, *tom-bons*, of very ample proportions about the waist and hips, tapering down gradually until they fit closely about the ankles. Over their long, cotton shirt some men wear the bulky sash, *cummerbund*, a short, decorated jacket of sheepskin, others a long coat of cloth. For head covering a man has his choice of turban, or bright colored tall but brimless hat; for foot covering, leather boots or curling-toed sandals.

Feminine costume depends for its interest on the texture and color of the material used in the long, shirt-like dress worn over the *tom-bons*. A variety of silks, as well as the calico and cashmere so commonly used by the peoples of Turkey and Persia are employed. On the back of the head is worn a tiny, round cap weighty with embroidery of gold that in no way conceals the many small braids into which the black hair is so carefully arranged. Like other women of the Moslem world the woman of Afghanistan is closely enveloped in an enormous, shroud-like garment when venturing forth from her own domain.

REFERENCES

Tilke, Oriental Costumes.
Zur Geschichte der Kostüme, plates 950, 707, 885, 891, 1053.
Northrup and Greene, Historic Costume Plates.
Giafferri, Feminine Costume of the World.
Racinet, Le Costume Historique, Vol. III.
Women of All Nations.

[28] *Ibid.*, Vol. I, p. 122.

CHAPTER XIX

NATIONAL COSTUMES OF THE FAR EAST

In MARKED contrast to the intricate, sophisticated, and tailored dress prevalent in Europe and America are the simple, natural, and draped costumes found in India—the *sārī* and the *dhoti*, and their derivatives, the *panung* of Siam, the *comboy* of Ceylon, and the *sarong* of Java. Varying chiefly in dimensions but all of similar shape, these colorful, decorated rectangles of cloth are wound about the body in a variety of interesting arrangements that have satisfied these peoples of the Far East for hundreds of years.

India.—The adherents of the different religious faiths of India —Hindus, Mohammedans, Sikhs, and Parsis—are distinguished by the cut and arrangement of their dress, while the residents of the south have a penchant for more brilliant colors than those of the north. Cottons and silks remarkable for fineness of texture with characteristic patterns, woven, embroidered, printed, or tie-dyed are used by all. In the colorful embroideries metal thread plays an important rôle, while tiny pieces of looking glass are ingeniously embroidered into many of the designs giving an interesting sparkle and sharp high lights.

Characteristic of the typical Hindu masculine costume are the long strips of cloth that are draped by the Hindu about his hips and waist as a loin cloth, about his head as a turban, and at times, about his shoulders as a cloak. The first mentioned garment, the *dhoti*, of white cotton, is wound around the loins, the ends passed backwards between the legs and tucked in at the waist,[1] like the *panung* of the Siamese.

For the turban a narrow strip of remarkably fine cotton or silk, plain or covered with a small tie-dye pattern, that measures from ten to fifty yards long, is wound around the head in various ways, one end always hanging down the back. This *pagri*, as it is termed, completely covers the head that is closely shaved with only a small tuft of hair left on top.

---

[1] GRANT, CHARLES, Article on "India," THE ENCYCLOPÆDIA BRITANNICA, Thirteenth Edition.

A third strip of cloth, the *chadar*, of cotton about three yards long, is wrapped about the shoulders or the waist as preferred. Formerly in cold weather, the Hindu gentleman was wont to throw across his shoulders long shawls, *doschella*, of fine Cashmere woven and worn in pairs so that the wrong side was never visible. Similar

FIG. 186. YOUNG INDIAN WOMEN. THE ONE AT THE LEFT IS A MOHAMMEDAN; THE ONE AT THE RIGHT IS A HINDU. Photo by Ewing Galloway, N. Y.

shawls, but single, imported from India, were the vogue with French and English beauties during the late eighteenth and early nineteenth centuries.

While some Hindu men wear the *kūrtā*, the long cotton shirt of the Mohammedan, the greater number prefer the short coat, *angharkā*, that reaches to the waist and opens on the left hand-side.[2]

---

[2] *Ibid.*

The most important article of attire for the Hindu woman is the *sārī*, a bright scarf measuring a trifle over a yard in width and about six yards in length, that is wound around the waist to form a full, long skirt then brought up over the left shoulder. The free end is carried over the head and allowed to fall over the right shoulder and side. The *sārī*, usually the product of the handloom of the household, is made of fine cotton, silk, or a mixture of the two fibres. Across one end and along both sides is woven a narrow border in gold threads, the other end, the one exposed to view on the right shoulder, having a rather wider border. The upper part of the body is clad in a cotton blouse, *cholee*, of such brevity that it fails to meet the *sārī* draped around the waist. The neck is V shaped and the sleeves are short just covering the elbow. In the north and central parts of India a fairly short and very full skirt, *lhenga,* is worn. The shiny, black hair is either knotted at the back of the head or arranged in several small braids which, gathered in one braid, fall down the back. When the *sārī* is not drawn over the head, a sheer veil, *orhna,* covers it.[3] Hats are entirely foreign to the native Hindu woman's costume.

The man of Moslem faith is clothed in a long white cotton shirt, *kūrtā,* which is fastened at the left-hand side with a button and loop, and has long sleeves buttoned at the wrist. His trousers, *pa'ejamas,* are of various styles; ankle-length and tight, or extremely full about the waist and knees but fitting closely from there down. Among the many coats considered necessary by the Mohammedan are the *anga,* a long, and wide-sleeved coat of white or colored cotton fastened with strings above the waist; the *saradi,* a sleeveless waistcoat that is worn over the *anga,* reversing the custom in the Occident; and the *chogā,* or overcoat that "hangs to below the knees" and like the *anga,* is fastened with a few loops above the waist. It is made of a great variety of fabrics,[4] cotton, rich brocades, or fine Cashmere from the Western frontier. Probably the most important part of his costume to the Mohammedan is his head-dress of which there are many varieties. The *pagri* of Hindu origin is now quite generally adopted by Moslem men. The *tarbush* is very similar to the *fez* of the Turk but with no tassel.

---

[3] *Ibid.*
[4] *Ibid.*

Another type of cap worn by the Mohammedan is of white cotton decorated with the exquisite all white Chikan embroidery.

The Moslem women wear the sleeveless *kūrta*, that reaches to the waist; the *angiyâ*, a short bodice with sleeves that extend half way between the shoulders and elbow, a garment not worn in the north; and trousers similar in cut to those of the men but of finer fabric. Very frequently the Moslem women wear the Hindu *sārī* of very fine, loosely woven cotton with designs in gold and silver threads. While silk is sometimes used for the *sārī* some cotton is always mixed with it as the Koran forbids the wearing of pure silk alone. The head is wrapped in a sheer veil, and when she goes

FIG. 187. SILVER ANKLETS WORN BY INDIAN WOMEN. Courtesy of the Metropolitan Museum.

beyond the threshold of her own home, the Moslem woman conceals her head and form in a voluminous, thick, shroud known as the *būrkā*, which has strips of lace across the eyes to make it possible for her to see her way.

Parsis men and women both wear the close-fitting *sadra*, or sacred shirt, and loose cotton trousers. The men add a short white cotton coat and the women a *sārī* that is draped over the head and right shoulder thus distinguishing the Parsi from the Hindu woman whose *sārī* covers the left shoulder.

The Sikh man is distinguished by the knot in which his hair is tied at the top of his head, as well as by his beard. His *pagri* is a very large turban and his *kūrtā*, roomy and loose, is held at the waist with a scarf. His full cotton trousers are fastened just below the knee, and over all is placed the *chogā*. Blue and white are the colors most favored by the Sikh.

The red leather shoe, often elaborately embroidered, worn throughout India has the upturned toe so characteristic of Eastern footwear. In one type of shoe the long, thin toe is fastened to the wearer's instep: in another the counter is folded so that it lies flat under the heel of the foot.

FIG. 188. A SIAMESE BELLE. © Board of Foreign Missions Presbyterian Church U. S. A.

From infancy to old age the woman of India, regardless of caste, is arrayed in jewelry of some form. Her money is put into jewels which form part of her dowry. The *tali*, a gold ornament strung on a slender cord, hangs about her neck and takes the place of the Occidental wedding ring. Ear-rings of heavy gold are usually so long that they reach to the shoulders. One or many necklaces, a rich pendant for the forehead, rings for fingers and toes, as well as bracelets, armlets, anklets, and in some districts, nose rings, are common to all classes. One writer says: "in the complex and highly organized national life of India, jewelry has passed from the condition of a desirable but useless ornament to that of a prime necessity, serving as a badge of caste, a favorite offering to the gods, and a most popular means of investing private fortunes. From the cradle to the grave, from the lowest rank to the highest, the racial taste for personal adornment in both men and women has always mounted to a passion among the various Indian peoples."[5]

Siam.—The national costume of Siam as worn by both sexes consists of a piece of cotton cloth measuring "about one yard in

[5] FRIEDLY, DURR, Article on "Indian Jewelry" in the *Bulletin of the Metropolitan Museum*, August, 1925, Vol. X, No. 8, p. 162.

width and three yards in length" so wrapped about the body that it forms a skirt to the knees, the ends coming to the front. These are then twisted together and drawn between the legs and tucked

Fig. 189. Javanese Women Wearing Batiked Sarongs. Photo by Ewing Galloway, N. Y.

into the waist at the back. With this *panung* men and women of the higher classes wear a simple jacket that opens in front as well as shoes and stockings.[6] The native woman of the lower class,

---

[6] Graham, W. A., Article on "Siam" in the Encyclopædia Britannica, Thirteenth Edition.

however, contents herself with a scarf, *pa-hom,* wound around the body and thrown over one shoulder.

Java.—The *sarong* of the Javanese is a colorful, highly decorative strip of cotton wound around the body to form a long, straight skirt with a deep fold in the front and held at the waist with a long silk scarf. The designs on the *sarongs* generally in deep, rich browns, blues, and reds, with sparkling bits of cream, are the products of the native craftsmen who are highly skilled in the craft of batik. With the *sarong* is worn the *kabaya,* a straight, white jacket that opens in front and has long sleeves. The woman's jacket is often lace-trimmed or embroidered. Over the shoulders is draped a fine cotton scarf, the *slendang.*

The hair, drawn softly back from the face, is without ornament of any kind, while unpretentious rings, ear-rings, and necklaces complete the woman's costume. The toe slippers are frequently embroidered.

Ceylon.—The Tamils and Singhalese of Ceylon wear garments that reflect much of the color and shape so characteristic of costume in India. The long, wrapped, and colorful skirt, *comboy,* is common to both sexes, the upper part of the body being covered with an abbreviated jacket which has equally short sleeves, puffed for the Tamils, and close-fitting for the Singhalese. The women on occasions of festivity add the Indian *sārī,* bringing one end of it up over the left shoulder and tucking it in at the waist.

The glossy, parted hair of the women is adorned with many elaborate silver ornaments and pins while necklaces of beaten gold and coins, as well as many bracelets, anklets, finger, toe, and ear-rings are considered necessary by all classes.

Burma.—In Burma, the land of Kipling's "Mandalay," simple white cotton jackets and long, straight strips of cotton or silk draped to form skirts serve as the chief body garments of both sexes. By the men the long strips of patterned material are wound about the waist and hips, the excess cloth being bunched up in the center front, in contrast to the arrangement followed by the women. With them the skirt laps across the front with the edge of the cloth falling straight down the left-hand side of the front.[7] The women's skirt or "*tamehn* is a simple piece of cotton or silk, almost square, four feet and a half long by five feet broad and woven in

7 ZUR GESCHICHTE DER KOSTÜME, plate 1058.

two pieces of different patterns. This is wound tightly over the bosom and fastened with a simple twist of the ends."[8]

As is customary in Oriental lands the hat is practically unknown, the parasol affording the necessary protection from the sun, and the simply-knotted hair of the women is adorned with combs

FIG. 190. A BURMESE MOTHER AND CHILD. Methodist Prints.

and wreaths of fresh flowers. The carrying of an umbrella is the prerogative of neither sex to the exclusion of the other. The selection of the material comprising this attractive adjunct to the wardrobe is not left to personal preference but carefully regulated by law, as is the color, the material and the length of the handle.[9]

---

[8] YOE, SHWAY, THE BURMAN, HIS LIFE AND NOTIONS, Vol. I, pp. 87–88. Copyright 1852, by the Macmillan Company. Reprinted by permission.
[9] *Ibid.*, Vol. II, p. 121.

Cambodia.—In Cambodia, in the southern part of French Indo-China, the national dress consists of a cotton coat and the *sampot*, a strip of gleaming silk of a variety of hues so wrapped around the waist and drawn up between the legs that the effect of trousers is obtained. In addition to the coat and *sampot*, the Cambodian woman drapes over her left shoulder a scarf of figured silk. From shoulder to waist on one side falls a series of gold chains that are always accompanied by large bracelets, anklets, and innumerable finger rings. A simple form of slipper that is comprised mainly of an elaborately embroidered toe piece is worn on the otherwise bare feet.

Annam.—To the north in Annam, the long chemise, *cai-ao*,[10] and the long black trousers, *caiquan*, worn by both sexes, betray a decided Chinese origin. The sleeves of the former garment, which is open at both sides from the waist to the bottom, and buttons on the right side like the Chinese coat, are long and close-fitting to the wrists. In north Annam the women add black skirts.

China.—The establishment in 1912 of a republican form of government in China brought with it attendant changes, one particularly that is regrettable from the point of view of those interested in costume. This is the abandonment of the colorful, richly embroidered robes worn by the former mandarins, Chinese governing officials, and their wives. A less picturesque dress and the European frock coat and trousers for court functions, have usurped the place of the long, straight robe with its exquisite embroideries and pectorals, *pou-fou*, indicative of the specific rank of the official wearing it. Squares of embroidery, about a foot in size on the front and back of the mandarin's robe designated to which branch of the government he belonged; a wild bird embroidered in very colorful threads indicated the wearer to be of the civil service, while a wild animal showed that he belonged to the army or navy. Motifs enclosed in circular frames indicated the wearers to be of princely or high ministerial rank. A round or elongated button at the apex of the crown of the round hat was an indication as to which of the nine ranks or grades the official belonged. Such colorful

---

[10] HARMUTH, LOUIS, A DICTIONARY OF WOMEN'S DRESS. The Fairchild Publishing Company.

stones as the coral, lapis lazuli, and sapphire as well as gold and silver were employed for these buttons. Attached to the back of the upturned brim of the fur and satin winter hat by a piece of jade, and bending down over the back of the neck was a peacock feather,

FIG. 191. A CHINESE MANDARIN AND HIS WIFE IN THEIR OFFICIAL ROBES.
Pauquet Frères.

xwa-lin, either single or double eyed. The mandarin's summer hat was of fine silk stretched on a conical frame of bamboo or fine straw, and practically covered by a large tassel of red silk which hung from the apex.[11] His boots were of black satin and about his neck hung the *chu-chu*, a long chain of one hundred and eight stones, as amber,

[11] DAVIS, J. T., THE CHINESE, p. 327. Harper and Brothers.

coral, and jade, which was "intended to remind the wearer of his native land."[12]

The mandarin's wife was clad in a robe somewhat similar. It too, had its square of embroidery to show her husband's place in officialdom as well as a profusion of allover embroidery of floral and dragon motifs. Her hair was drawn severely back from the forehead and fastened at the back of the head by elaborate pearl ornaments. The head-dress was a tall, ornate and bejeweled affair standing out from the head. A fashion peculiar to the Chinese was the custom followed by all gentlefolk of allowing their finger nails to grow as long as possible, sometimes to the length of several inches, and of wearing on each finger to protect these indications of their freedom from all manual efforts, a shield of gold or jade.

The costume of the ordinary citizen of the republic differs from that worn during the empire only in the length of the sleeves and the jacket. His customary attire consists of long trousers, wide at the bottom and flapping against his ankles as he walks, and a short, dark blue jacket, or a long robe, both of which fasten in a characteristic and unusual line from the center front across the chest, and under the right arm with buttons and loops. Over the robe or the jacket is worn a sleeveless coat which generally fastens in a straight line down the center front. Gentlemen of wealth wear a wide sleeved jacket, *ma-coual*, of rich satin or one of fur in winter, over an ankle-length silken robe. The long queue, imposed upon the Chinese by their Manchu conquerors, (1644–1912) as a mark of submission,[13] has not been generally worn since the establishment of the republic, the Occidental hair-cut having superseded it. A round cap, long stockings of silk or cotton, slippers of cloth with soles of felt, a necklace of beads, a fan, purse, snuff box, watch, and chop sticks are the necessary accessories of the gentleman's costume.

Rich silks in a variety of weaves and colors, blue being the dominating hue, are fashioned into knee-length or shorter coats, *ma-coual*, a long robe, *haol*, and long trousers for the daintily formed Chinese woman. The coat has a narrow standing collar and

---

[12] GRAY, J. H., CHINA, Vol. I, p. 28. Copyright 1878 by the Macmillan Company. Reprinted by permission.

[13] DOOLITTLE, J., SOCIAL LIFE IN CHINA, p. 517. Sampson Low, Marston and Company, Ltd.

opens generally under the right arm as does the man's. The trousers are tied at the ankles in North China to show the tiny feet, and are left unconfined in South China. In public, or when receiving guests in her home. a woman of the upper classes places over her trousers a skirt composed of two pieces of silk lapped in front and back, and elaborately embroidered. Her underwear of silk or linen,

FIG. 192. A CHINESE FAMILY. Methodist Prints.

is of a cut identical with that of her outer garments. Short stockings of heavy white cotton material made with a seam up the front are worn with embroidered cloth or satin slippers. These usually have a rather thick sole, no heels, and are entirely hand-made. [It is said that except in cities where foreign influence is very strong, the ancient custom of binding the feet of young girls over the age of five or six years still prevails.]

Until the time of her marriage the Chinese girl wears her hair flowing over her shoulders[14], but just before the important event the thick, black hair, frequently brushed with a preparation of slippery bark, is brought straight back from the face and held in place by jeweled pins of precious metal, tortoise shell, or ivory which one authority states appeared in China as early as 1122 B. C.[15] A band of embroidered silk is placed across the forehead and ears. Elaborate ear-rings of jade, pearl, or the brilliant feathers of the king-fisher bird, as well as necklaces and rings of the same, and a dainty fan complete the typical costume of the Chinese woman. The final touches to her toilette are given by applying rouge and whitening to her cheeks, and by penciling her finely drawn eyebrows.

FIG. 193. GOLD EAR-RINGS OF THE MING PERIOD.
Courtesy of the Metropolitan Museum.

The Manchu woman wears the ankle-length robe, and a unique head-dress which is an elaborate structure standing eight to ten inches above her head. It consists of a golden bar several feet in length extending from right to left, wound with loops of black satin and decorated with embroidery, flowers, and jewels. Formerly the crossbar was wound with the wearer's own silky black hair.

In cold weather the garments of Chinese men and women are heavily padded with silk waste or cotton, or, for the wealthy, lined with fur. The weight of the silk for the various garments is suited to the different seasons, a thin, gauze-like silk being used during the very hot summer months, and a heavy one for the colder days. Clever tailors take infinite pains in the fashioning of the handsome textiles into straight line garments that have followed the same silhouette for centuries and spend many months on the embroidery for a coat, the designs being symbolic of Chinese faiths and customs.

[14] DAVIS, J. T., THE CHINESE, p. 327. Harper and Brothers.
[15] GRAY, J. H., CHINA, Vol. I, p. 370. Copyright 1878 by the Macmillan Company. Reprinted by permission.

On the bestowal of its name after the first month of its birth, the Chinese child is clad in wide, baggy trousers that reach to the wee ankles, a long coat of satin or blue cotton, and a diminutive jacket that extends to the hips. If the child's parents are wealthy the jacket is lined throughout with fur, otherwise he must depend for warmth on many layers of wadded and quilted coats. As a concession to the interests and pleasures of childhood, the first shoes and mittens are quaintly cut in the shapes of animals' heads. The chief distinction between the clothes of boys and girls lies in the slightly more elaboration of the clothing of the latter. The girl's hair too, receives greater attention. Her head is shaved when she is a few weeks old, small tufts of hair being left on the top and sides. When she attains the advanced age of four years it is allowed to grow and is braided with gay red cords. Across the forehead it is cut in a straight fringe.

Mongolia.—Decidedly eccentric to the western observer appear many features of the dress of the Mongols, the northern neighbors of the blue-coated Chinese. Baggy trousers and long, roomy, beltless coats of plain or elaborately embroidered silk, of sombre coloring for daily wear, are the main articles of the attire of both men and women of Mongolia. In the northern part of the province this coat is thickly quilted, reaches from neck to ankles and has curious close sleeves that extend to the knees and end in a flaring, turned back cuff. In the women's garments the sleeves are "puffed at the shoulder and filled with something hard and solid that lifts the puffs some inches above the shoulders."[16]

Particularly characteristic are the knee-high, soft red leather boots that have decidedly turned-up toes and are profusely decorated with embroidery and appliqué. The slow, ungainly walk of the Mongols is attributed to these boots which are worn many sizes too large for the foot in order that several layers of thick cotton stockings may be worn in the cold weather.

The man's hat, with upturned brim of fur and jeweled ornament of the top of the crown, is perched saucily on his head and held in place with a strap passing behind the ears and under the chin. The same type of headgear tops the most extraordinary hair arrangement of the northern Mongolian women. A jeweled, silver

---

[16] FRANK, HARRY, WANDERING IN NORTHERN CHINA, p. 40. The Century Company.

skull cap is placed over the oiled and parted hair which is "wound in single strands round two horns that are thin and flat but wider and larger than those of the water buffalo."[17] These curved horns extend beyond the shoulders, and are banded at intervals with

FIG. 194. A MONGOLIAN WOMAN WITH TYPICAL HEAD-DRESS AND PADDED SLEEVES. Photo from Brown Brothers.

FIG. 195. TWO TYPICAL KOREAN MEN. NOTE THE UNUSUAL HEAD COVERING. Methodist Prints.

cross pieces of silver and "from the ends . . . are suspended braids or cords reaching to the waist."[18] The less ridiculous head-dress of southern Mongolian women consists of the fur-brimmed hat worn over a jewel-studded cap from the sides of which and over the

[17] *Ibid.*, p. 40.
[18] *Ibid.*, p. 40.

temples fall numerous waist-length chains of jewels, coral, turquoise, and pearls.

Korea.—As blue is the prevailing color in Chinese costume, white is that in the clothing of the Koreans, men as well as women. Men of all classes are clothed in a form of "waistcoat shirt," voluminous trousers that are secured about the ankles with cords, and an ever present overcoat called *turamaggie*,[19] that extends to within about eight inches of the ground and is curiously fastened with ties on the right breast. This coat is of costly, delicate white silk when worn by men of high degree, but of grass cloth or calico for the lower classes. From the silken sash which binds the high waist hang two small, tasselled cases containing a pair of chop sticks and a small knife. The feet are encased in thick white socks with narrow, upturned toes, that are held in place with the same winding cords that fasten the trousers, and then in low leather slippers that offer no support for the instep.

The article of men's attire which compels interest is the very unique hat. Its shape calls to mind the tall beaver of the Welsh, but there all resemblance ends. The Korean hat has a diminutive brim of fine bamboo and a crown of loosely braided horse hair showing within the tightly coiled hair of the wearer. This weird head-dress is held on with black ribbons tied under the chin or, in the case of men of wealth, with a chain of small pieces of slender bamboo and amber beads.[20] When he has entered the state of matrimony the Korean man is permitted to twist his hair, which until then is worn in a long queue, into a knot on the top of his head where it is confined by a four inch strip of black horsehair that tightly and completely encircles the head.[21] Then in order to protect the precious knot from evil spirits he dons the tall, transparent-crowned hat removing it neither day nor night. In rainy weather it is protected by a cone-shaped hat of yellow oiled paper or silk which can be folded and carried in the waistcoat until needed.

The Korean woman's dress is much like that of her husband: full trousers, and ample petticoat plaited at the top into a broad band placed well up under the arms where it just misses meeting a

---

[19] *Ibid.*
[20] *Ibid.*
[21] HAMILTON, ANGUS, KOREA, p. 40. Charles Scribner's Sons.

long-sleeved, round-necked, and extremely short jacket. These garments, of white for married women and of bright colors for unmarried women and children, are entirely covered for street wear by a green or red silk cloak that is drawn over the head to conceal the face from view. The long wide sleeves of this *chang-ot*[22] are never used for the arms, but hang idly from the side of the head. The white socks, slippers, and fan are replicas of those used by the

FIG. 196. A YOUNG KOREAN PRINCESS.
Methodist Prints.

men, and the glossy hair is parted in the center and drawn into a knot low on the back of the head and ornamented with a scarlet rosette. Finger rings and a pin or button of amber to fasten her small jacket seem to appease any craving she may have for jewelry.

Japan.—A costume that contrasts strangely with that of European peoples today is that which has been the prevailing type worn for several centuries in Japan. The Japanese nation, shut off until 1856 from intercourse with other peoples, has been able to preserve intact its conventions and traditions. There is a tendency at present, however, on the part of the Japanese to discard their national dress in favor of the less picturesque but more comfortable clothes of the Europeans. The more conservative men and women of the interior persist in clinging to their kimonos which are generally exquisite examples of line and color.

The Japanese man is, traditionally, attired in a dark kimono which is the same, practically, as that worn by the feminine members of the household, the chief difference being found in the shorter sleeves for the men. Tucks at the waist line lift it to the convenient ankle-length. For daily wear a wide sash, *heko-obi*, is

[22] *Ibid.*, p. 28.

wound around the waist two or three times and tied at the back in
a loose bow, while for formal occasions this is replaced by one of
stiff silk, *kaku-obi*, tied in a double knot.

The construction of the kimono is a comparatively simple
matter; four straight strips of the eighteen-inch-wide silk are sewn
together by hand to form the back and two fronts, and two straight
strips for the long, bag-like sleeves, *furisode*, which are sewn along
the bottom and part way up the outer edge, leaving an opening for
the hand. A V-shaped neck line is made by the straight roll collar,

Fig. 197. A Japanese Family. Methodist Prints.

yeri, which follows the line of the front of the kimono that is lapped
left over right.

The underwear consists of a loin cloth of muslin, a shirt of silk
or cotton, *juban*, and an under kimono, *shitagi*, to which is attached
a collar that extends beyond the outer kimono. For extra warmth
in winter, a padded, knee-length jacket, *dogi*, as well as additional
kimonos are worn. On formal occasions a pair of loose trousers,
hakama, is worn over the outer kimono. The *hakama*, much in
appearance like a divided skirt, and made of rather stiff silk of
a dark color, are open half way down the sides and have the fullness at the top arranged in plaits, six in front and two in back,
and attached to a stiff belt. To this belt are fastened cords

which hold the *hakama*[23] in place by passing over the *obi* and tying in back.

The *haori* or coat of black silk is similar to that worn by the women, both in cut and detail. When traveling, the men wear basket-shaped hats of straw, *kasa*, at other times shading their heads with fans or parasols. The elaborate hair cuts of olden times have given way to that of European style.

FIG. 198. JAPANESE WOMEN IN KIMONOS.
Methodist Prints.

The woman's kimono may be worn touching the floor or shorter, the extra length being held at the waist by a cord or sash of soft silk. Over this strip of silk is worn the most important accessory of the woman's costume, the *obi*. This sash of brocade richly embroidered along its entire length, lined with contrasting colors, and sometimes interlined with canvas or cotton, measures twelve to fifteen inches in width, and four to six yards in length. It is folded lengthwise, the two edges turning upward and wound twice around the body; then the two ends at the back are tied in a very complicated flat knot, or in a butterfly bow. The latter arrangement is worn only by maidens and brides. In order to hold up the upper loop a small cushion, *obiage*,[24] is fastened inside it by a silk cord which passes through the knot and is tied in front over the *obi*.

Extending beyond the roll collar of the kimono is the brightly colored, richly embroidered collar, *han-yeri*, of the fine crepe short chemise, *shito-juban*. Beneath this is worn a short petticoat, *yumoji*, in the form of a rectangular piece of soft cotton wound

[23] GUNSAULUS, H., JAPANESE COSTUME, p. 12. Leaflet No. 12. The Field Museum of Natural History.

[24] *Ibid.*, p. 7.

around the hips. Over the *shito-juban* is placed the long petticoat, *koshimaki*, of gayly colored, patterned crepe or fine wool.

Out-of-doors the Japanese woman frequently wears a knee-length coat, *haori*, made like the kimono, of silk and with added fulness at the sides in the form of gores, and without the double-breasted cut of the kimono. The *haori* fastens directly in front by means of tiny silken cords. The wearer's crest is found on the *haori*, and in the same positions as on the kimonos, in the center of the back, at the top of the sleeves and on each side of the front at the chest, embroidered or stenciled.

Tradition and convention regulate the woman's coiffure as well as the color of her kimono. The married woman wears her hair in one large puff at the top of her head, the size of the puff diminishing as her age increases, while her unmarried sister secures hers in two loops. The hair is stiffened with oil of camellia and held in place with a comb and lacquered pins whose number, size and variety vary with the wearer's age. The intricate arrangement of this head-dress necessitates the services of a professional hair dresser two or three times a week, and a wooden headrest instead of a pillow for sleeping. As a hat would endanger this frail structure, a scarf, or in winter a square of challie, *zukin*, wrapped around the head in the form of a hood constitutes the head covering for out-of-door wear. The lack of hats for protection against the sun makes the parasol the indispensable accessory in the Japanese wardrobe, as is the fan, which, when not in use is tucked away in the folds of the *obi*. A dainty silk vanity case, stenciled or embroidered and containing a tiny paper handkerchief, is concealed in the bosom of the kimono.

The foot covering, about the same for both sexes, consists of white cotton stockings, *tabi*, which reach slightly above the ankle and have separate divisions for the great toes. The *tabi* are fastened at the back by means of hooks and have slightly stiffened soles. Within doors these are the only covering of the feet as in Japan it is not customary to wear any type of shoe in the house. The sandals, *zori*, have soles made of rawhide, braided rushes, or hemp, and sometimes slight heels. They are securely held to the foot by cords that pass between the first and second toes, cross at the instep and fasten at the side of the heel. For inclement weather high wooden clogs, *gheta*, are used.

Silk and fine cotton materials of various interesting weaves and weights are employed for the majority of the garments, cotton in allover patterns or stripes being preferred for every day wear. The kimono worn on formal occasions in winter is made of heavy crepe silk, plain or brocaded, and for additional warmth padded with floss silk. Many thicknesses of padding are placed at the bottom. Very loosely woven thin silks, particularly known as of the screen weave, are used for the formal summer costumes. While interesting designs with motifs from nature are painted, embroidered, or woven around the bottom of the kimono inside as well as outside, since the fall of the Shogunate the lavishly embroidered kimono is seen only on the stage. The singing girls, *geisha*, and the courtesans are attired in brilliantly colored kimonos, but the young gentlewomen wear soft, subdued colors and the matrons quite sombre gray, brown, and blue, really brilliant coloring being found in the lining of the kimono and in the undergarment, *kosh-imaki*.

Young Japanese boys and girls are but charming small editions of their elders. When very young they are apparelled in cottons and silk crepes with the largest of designs and the gayest of colors— yellow, bright blue, green, and the favorite red. As soon as he is able to run about alone, the boy adopts the more sombre colors while his sister revels in the brightest ones until well in her teens. From babyhood their kimonos are identical in cut with those of their elders, the young girl's kimono having the extra length sewn in a tuck at the hip: that of the boy having lengthwise tucks at the shoulder to be let out as need arises. The *tabi, zori*, and *gheta* are worn as soon as the children are able to toddle about.

Ainu Dress.—Inhabiting the Island of Yezo, one of the northern islands of the Japanese Empire, are the Ainu, a people said to be the "last representatives of the original races that inhabited Japan."[25] Most worthy of attention and interest is the kimono worn there by men and women alike. Shaped like that of the Japanese, but shorter, and with a variation in the cut of the sleeve, this kimono is made of elm bark fibre and has as decoration appliqué of dark blue cotton cloth in distinctive geometric designs. Scroll-

[25] HARMUTH, LOUIS, A DICTIONARY OF WOMEN'S WEAR. The Fairchild Publishing Company.

like embroidery is worked over the appliqué connecting the different parts of the motifs. The sash, or *obi*, used to hold the kimono at the waist is similar to but narrower than the regular Japanese one.

Fig. 199. An Ainu Kimono with Characteristic Decoration in Appliqué. Courtesy of the American Museum of Natural History.

Both men and women wear ankle-length, tight trousers and high sandals. The women wear close-fitting caps over their short, unbound hair, and many ropes of beads around the neck.

The Philippines.—The whims of fashion are felt to some extent even in the far isles of the Philippines, though it is chiefly the length and width of the skirts of feminine dress that are subject to its vagaries, the other parts of the national dress remaining quite generally untouched.

FIG. 200. A NATIVE PHILIPPINE GIRL IN COSTUME. NOTE THE CRISPNESS OF THE SLEEVES OF THE CAMISA. Courtesy of the American Museum of Natural History.

While dependent on Asia and America for the silk and cotton employed in the clothing, the Philippino woman utilizes the leaf of the native pineapple for the manufacture of the sheer, delicate cloth, *rengue*, from which are made the square scarf, *pañuelo*, and the bodice, *camisa*, with its enormous sleeves that stand crisply above the shoulders and barely reach to the elbow. The *pañuelo*, about a foot or so square, folded first diagonally, then in several narrow folds, is placed over the shoulders with the point falling between the shoulder blades, and the two ends fastened together at the front of the waist. As this crisp, starched fichu leaves the neck quite open in front, the wearing of jeweled necklaces, particularly in the evening, is quite customary. The sleeves, likewise starched, are extremely short and permit the wearing of bracelets on both arms.

The skirt, *saya*, of this costume reaches to the floor and extends in back in the form of a long, pointed train that for walking and dancing is thrown in a variety of graceful ways over the left forearm. Silk is the fabric most commonly used for the skirt and it must harmonize in color with the *camisa* and *pañuelo*, while black net takes the place of the thin black silk which formerly was used for the three-quarter-length overskirt, *tapis*, that veils the bright-hued skirt. Both *tapis* and *pañuelo* are embroidered by hand or by machine in the native factories in floral motifs with bright floss silks. Colored beads and imitation pearls are frequently intertwined in the decoration of these articles.

The peasant women substitute a square of silk for the crisp *pañuelo* and black silk for the embroidered net of the *tapis*, and are content with a shorter train than are their compatriots of wealth and leisure.

Careful attention is paid to the oiling and smoothing of the glistening black hair that is simply dressed on the top of the head, and is disarranged by no hat, a parasol providing the necessary protection from sun and rain.

A blouse of *rengue* cloth, in cut much like that worn by the Chinese, and long trousers formed the costume of the Philippine man before the coming of the Europeans: now the shirt, coat, and trousers of the latter are quite general.

Hawaii.—Extreme simplicity characterized the body covering of the Polynesians inhabiting the islands of what is now known as the Territory of Hawaii. The material from which their garments were made, like that of the inhabitants of other islands of the Pacific and South Seas, was derived from trees. A form of cloth known as *kapa*, or *tapa*, was manufactured by the women from the bark of certain trees of the islands and dyed in a variety of colors.[26] The

[26] CASTLE, W. R., HAWAII, PAST AND PRESENT, p. 22. Dodd, Mead and Company.

men used narrow strips of *tapa* as girdles about their loins, while the women wound yard lengths about waist and hips as skirts. The upper part of the body was left uncovered except for the occasional *tapa* cloak,[27] but adorned with flowers, feathers, and strings of shells about the neck.

REFERENCES

GIAFFERRI, FEMININE COSTUME OF THE WORLD.
RACINET, LE COSTUME HISTORIQUE, Vol. III.
GUNSAULUS, JAPANESE COSTUME.
HAMMERTON, PEOPLES OF ALL NATIONS.
TILKE, ORIENTAL COSTUMES.
ZUR GESCHICHTE DER KOSTÜME, plates 885, 1034, 1124, 1058, 1131, 1174, 215, 1010, 1107, 915.
WILLIAMS, THE MIDDLE KINGDOM.
GRAY, CHINA.

[27] *Ibid.*, p. 22.

CHAPTER XX

NATIONAL COSTUME IN THE WESTERN WORLD—THE ESKIMOS, MEXICANS, AND INDIANS OF NORTH AND SOUTH AMERICA

THE results of extensive research by ethnologists and historians into the manners and customs of the early dwellers on the continents of North and South America, and the extensive collections displayed by so many museums throughout the country, furnish excellent material for the student of costume, the illustrator, and the designer with imagination who wishes to create for the modern American woman a costume of truly American inspiration.

As was the case with all primitive peoples, climate was a determining factor as to the abundance or scantiness of the body covering of the native American tribes, while the material at hand determined largely the shape of the garments and their decoration. In North America alone dress varied from an entire suit of fur worn by the Eskimo of the Arctic region, to a mere breech cloth of native woven cotton that encircled the loins of the Maricopa Indian living in what is now the southwestern United States.

The Eskimo Dress.—Secluded in the land of snow and ice, away from the influence of the changing customs of the people of the south, the present-day Eskimo doubtless preserves in his dress the very features which characterized that of his fathers for a great length of time. Thus uninfluenced by the whims of fickle fashion, the cut and material of masculine and feminine Eskimo dress remained the same year after year. The garments, alike for men and women, as well as for children, are fashioned from the skin of the native seal, caribou, or reindeer and ornamented with bands of bear, fox, or dog fur.

The costume of every Eskimo consists of four articles: shirt, tunic, trousers, and a pair of high boots, each designed for warmth and protection against the rigors of the climate. In Greenland skins of birds are sewn together for the shirt, *timiak*,[1] with the soft

---

[1] NANSEN, F., ESKIMO LIFE, p. 22. Longmans, Green and Company.

down worn next to the body. Black dog fur edges the bottom of the
long sleeves and the round, close neck to which is attached a hood
to be drawn up over the head when the wearer is out-of-doors. The
tunic, *anork,* of the men, reaching to about the waist, is of sealskin

FIG. 201. THE FUR GARMENTS OF AN ESKIMO MAN AND WOMAN.
Photo from Brown Brothers.

or gay cotton material brought in by the traders. It is very similar
to the *amout*[2] of the women which differs from it mainly in the
possession of a warmly lined fur hood in which the infant or very
young child is carried, so warm and cozy that he feels no need for

[2] *Ibid.,* p. 24.

clothing of his own until able to run about alone. Both sexes wear
hairy sealskin trousers tucked into high boots that reach well over
the knees or even higher for the women. The boots, *kamiks*, of the
hairless skin are a source of much pride to the feminine wearer who
indulges her artistry in the decoration of their tops with bands of

Fig. 202. A Native of Greenland. The Deep Collar Is of Beads. Photo from Brown
Brothers.

embroidery, feather trimmings, or intricate geometric patterns cut
from painted or dyed skins. Short socks of skin with the hair
turned inwards are worn inside the roomy, water-tight *kamiks*.[3]
Bright-hued beads in strings of various lengths or in the shape of a
shoulder collar six or eight inches wide contribute color and
interest to the costume of the women.

[3] *Ibid.*, p. 23.

The *parkeh*[4] of the Alaskan Eskimo is an outer garment or tunic of seal or reindeer skins much longer and fuller than the *anork* worn in Greenland. Just above the wide band of fox fur which edges the botton of this three-quarter length tunic is a broader band made of skins skillfully cut and sewed in designs that are remarkable for their sparkle and interest in dark and light. The attached fox-edged hood is another feature of this garment. The tunic of the Eskimo woman of Point Barrow is cut with rounded tabs or aprons in both front and back, while her relative in the region of the Hudson Bay cuts the tabs narrow and lance shaped.[5] The very long trousers are met slightly above the ankles by sealskin or walrus-hide *mukleks* fashioned much like the Indian moccasin.[6]

Costumes of the North American Indians.—The skin or cloth trousers and coat worn by the North American Indian of today reflect in cut the European influence which began with the coming to this continent of the white settlers. Gay calicoes, vividly colored broadcloths and ribbons are now employed by the braves and squaws on the government reservations; the glass beads of the newcomers now decorate their garments and moccasins instead of the old-time quills of the porcupine and the native wampum.

When tramping the virgin forests and broad, rolling plains, the early Indian derived his clothing as well as his food from the roving herds of deer, mountain goat, and buffalo, letting the natural shape of the tanned skin determine to a large extent the shape of the scant garment he donned for protection against the cold, or on ceremonial occasions. In general, the dress customarily worn by the Indians of the Plains consisted of a breech cloth of leather and, when needed, a large robe of the skins of the deer, or moose. Men of achievement and distinction in the tribes wore shirts made of two deerskins sewn together to form shoulder seams but open at the sides, much like the *poncho* of the South American Indian of today, and belted with a buckskin sash. On the shoulders were bands decorated with porcupine quills. High, close-fitting leggings of deer-

---

[4] DEVINE, E. I., ACROSS WIDEST AMERICA, p. 189. Benziger Brothers.
[5] THE NORTH AMERICANS OF YESTERDAY, by F. S. DELLENBAUGH, p. 159. G. P. Putnam's Sons, New York. Quoted by permission of the publishers.
[6] DEVINE, E. I., ACROSS WIDEST AMERICA, p. 189.

skin were similarly embroidered and fringed along the seams. Moccasins of buckskin worn for hunting or on long travels, were, like the leggings, ornamented with quill work as well as bright beads along the flaps and seams.

FIG. 203. SIOUX INDIAN WOMEN. Photo from Brown Brothers.

The dressing of the hair varied with the location of the tribe. It was a very general custom to crop the hair close to the head leaving a ridge of hair at the center from forehead to neck. "Again in the north the hair was gathered into a knot at the back of the head. In the south, on the other hand, the knot was drawn up on top of the head. In the upper Mississippi valley and around the

Great Lakes the men wore the hair long and braided."[7]　While in cold weather it was customary with some tribes to wear a broad band of calf skin bound around the forehead, a hat was not worn by the Indian. The Menominee on the shores of Lake Michigan used

FIG. 204.　A SIOUX INDIAN. NOTE THE HEAD FEATHERS AND THE MOCCASINS.

FIG. 205.　CROW INDIANS. THE CHILD'S DRESS IS DECORATED WITH ELKS' TEETH.

Courtesy of the Museum of the American Indian, Heye Foundation.

as a head-dress the entire skin of an otter. Chiefs and men of achievement had their heads encircled by bands of leather into which were fastened the feathers of the eagle and the turkey.

Two skins of the buffalo, the mountain sheep, or the deer, sewn edge to edge or suspended from the shoulders by straps formed the dress of the Plains Indian woman who indulged her taste for

[7] WISSLER, CLARK, INDIAN COSTUMES IN THE UNITED STATES, pp. 8–9. American Museum of Natural History Guide Leaflet Series.

ornamentation by sewing to the upper part of this garment several hundred elk teeth, adding at the sides and bottom rattles made of deer hoof, or fringe, or elaborating it with quill work. A huge buffalo robe worn hair side in, exposing to view the elaborately painted skin side, served the women as well as the men necessary protection in winter. The woman's leggings of painted and beaded skins reached to the knee where they were bound securely. At the ankle they met the decorated moccasin.[8] Two braids bound at the ends with thongs, and a part extending from forehead to the nape of the neck characterized the hair dressing of the woman of the Plains who evolved her jewelry from shells, bones, and claws of animals procured by the fishermen and hunters of her tribe.

While skins, particularly those of the deer and rabbit, were utilized in the shirts, robes, and moccasins of the Indian dwelling in what are now the southwestern states of the United States, cloth woven from the native grown cotton, made from willow bark, or the fiber of the yucca plant, was extensively used for the ordinary garments, breech cloth and skirt, worn in that part of the country. The bodies and faces of both sexes were painted red, white or black, suiting tribe and occasion.

A straight, loose shirt of deerskin or cloth covered the upper part of the body which was further protected on cold days by a shawl-like wrap of deerskin or rabbitskin which is today replaced among the Navajo and the Hopi Indians by blankets of native manufacture and bold, woven pattern. Both sexes had moccasins of deerskin; after the introduction and use of the horse, of untanned raw hide. As a rule, this foot covering was worn only in the snow or on trails of great roughness. Another fashion which was followed by men and women alike was that of wearing the hair free, a head band being used occasionally. The Hopi were exceptions to this rather general custom cutting it fairly short at the sides and twisting the long back hair into a knob at the back of the head. The married women of the Hopi parted the hair, then wound the long strands with strips of colored cotton, the unmarried women signifying their status by enormous whorls or loops of hair that stood out from the head above the ears. For necklaces and earrings, turquoise, seeds, shells, beads, and later silver were used.

---

[8] *Ibid.*, pp. 18–19.

Both Navajo and Hopi women had a somewhat different mode of dress from that of the other Indians in that section of the country. Their main garment was a simple cotton strip draped across the front and back of the body and fastened at the right shoulder. The left shoulder was uncovered. This primitive garment, confined at the waist by a sash, extended slightly over the knees, and left legs and arms bare.

FIG. 206.   THE HAIR ARRANGEMENT OF THE   FIG. 207.   AZTEC WOMEN HUEPILLI AND
         HOPI INDIAN WOMAN.   CUEITL.
         Courtesy of the American Museum of Natural History.

Mexican Dress.—While the Spanish left their imprint on Mexican dress after the entrance into Mexico City in 1519 of Cortez and his Spanish troops and his final conquest of the country, it is the dress of the earlier ruling people, the Aztecs, that is more strongly reflected in the garments of the modern Mexican Indian. The gaily striped rectangle of wool cloth, the *zarape*, which the peon throws over his shoulders, is doubtless a descendant of the *timatli* of the Aztecs, which Biart describes as "a piece of cloth four feet long, which enveloped the body and two corners of which were knotted upon the breast and shoulders."[9] The kinship of the long cloth girdle of the Huichol Indian and the large girdle, *maxatl*, that the Aztec wound about his loins seems apparent. Likewise the influence of the Aztec woman's sleeveless blouse, *huepilli*, and the length of colorful cloth, *cueitl*, that she wrapped about her waist and hips for a skirt is seen today in the dress of the modern Tehuan woman. This early *cueitl* was woven from cotton or the thread of the palm tree.[10]

The Aztec woman revelled in rich jewels for her personal adornment: brilliant turquoise, emeralds, amethysts, and gold gleamed against her tawny skin, and in the case of the woman of wealth, on the straps of her leather sandals.[11]

Particularly skilled in the art of handling feathers, the Aztecs provided for their chief's adornment on gala occasions broad mantles made from brilliant birds' feathers. These were accompanied by collars and necklaces of turquoise.[12]

The Tehuan Indians who occupy the Isthmus of Tehuantepec have retained, together with the old customs of the Aztecs, a great deal of the ancient

Fig. 208.   A Tehuan Indian Woman Wearing the Huepilli. Photo by Brown Brothers.

dress. With their short, sleeveless blouse of silk or cotton heavily and brightly embroidered in designs that antedate the Conquest, the women wear the ancient style of wrapped skirt of blue or red

[9] Biart, Lucien, The Aztecs, pp. 292–294. A. C. McClurg and Company.
[10] *Ibid.*
[11] *Ibid.*
[12] The North Americans of Yesterday by F. S. Dellenbaugh, p. 136. G. P. Putnam's Sons, New York. Quoted by permission of the publishers.

cotton. About the bottom of the straight skirt now worn for festive occasions is a wide, plaited ruffle of stiffly starched lace. Unusual, to say the least, is the white head-dress, *huepilli*, which both matrons and maidens don with their holiday attire. It consists of a short garment with a deep plaited flounce of starched cotton lace. The flounce is arranged over the head forming a broad frame for the face, and falling with the rest of the garment down the back. It is said that the *huepilli* was originally a baby's shirt that was worn for luck by the person who rescued the child from drowning.

Five and ten dollar gold pieces of the United States coinage are worn by wealthy Tehuan women in long strings about their necks together with small pendants of pearls arranged in the form of doves' wings. A silk or cotton kerchief, embroidered or fringed is used as a shawl for the shoulders. Rarely are shoes or sandals seen on the feet of Tehuans, male or female, the former being happy in his simple costume of white or colored trousers and coat, gaudy *zarape*, and broad *sombrero*.[13]

The *sombrero* is the national headgear of Mexico: of straw for the peon; of expensive white or gray felt for the gentleman who has his hat faced with silver laces, and banded with silver about the imposing crown. A brim of considerable width, sometimes as much as two feet, is its distinctive feature. With this decorative hat the Mexican of means and station wears dark trousers, short jacket of black cloth, and ruffled shirt. Small silver buttons placed close together accent the side seams of the trousers and outline the fronts of the jackets that are elaborately embroidered in threads of gold and silver. The whole dress recalls that worn in some parts of Spain today.

---

[13] COREY, HERBERT, THE ISTHMUS OF TEHUANTEPEC. The *National Geographic Magazine*, May, 1924.

The Mexican woman of Spanish ancestry retains for occasional wear the black lace *mantilla*, large tortoise-shell comb, and full skirts of her Spanish ancestresses, while her poorer sister arranges a long veil, *rebozo*, of thin and dark colored cotton about her head and shoulders, and wears a simple blouse and full skirt.

South American Costumes.—Gaudy hues figure conspicuously in the dress of the South American peoples, reflecting not only the love of color of the native Indians, but also that of the Spanish and Portuguese descendants of the early settlers from across the Spanish Main. Wool and cotton are the chief textiles from which the simple garments are made, the latter from the native-grown product, the former chiefly from the hair of the llama and alpaca. Silks and velvets are of course extensively used in the dress of the upper and wealthy classes who follow faithfully the current fashions of the Continent. The cholas, and Indians, cling to the *poncho* and the *rebozo*, the former particularly distinctive of South American dress.

Fig. 210.   A Mexican in Riding Costume. Photo by Burton Holmes, from Ewing Galloway.

Peru.—The Indian of Peru is an extremely colourfully clad individual in collarless, but skirted coat of green, knee breeches of black, and decorative straw hat with abundant trimmings of gay ribbons. Crude sandals and woolen stockings that are guiltless of feet clothe his lower extremities. Like the majority of South Americans he wears his hair long.

Not to be outshone by the finery of her husband, the Inca Indian woman combines a red bodice with a short skirt of red or green, and covers her head with a large, embroidered handkerchief that covers just the top and back of her head. Of equally brilliant color as skirt and bodice is her mantle, *lliclla*, that is fastened at the chest.

Indians of other tribes cling to the *poncho*, a square of rough woolen cloth with a hole in the center for the head, reaching a little below the waist, and of bright hue for both men and women, the latter wearing extremely bright-hued skirts, and enormous round felt hats encircled by bands of gold or silver. The men are content with headgear of slightly smaller dimensions worn atop close caps of brilliant colored cloth with tabs over each ear. Characteristic of the head-dress of Indian women in southern Peru is the head shawl tied over a large pancake hat.[14]

Chile.—The most interesting, for our purpose, of the Indians in Chile are the Araucanians whose men wear the "*chirapá*, or bloomers evolved from a blanket wrapped round the legs and tucked through the belt, the same type of trousers formerly worn by the Argentine gaucho."[15] This nether garment is accompanied by a simple shirt and a striped *poncho* of guanaco wool. This latter garment, though shorter, is worn by the women, when out-of-doors, over their blue wool dress that is pinned at the shoulders and belted at the waist. In addition they have the *ichella*, "a long cloak, with fringe at the bottom fastened over the breast with a long pin, at the end of which is an enormous round silver disk that is elaborately ornamented and worn by every woman."[16] Heavy necklaces and large ear pendants of silver are noticeable ornaments. Their long black hair hangs in two braids down the back, and the head is swathed in an embroidered cloth.

While the native Chilean has her garments cut in strictly modern European fashion, her head-dress never varies; it is the *manta*, a large square of thin black material drawn over the head and shoulders, pinned, and allowed to fall over and conceal most of the dress. Of silk or lace for the high-born, of cashmere or alpaca for the lowly, this distinctly national article of dress is doubtless a development of the Spanish *mantilla*.

---

[14] BINGHAM, H., IN THE WONDERLAND OF PERU. *National Geographic Magazine*, April, 1913.

[15] ADAMS, H. C., A LONGITUDINAL JOURNEY THROUGH CHILI, *National Geographic Magazine*, September, 1922.

[16] HARMUTH, L., A DICTIONARY OF WOMEN'S WEAR. Fairchild Publishing Company.

Argentina.—But little of picturesque costume is evident to-day in the Argentine, that of the gaucho, the "cowboy of the pampas," practically alone retaining its former distinctive features, chief of which is the *chiripá*, a square of colored cloth or blanket wound about the waist and legs and fastened by a massive belt of solid silver. The *chiripá* is usually worn to-day over white cotton trousers that are tucked into the tops of high boots of very soft leather armored with enormous spurs. Over his cotton shirt is a short, embroidered jacket which with a large felt hat and bright-hued kerchief tied about the throat add potent touches to a thoroughly interesting attire.

Bolivia.—Characteristic of the dress of most of the Indians of Bolivia and showing traces of Spanish dress of the time of the Conquest, are the loose trousers, checked or striped, bright cotton shirt, similarly patterned *poncho*, and stiff felt hat worn over a close, knitted cap. The majority of the women are garbed in embroidered chemise, small bodice, many short and full, bright skirts, shawl, *rebozo*, over the shoulders, and tiny hats of felt or Panama straw with extremely high crowns. The hair is arranged in two large braids or many small ones de-corated with ornaments of silver.[17]

FIG. 211. A CHOLITA FROM BOLIVIA
Photo by Brown Brothers.

Ecuador.—The poncho, straw hat with broad brim, together with linen trousers and loose white shirts are to be found as the comfortable, and suitable costume of the men residing in the hot climate of Ecuador. The women are clad with equal simplicity in loose blouses, full skirts, and broad-brimmed hats of straw.

[17] *Ibid.*

REFERENCES

RACINET, LE COSTUME HISTORIQUE, Vol. II.
GIAFFERRI, HISTORY OF FEMININE COSTUME OF THE WORLD.
CATLIN, THE NORTH AMERICAN INDIANS.
CURTIS, NORTH AMERICAN INDIANS.
DELLENBAUGH, NORTH AMERICANS OF YESTERDAY.
NANSEN, ESKIMO LIFE.
WISSLER, INDIAN COSTUMES IN THE UNITED STATES.
National Geographic Magazine.

HISTORICAL TABLE AS GUIDE FOR HISTORY OF COSTUME

FRENCH RULERS

Capetian

Hugh Capet	987– 996
Robert II	996–1031
Henri I	1031–1060
Anna of Russia	
Philippe I	1060–1108
Bertha of Holland	
Bertrade of Montfort	
Louis VI	1108–1137
Adelaide of Savoy	
Louis VII	1137–1180
Eleanor of Aquitaine	
Constance of Castile	
Alice of Champagne	
Philippe II	1180–1223
Isabelle of Artois	
Ingeborg of Denmark	
Marie of Meran	
Louis VIII	1223–1226
Blanche of Castile	
Louis IX	1226–1236
Marguerite of Provence	
Philippe III	1270–1285
Isabella of Aragon	
Marie of Brabant	
Philippe IV	1285–1314
Jeanne of Navarre	
Louis X	1314–1316
Margaret of Burgundy	
Clemence of Hungary	
Jean I	1316–1316
Philippe V	1316–1322
Jeanne of Meran	

ENGLISH RULERS

Saxon

975– 979	Edward the Martyr
979–1016	Ethelred I
1016–1017	Edmund

Dane

1017–1035	Canute
1035–1040	Harold I
1040–1042	Hardicanute

Saxon

1042–1066	Edward the Confessor
1066	Harold II

Norman

1066–1087	William I
	Mathilda of Flanders
1087–1100	William II
1100–1135	Henry I
	Mathilda of Scotland
	Adelaide of Louvain
1135–1154	Stephen
	Mathilda of Boulogne

Plantagenet

1154–1189	Henry II
	Eleanor of Aquitaine
1189–1199	Richard I
	Berengaria of Navarre
1199–1216	John
	Hadwissa of Glouster
	Isabella of Angoulême
1216–1272	Henry III
	Eleanor of Provence
1272–1307	Edward I
	Eleanor of Castile
	Margaret of France
1307–1327	Edward II
	Isabella of France

FRENCH RULERS		ENGLISH RULERS	
Charles IV	1322–1328	1327–1377	Edward III
Blanche			Philippa of Hainault
Maria of Luxemburg			
Jeanne of Evreaux			
Valois			
Philippe VI	1328–1350		
Jeanne of Burgundy			
Blanche of Navarre			
Jean II	1350–1364		
Bonne of Luxemburg			
Jeanne of Auvergne			
Charles V	1364–1380	1377–1399	Richard II
Jeanne of Bourbon			Anne of Bohemia
			Isabella of France
Charles VI	1380–1422	Lancaster	
Isabella of Bavaria		1399–1413	Henry IV
			Mary de Bohun
			Joan of Navarre
		1413–1422	Henry V
			Katherine of Valois
Charles VII	1422–1461	1422–1461	Henry VI
Marie of Anjou			Margaret of Anjou
		York	
Louis XI	1461–1483	1461–1483	Edward IV
Margaret of Scotland			Elizabeth Woodville
Charlotte of Savoie		1483–1483	Edward V
Charles VIII	1483–1498	1483–1483	Richard III
Anne of Britanny			Anne Neville
Valois Orleans		Tudor	
Louis XII	1498–1515	1483–1509	Henry VII
Anne of Brittany			Elizabeth of York
Mary Tudor		1509–1547	Henry VIII
Francois I	1515–1547		Katherine of Aragon
Claude of France			Anne Boleyn
Eleanor of Portugal			Jane Seymore
			Anne of Cleves
			Katherine Howard
			Katherine Parr
Henri II	1547–1559	1547–1553	Edward VI
Catherine de Medici		1553–1553	Jane Grey
		1553–1558	Mary
			Philip II of Spain
		1558–1603	Elizabeth
Francois II	1559–1560		
Mary Stuart			
Charles IX	1560–1574		
Elizabeth of Austria			
Henri III	1574–1589		
Louise of Lorraine			
Bourbon		Stuart	
Henri IV	1589–1610	1603–1625	James I
Marguerite of Valois			Anne of Denmark
Marie of Medici			

FRENCH RULERS

Louis XIII	1610–1643
Anne of Austria	
Louis XIV	1643–1715
Marie Theresa	
Louis XV	1715–1774
Marie Leczinska	
Louis XVI	1774–1789
Marie Antoinette	
The Revolution	1789–1792
First Republic	1792–1795
Directoire	1795–1799
Consulate	1799–1804
First Empire	1804–1814
Napoleon	
Josephine	
Marie Louise	
Restoration, House of Bourbon	
Louis XVIII	1814–1824
Maria of Sardinia	
Charles X	1824–1830
Maria Theresa of Sardinia	
Louis Philippe	1830–1848
Marie Amelia of the Two	
Sicilies	
Second Republic	1848–1852
Second Empire	
Napoleon III	1852–1870
Eugénie	
Third Republic	1870–

ENGLISH RULERS

1625–1649	Charles I
	Henrietta Maria
Commonwealth	
1649	Commonwealth declared
1653–1658	Oliver Cromwell
1658–1660	Richard Cromwell
Stuart	
1660–1685	Charles II
	Katherine of Portugal
1685–1689	James II
	Anne Hyde
	Mary of Modena
1689–1702	William II of Orange
	Mary II (Stuart)
1702–1714	Anne
	George of Denmark
Hanover	
1714–1727	George I
	Sophia of Brunswick
1727–1760	George II
	Caroline of Anspach
1760–1820	George III
	Charlotte Sophia of Mecklenburg-Strelitz
1820–1830	George IV
	Caroline of Brunswickwolfenbüttel
1830–1837	William IV
	Adelaide of Saxe-Meiningen
1837–1901	Victoria
	Albert of Saxe-Coburg and Gotha
Saxe-Coburg	
1901–1910	Edward VII
	Alexandra of Denmark
Windsor	
1910–1936	George V
	Mary of Teck
1936–1936	Edward VIII
1936–1952	George VI
	Elizabeth
1952–	Elizabeth II
	Philip

PAINTERS WHOSE WORKS ILLUSTRATE HISTORIC COSTUME

ITALIAN

Giotto	1276–1336	Michelangelo	1475–1564
Brunelleschi	1370–1446	Rossellino	1427–1478
Fra Angelico	1387–1455	Titian	1477–1576
Masaccio	1401–1428	Giorgione	1478–1510
Fra Filippo Lippi	1406–1469	Palma Vecchio	1480–1528
Piero della Francesca	1416–1492	Lorenzo Lotto	1480–1556
Giovanni Bellini	1430–1516	Raphael	1483–1520
Andrea Mantegna	1431–1516	Andrea del Sarto	1486–1531
Botticelli	1444–1510	Correggio	1489–1534
Perugino	1446–1524	Tintoretto	1518–1594
Ghirlandajo	1449–1494	Giovanni Moroni	1525–1578
Leonardo da Vinci	1452–1514	Paolo Veronese	1528–1588
Pinturicchio	1454–1513	Caravaggio	1569–1609
Carpaccio	1460–1522	Pietro Longhi	1702–1762

FLEMISH

Hubert van Eyck	c. 1370–1426	Jan Mabuse	1474–1555
Jan van Eyck	1387–1440	Lucas van Leyden	1494–1533
Roger van der Weyden	1400–1464	Frans Pourbus	1570–1622
Paul Cristus	1400–1473	Peter Paul Rubens	1577–1640
Hans Memling	1430–1494	Anthony Van Dyck	1599–1631
Hugo van der Goes	1420–1482	David Teniers	1610–1690
Gheerardt David	1460–1523	Sir Peter Lely (van der	
Quentin Matsys	1466–1530	Faes)	1618–1680

DUTCH

Frans Hals	1580–1666	Pieter de Hooch	1629–1677
Justus Sustermans	1597–1681	Jacob van Ruisdael	1629–1682
Rembrandt van Rijn	1606–1669	Johannes Vermeer	1632–1675
Gerard ter Borch	1617–1681	Nicolaes Maes	1632–1693
Aalbert Cuyp	1620–1691		

GERMAN

Albert Dürer	1471–1528	Bartholomaeus Bruyn	1493–1557
Hans Holbein	1497–1543	Anton Mengs	1728–1774
Lucas Cranach	1472–1553		

SPANISH

Alonzo Coello	d. 1590	Francisco Goya	1746–1828
Domenico Theotocopuli		Mariano Fortuny	1841–1874
(El Greco)	1548–1625	Joacquin Sorolla y Bastida	1862–1923
Diego Velasquez	1599–1660	Ignacio Zuloaga	1870–
Bartolome Murillo	1618–1682		

318

FRENCH

Jean Fouquet	c. 1420–1480	Jean L. Gericault	1791–1824
François Clouet	1500–1572	Jean B. C. Corot	1796–1875
Nicolas Poussin	1594–1665	Paul Delaroche	1797–1856
Claude Lorrain	1600–1682	Ferdinand Delacroix	1798–1863
Charles LeBrun	1619–1690	Eugène Isabey	1804–1886
Nicolas Le Largillière	1656–1746	Honoré Daumier	1808–1879
Hyacinthe Rigaud	1659–1743	Théodore Rousseau	1812–1867
Antoine Watteau	1684–1721	Jules Dupré	1812–1889
Jean Nattier	1685–1766	Jean Messonier	1813–1891
Nicolas Lancret	1690–1743	Jean François Millet	1814–1875
Jean Chardin	1699–1779	Gustave Courbet	1819–1877
François Boucher	1703–1770	Camille Pissarro	1831–1903
Quentin de la Tour	1704–1788	Edouard Manet	1832–1883
Charles André Van Loo	1705–1765	Leon Bonnat	1833–1922
Jean B. Greuze	1725–1805	Hilaire G. Edgar Degas	1834–1917
François Drouais	1727–1775	Henri Fantin-Latour	1836–1904
Jean H. Fragonard	1732–1806	Carolus Duran	1837–1917
Jacques L. David	1748–1825	Alfred Sisley	1839–1889
François Gérard	1770–1837	Paul Cézanne	1839–1906
Mme. E. Vigée Lebrun	1775–1842	Claude Monet	1840–1926
Pierre Prud'hon	1758–1823	Firmin A. Renoir	1841–1919
Jean A. D. Ingres	1780–1867	Georges Seurat	1859–1891

ENGLISH

William Hogarth	1697–1764	John Hoppner	1758–1810
Sir Joshua Reynolds	1723–1792	John Opie	1761–1807
Thomas Gainsborough	1727–1788	Sir Thomas Lawrence	1769–1830
George Romney	1734–1802	John Lavery	1857–
Sir Henry Raeburn	1756–1823		

AMERICAN

Joseph Blackburn	1708–1765	George H. Boughton	1833–1905
John S. Copley	1737–1815	J. McNeil Whistler	1834–1903
Gilbert Stuart	1755–1828	William M. Chase	1849–1916
John Trimbull	1756–1843	John S. Sargent	1856–1925
Thomas Sully	1783–1872		

BIBLIOGRAPHY OF HISTORY OF COSTUME

Academic

ENCYCLOPÆDIA BRITANNICA: ROBES; UNIVERSITIES.

HARRADEN, R. B. COSTUMES OF THE UNIVERSITY OF CAMBRIDGE, London: R. Ackermen, 1815.

HAYCROFT, F. W. THE DEGREES AND HOODS OF THE WORLD'S UNIVERSITIES AND COLLEGES. London: Cheshunt Press Ltd., 1924.

LEONARD, G. C. THE CAPS AND GOWNS IN AMERICA. Albany: Catrell and Leonard, 1896.

Accessories

Combs

CHILD, THEODORE. WIMPLES AND CRISPING PINS. New York: Harper and Brothers, 1895.

WINTER. DIE KÄMME ALLER ZEITEN. Leipzig: Degener, 1907.

Corsets

LEOTY, ERNEST. LE CORSET À TRAVERS LES ÂGES. Paris: P. Ollendorff 1893.

Crinoline

RHEAD, G. W. CHATS ON COSTUME. New York: F. A. Stokes and Co., 1906.

PHILPOTT. CRINOLINE. London: Philpott, 1864.

LORD, W. B. THE CORSET AND THE CRINOLINE. London: 1865.

Fans

FLORY, A. M. A BOOK ABOUT FANS. New York: The Macmillan Company, 1895.

PERCIVAL, MACIVOR. THE FAN BOOK. London: T. F. Unwin, 1920.

RHEAD, G. W. HISTORY OF THE FAN. London: K. Paul, Trench, Trieber and Company, Ltd., 1910.

UZANNE, L. O. LES ORNAMENTS DE LA FEMME. Paris: Librairies-imprimeries, 1892.

Furs

DAVY, RICHARD. FURS AND FUR GARMENTS. London: Roxburghe Press, n.d.

General

BOEHN, MAX VON. MODES, MANNERS, ORNAMENTS. New York: E. P. Dutton and Company, 1914.

LESTER, K. M. AND OERKE, B. V. ACCESSORIES OF DRESS. Peoria: Manual Arts Press, 1940.

Gloves

BECK, S. W. GLOVES, THEIR ANNALS AND ASSOCIATIONS. London: Hamilton, Adams and Company, 1883.

Head Dress

CHILD, T. WIMPLES AND CRISPING PINS. New York: Harper and Brothers, 1895.

RHEAD, G. W. CHATS ON COSTUME. London: T. F. Unwin, 1910.

DE VILLERMONT, MARIE. HISTOIRE DE LA COIFFURE FÉMININE. Paris: Renouard Laurens, Ed., 1892.

Jewelry

BURGESS, F. W. ANTIQUE JEWELRY AND TRINKETS. New York: G. P. Putnam's Sons, 1919.

EVANS, JOAN. ENGLISH JEWELRY FROM THE FIFTH CENTURY TO 1800. London: Methuen and Company, 1921.

HEATON, H. A. BROOCHES OF MANY NATIONS. Murray, Nottingham Book Company, 1904.

LUTHMER, F. ORNAMENTAL JEWELRY OF THE RENAISSANCE. London: H. Sotheran, 1882.

PERCIVAL, M. CHATS ON OLD JEWELRY. London: T. F. Unwin, 1912.

SMITH, C. JEWELRY. London: Methuen and Company, 1908.

VEVER, H. LA BIJOUTERIE FRANÇAISE AU XIX SIÈCLE. Paris: H. Floury, 1906–1908.

WILLIAMS, C. R. GOLD AND SILVER JEWELRY AND RELATED OBJECTS New York: New York Historical Society, 1924.

Shoes and foot-wear

DUTTON, W. H. BOOTS AND SHOES OF OUR ANCESTORS. London: Chapman and Hall Ltd., 1898.

HALL, J. S. BOOK OF THE FEET. New York: 1847.

REDFERN, W. B. ROYAL AND HISTORICAL GLOVES AND SHOES. London: Methuen and Company, 1904.

RHEAD, G. W. CHATS ON COSTUME. New York: F. A. Stokes Co., 1906.

WRIGHT, THOMAS. ROMANCE OF THE SHOE. London: C. J. Farncombe and Sons, Ltd., 1922.

Umbrellas

UZANNE, L. O. THE SUNSHADE, THE GLOVE, THE MUFF. 1883.

Afghanistan

HAMILTON, ANGUS. AFGHANISTAN. Boston: J. B. Millet Company, 1910.

Albania

BAILEY, W. F. SLAVS OF THE WAR ZONE. New York: E. P. Dutton and Company, 1916.

TILKE, M. COSTUMES OF EASTERN EUROPE. New York: E. Weyhe, 1926.

American Indians

CATLIN, GEORGE. MANNERS AND CUSTOMS OF THE AMERICAN INDIANS. London: Chatto and Windus, 1876.

CURTIS, E. S. THE NORTH AMERICAN INDIAN. Cambridge: University Press, 1907–1925

DELLENBAUGH, F. S. NORTH AMERICAN INDIANS OF YESTERDAY. New York: G. P. Putnam's Sons, 1900.

HARVEY, F. FIRST FAMILIES OF THE SOUTHWEST. Kansas City, Mo.: F. Harvey, 1913.

HODGE, F. W. HANDBOOK OF THE AMERICAN INDIANS. Washington: Government Printing Office, 1907–1910.

HOUGH, W. RACIAL GROUPS AND FIGURES IN THE NATURAL HISTORY MUSEUM BUILDING OF THE UNITED STATES NATIONAL MUSEUM. Washington: Government Printing Office, 1922.

National Geographic Magazine: September, 1927.

STARR, F. INDIANS OF SOUTHERN MEXICO. Chicago: F. Starr, 1899.

VERRILL, A. H. THE AMERICAN INDIAN, New York: D. Appleton and Company, 1927.

WISSLER, CLARK. INDIAN COSTUMES IN THE UNITED STATES. New York: American Museum of Natural History, 1926.

Arabia

BURTON, SIR RICHARD. A PILGRIMAGE TO MECCA. New York: Longmans, Green and Company, 1856.

STRACHEY, L. MEMORIES OF AN ARAB PRINCESS. New York: Double-day, Page and Company, 1907.

Assyria

HOPE, THOMAS. COSTUME OF THE ANCIENTS. London: Bulmer and Company, 1812.

HOUSTON, M. G. and HORNBLOWER, F. ANCIENT EGYPTIAN, ASSYRIAN, AND PERSIAN COSTUME. London: A. and C. Black, 1920.

LUTZ, H. F. TEXTILES AND COSTUMES AMONG THE PEOPLES OF THE ANCIENT NEAR EAST. Leipzig: Hindrichs, 1923.

Austria

HOLME, CHARLES. PEASANT ART IN AUSTRIA AND HUNGARY. London: "The Studio," Ltd., 1911.

McCRACKEN, W. D. THE SPELL OF THE TYROL. Boston: L. C. Page and Company, 1914.

Bibliography

BROOKLYN PUBLIC LIBRARY. READING AND REFERENCE LIST ON COSTUME.

CLARK, M. E., AND OTHERS. ART IN HOME ECONOMICS. Chicago: The University of Chicago Press, 1925.

DETROIT PUBLIC LIBRARY. COSTUME, A LIST OF BOOKS.

EVANS, MARY. COSTUME SILHOUETTES. Philadelphia: J. B. Lippincott Company, 1923.

KELLY AND SCHWAB. HISTORIC COSTUME. London: T. B. Batsford. Ltd., 1925.

RACINET, A. LE COSTUME HISTORIQUE. Paris: Firmin-Didot et Cie., 1888.

TRAPHAGEN, ETHEL. COSTUME DESIGN AND ILLUSTRATION. New York: John Wiley and Sons, Inc., 1918.

Bulgaria

FOX, FRANK. BULGARIA. London: A. and C. Black, 1915.

MONROE, W. S. BULGARIA AND HER PEOPLE. Boston: L. C. Page Company, 1914.

National Geographic Magazine: November, 1908, December, 1908, November, 1912, April, 1915, October, 1915.

TILKE, MAX. COSTUME OF EASTERN EUROPE. New York: E. Weyhe, 1926.

Byzantium

NORRIS, HERBERT. COSTUME AND FASHION. London: J. M. Dent and Son, 1925.

ZUR GESCHICHTE DER KOSTÜME. Munich: Braun und Schneider.

Children

BROOKE, I. ENGLISH CHILDREN'S COSTUME. London: A. and C. Black, 1930.

EARLE, A. M. CHILD LIFE IN COLONIAL DAYS. New York: The Macmillan Company, 1922.

GODFREY, E. ENGLISH CHILDREN IN OLDEN TIMES. London: Methuen and Company, 1907.

JACKSON, M. WHAT THEY WORE: A HISTORY OF CHILDREN'S DRESS. George Allen and Unwin, Ltd., London.

MACQUOID, P. FOUR HUNDRED YEARS OF BEAUTIFUL CHILDREN. London: The Medici Society, Ltd., 1923.

MENPES, D. WORLD'S CHILDREN. London: A. and C. Black, 1903.

MILLER, O. T. LITTLE PEOPLE OF ASIA. New York: E. P. Dutton and Company, 1887.

SAUERLANDT, MAX. KINDERBILDNISSE AUS FÜNF JAHRHUNDERT. Leipzig: 1921.

China

BALL, J. D. THINGS CHINESE. New York: Charles Scribner's Sons, 1904.

GRAY, J. H. CHINA. New York: The Macmillan Company, 1878.

National Geographic Magazine: August, 1900, September, 1905, February, 1908, April, 1908, September, 1908, February, 1910, September, 1910, October, 1912, May, 1913, June, 1913, October, 1913.

RACINET, A. LE COSTUME HISTORIQUE. Paris: Firmin-Didot et Cie., 1888.

TILKE, MAX. ORIENTAL COSTUMES. New York: Brentano, 1922.

WILLIAMS, S. W. THE MIDDLE KINGDOM. New York: Charles Scribner's Sons, 1883.

Czechoslovakia

HAIRE, F. A. THE FOLK COSTUME BOOK. New York: A. S. Barnes, 1926.

National Geographic Magazine: February, 1917, June, 1927.

UPRKA, JOZA. PEASANTS' FURS IN CZECHOSLOVAKIA. Kromeriz, n.d.

Dalmatia

National Geographic Magazine: May, 1908, December, 1908, January, 1928.

TILKE, MAX. COSTUMES IN EASTERN EUROPE. New York: E. Weyhe, 1926.

Denmark

DANSKE-NATIONALDRAGTER. Nolding: P. Blichers Forlag, 1915.

Ecclesiastical Costume

DUCKETT, SIR G. F. MONASTIC AND ECCLESIASTICAL COSTUME. Lewes: Farncombe Company, 1892.

LaCROIX, PAUL. MILITARY AND RELIGIOUS LIFE IN THE MIDDLE AGES. London: 1874.

MACALISTER, R. A. S. ECCLESIASTICAL VESTMENTS. London: Stock, 1896.

NAINFA, J. H. COSTUME OF THE PRELATES OF THE CATHOLIC CHURCH. Baltimore: J. Murphy Company, 1926.

PLANCHÉ, J. R. CYCLOPÆDIA OF COSTUME. London: Chatto and Windus, 1876–79.

PUGIN, A. W. N. GLOSSARY OF ECCLESIASTICAL ORNAMENT. London: H. G. Bohn, 1846.

STRUTT, J. THE REGAL AND ECCLESIASTICAL ANTIQUITIES OF ENGLAND. London: H. G. Bohn, 1842.

Egypt

ERMANN, ADOLF. LIFE IN ANCIENT EGYPT. New York: The Macmillan Company, 1894.

HOPE, THOMAS. COSTUME OF THE ANCIENTS. London: Bulmer and Company, 1841.

HOUSTON, M. G. and HORNBLOWER, F. ANCIENT EGYPTIAN, ASSYRIAN, AND PERSIAN COSTUME. London: A. and C. Black, 1920.

TILKE, MAX. ORIENTAL COSTUMES. New York: Brentano, 1922.

WILKINSON, J. G. MANNERS AND CUSTOMS OF THE ANCIENT EGYPTIANS. New York: Dodd, Mead and Company, 1879.

England

ASHDOWN, E. J. BRITISH COSTUME. Boston: Thomas Nelson and Sons, 1910.

BROOKE, IRIS. ENGLISH COSTUME. London: A. and C. Black, Ltd., 1935 and 1936.

CALTHROP, D. C. ENGLISH COSTUME. London: A. and C. Black, 1906.

CLINCH, GEORGE. ENGLISH COSTUME. Chicago: A. C. McClurg, 1910.

DRUITT, HERBERT. COSTUMES ON BRASSES. Philadelphia: G. W. Jacobs 1907.

FAIRHOLT, F. W. COSTUME IN ENGLAND. London: G. Bell and Sons, 1916.

HOLDEN, ANGUS. ELEGANT MODES IN THE NINETEENTH CENTURY. London: G. Allen and Unwin, 1935.

HUGHES, TALBOT. DRESS DESIGN. New York: The Macmillan Company, 1913.

KELLY, F. M. AND SCHWAB, R. HISTORIC COSTUME. London: B. T. Batsford, Ltd., 1925.

NORRIS, HERBERT. COSTUME AND FASHION. London: J. M. Dent and Son, 1925.

PARSONS, F. A. THE PSYCHOLOGY OF DRESS. New York: Doubleday, Page and Company, 1920.

PLANCHÉ, J. R. HISTORY OF BRITISH COSTUME. London: G. Bell and Sons, 1907.

PRICE, J. M. DAME FASHION. New York: Charles Scribner's Sons, 1913.

SHAW, HENRY. DRESSES AND DECORATIONS OF THE MIDDLE AGES. London: G. H. Bohn, 1858.

SMITH, C. H. THE ANCIENT COSTUME OF GREAT BRITAIN AND IRELAND. London: J. Dowling.

STRUTT, JOSEPH. DRESS AND HABITS OF THE PEOPLE OF ENGLAND. London: G. H. Bohn, 1842.

Eskimo

NANSEN, FRIEDTJOF. ESKIMO LIFE. New York: Longmans, Green and Company, 1893.

France

BOUTET, H. LES MODES FEMININES DU XIX SIÈCLE. Paris: 1902.

CHALLAMEL, A. HISTORY OF FASHION IN FRANCE. New York: Scribner and Welford, 1882.

CANZIANI, ESTELLA. COSTUMES, TRADITIONS, AND SONGS OF SAVOY. London: Chatto and Windus, 1911.

DEMAY, G. LE COSTUME AU MOYEN ÂGE. Paris: Dumoulin et Cie, 1880.

ENLART, C. MANUEL D'ARCHÉOLOGIE FRANÇAISE. Le Costume. Paris: A. Picard et Fils, 1902.

FISCHEL, OSKAR, AND BOEHN, MAX. MODES AND MANNERS OF THE NINETEENTH CENTURY. New York: E. P. Dutton and Company, 1909.

GIAFFERRI, P. L. LE HISTOIRE DU COSTUME FEMININE FRANÇAISE. Paris: Editions Nilsson, 1922.

JACQUEMIN, RAPHAEL. HISTOIRE GENERAL AU COSTUME. Paris: 1866.

KEIM, A. LE COSTUME DU PAYS FRANCE. Paris: Editions Nilsson, 1929.

LACROIX, PAUL. COSTUMES HISTORIQUES. Paris: Administration le librairie, 1852. MANNERS, CUSTOMS AND DRESS DURING THE MIDDLE AGES AND THE RENAISSANCE PERIOD. London: Chapman and Hall, 1876.

LESTER, K. M. HISTORY OF COSTUME. Peoria: Manual Arts Press, 1925.

MERCURI, PAOLO. COSTUMES HISTORIQUES. Paris: A. Lévy, Fils, 1860.

National Geographic Magazine: September, 1914, November, 1915, July, 1923.
PARSONS, F. A. THE PSYCHOLOGY OF DRESS. New York: Doubleday, Page and Company, 1920.
PAUQUET FRÈRES. MODES ET COSTUMES HISTORIQUES. Paris: Bureau des Modes et Costumes Historiques, 1875.
PITON, CAMILLE. LE COSTUME CIVIL EN FRANCE. Paris: E. Flammarion, n.d.
PRICE, J. M. DAME FASHION. New York: Charles Scribner's Sons, 1913.
QUICHERAT. J. HISTOIRE DU COSTUME EN FRANCE. Paris: Hachette et Cie., 1875.
RACINET, A. LE COSTUME HISTORIQUE. Paris: Firmin-Didot et Cie., 1888.
RENAN, AVERY. LE COSTUME EN FRANCE. Paris: Librairie-imprimeries, 1890.
ROBIDA, A. "YESTER-YEAR," TEN CENTURIES OF TOILETTE. New York: Charles Scribner's Sons, 1891.
ROUX, J. C. T. LE COSTUME EN PROVENCE. Paris: A Lemerre, 1907.
UZANNE, L. O. FASHIONS IN PARIS. London: Heinemann, 1901.
VIOLLET-LE-DUC, E. E. DICTIONNAIRE DU MOBILIER FRANÇAIS. Paris: 1858.

General Books on Costume
DAVENPORT, MILLIA. THE BOOK OF COSTUME. New York: Crown Publishing Company, 1948
GIAFFERR., P. L. FEMININE COSTUME OF THE WORLD. Paris: Editions Nilsson, 1926.
HOTTENROTH, F. LE COSTUME CHEZ LES PEUPLES ANCIENS ET MODERNS. Paris: A. Guérine, 1896.
KRETSCHMER, A. COSTUMES OF ALL AGES, ANCIENT AND MODERN. Leipzig: 1887.
PLANCHÉ, J. R. CYCLOPÆDIA OF COSTUME. London: Chatto and Windus, 1876–79.
RACINET, A. LE COSTUME HISTORIQUE. Paris: Firmin-Didot et Cie., 1888.
RHEAD, C. W. CHATS ON COSTUME. London: T. F. Unwin, 1906.
ROBIDA, A. "YESTER-YEAR," TEN CENTURIES OF TOILETTE. New York: Charles Scribner's Sons, 1891.
VECELLIO, C. COSTUMES ANCIENS ET MODERNS. Paris: 1860.
WEBB, W. M. HERITAGE OF DRESS. New York: McClures, 1908.
WORTH, J. P. CENTURY OF FASHION. Boston: Little, Brown and Company, 1928.
ZUR GESCHICHTE DER KOSTÜME. Munich: Braun und Schneider.

Germany
KRETSCHMER, ALBERT. COSTUMES NATIONAUX ALLEMANDS. Leipzig: 1870.
PETTIGREW, D. W. PEASANT COSTUME OF THE BLACK FOREST. London: A. and C. Black, Ltd., 1937.

Greece
ABRAHAMS, E. B. GREEK DRESS. London: John Murray, 1908.
BLÜMNER, H. HOME LIFE OF THE ANCIENT GREEKS AND ROMANS. New York: Funk, Wagnalls and Company, 1893.
EVANS, M. M. GREEK DRESS. New York: The Macmillan Company, 1893.
GUHL, E. K. AND KONER, W. D. THE LIFE OF THE GREEKS AND ROMANS. London: Chatto and Windus, 1875.

GULICK, C. B. LIFE OF THE ANCIENT GREEKS. New York: D. Appleton and Company, 1911.

HAWES, A. H. AND H. B. CRETE, THE FORERUNNER OF GREECE. New York: Harper and Brothers, 1916.

HEUZY, LEON. HISTOIRE DU COSTUME ANTIQUE. Paris: Edouard Champion, 1922.

HOPE, THOMAS. COSTUME OF THE ANCIENTS. London: Bulmer and Company, 1841.

METROPOLITAN MUSEUM, THE DAILY LIFE OF THE GREEKS AND ROMANS. New York: The Metropolitan Museum of Art, 1924.

National Geographic Magazine: March, 1913, October, 1925, September, 1916.

TUCKER, T. G. LIFE IN ANCIENT ATHENS. New York: The Macmillan Company, 1907.

Hawaii

ALEXANDER, W. D. HISTORY OF HAWAII. New York: The American Book Company, 1891.

CASTLE, W. R. HAWAII, PAST AND PRESENT. New York: Dodd, Mead and Company, 1913.

Hungary

HOLME, CHARLES. PEASANT ART IN AUSTRIA AND HUNGARY. London: "The Studio," Ltd., 1911.

MALONYAI DEZSÖ. A MAGYAR NÉP MÜVÉSZETE. Budapest: 1907–12

MANN, K. PEASANT ART IN EUROPE. London: A. and C. Black, Ltd., 1935.

MITTON, G. E. A. HUNGARY. London: A. and C. Black, 1914.

India

BALFOUR, EDWARD. THE CYCLOPÆDIA OF INDIA AND EASTERN AND SOUTHERN ASIA. London: Bernard Quaritch, 1885.

GRANT, CHARLES. INDIA. The Encyclopædia Britannica, Thirteenth Edition.

KELLY, R. T. BURMA. London: A. and C. Black, 1905.

TILKE, MAX. ORIENTAL COSTUMES. New York: Brentano, 1922.

WATSON, J. F. THE TEXTILE MANUFACTURES AND COSTUMES OF INDIA. London: Eyre and Spottiswoode, 1866.

YOE, S. THE BURMAN, HIS LIFE AND NOTIONS. New York: The Macmillan Company, 1852.

Ireland

JOYCE, P. W. THE SOCIAL HISTORY OF ANCIENT IRELAND. New York: Longmans, Green and Company, 1903.

Italy

CALDERINI, EMMA. IL COSTUME POPULARE IN ITALIA. Milan: Sperling and Kupfer, 1934.

FLOERKE, HANS. DIE MODEN DER ITALIENSCHEN RENAISSANCE. Munich: George Muller, 1917.

HOLME, CHARLES. PEASANT ART IN ITALY. London: "The Studio," Ltd., 1913.

PARSONS, F. A. THE PSYCHOLOGY OF DRESS. New York: Doubleday, Page and Company, 1920.

PINELLI, B. ETCHINGS OF ITALIAN COSTUME. Rome: 1844.

VECELLIO, C. COSTUMES ANCIENS ET MODERNS. Paris: Firmin-Didot et Cie, 1860.

Japan

BACON, A. M. JAPANESE GIRLS AND WOMEN. New York: Houghton Mifflin Company, 1912.

CHAMBERLIN, B. H. THINGS JAPANESE. London: John Murray, 1905.
GUNSAULUS, H. C. JAPANESE COSTUME. Chicago: Field Museum of Natural History, 1923.
KNOX, G. W. JAPANESE LIFE IN TOWN AND COUNTRY. New York: G. P. Putnam's Sons, 1904.
PRIEST, A. JAPANESE COSTUME. New York: Metropolitan Museum of Art, 1935.
VICTORIA AND ALBERT MUSEUM. GUIDE TO THE JAPANESE COLLECTION. Part II—Costume. London, 1920.

Jewish Costume
DE QUINCY, THOMAS. TOILETTE OF THE HEBREW LADY. Hartford: E. V. Mitchell, 1926.
DICTIONARY OF THE BIBLE. New York: Charles Scribner's Sons.
JEWISH ENCYCLOPÆDIA. New York: Funk, Wagnalls and Company, 1903.
MILLER, M. AND MILLER, J. L. ENCYCLOPÆDIA OF BIBLE LIFE AND APPAREL. New York: Harper & Brothers, 1944.
SMITH, W. M. DICTIONARY OF THE BIBLE. Hartford: J. B. Burr and Company, 1868.

Korea
HAMILTON, ANGUS. KOREA. New York: Charles Scribner's Sons, 1904.

Lace
BROOKE, M. L. LACE AND LACE MAKING. London: G. Routledge and Son, 1923.
CLIFFORD, C. R. THE LACE DICTIONARY. New York: Clifford and Lawton, 1913.
ENCYCLOPÆDIA BRITANNICA.
LEFÉBURE, ERNEST. EMBROIDERY AND LACE. London: H. Grevel, 1888.
LOWES, E. L. CHATS ON OLD LACE. London: T. F. Unwin, 1919.
MOORE, N. H. THE LACE BOOK. New York: F. A. Stokes Company, 1904.
PALLISER, MRS. BURY. THE HISTORY OF LACE. London: S. Low Marsden and Company, 1928.
POLLEN, MRS. J. H. SEVEN CENTURIES OF LACE. London: Heinemann, 1903.
RICCI, ELISA. OLD ITALIAN LACES. Philadelphia: J. B. Lippincott Company, 1913.
SHARP, MARY. POINT AND PILLOW LACE. New York: E. P. Dutton and Company, 1913.
WRIGHT, THOMAS. THE ROMANCE OF THE LACE PILLOW. Olney Bucks: H. H. Armstrong, 1919.

Mexico
BIART, LUCIEN. THE AZTECS. Chicago: A. C. McClurg, 1892.
DELLENBAUGH, F. S. THE NORTH AMERICANS OF YESTERDAY. New York: G. P. Putnam's Sons, 1917.
GARCIA, CUBAS A. THE REPUBLIC OF MEXICO. Mexico: 1876.
SPENCE, LEWIS. MEXICO OF THE MEXICANS. New York: Charles Scribner's Sons, 1917.

Military costume
LACROIX, PAUL. MILITARY AND RELIGIOUS LIFE IN THE MIDDLE AGES. London: 1874.
LUARD, JOHN. HISTORY OF THE DRESS OF THE BRITISH SOLDIER. London: Clowes and Sons, 1852.
PLANCHÉ, J. R. CYCLOPÆDIA OF COSTUME. London: Chatto and Windus, 1876–79.

Sigel, G. A.   Deutschlands Heer und Flotte in Wort und Bild. 1900.

Montenegro
DeWindt, Harry.   Through Savage Europe.   Philadelphia: J. B. Lippincott Company, 1907.
Henderson, P. E.   A British Officer in the Balkans.   Philadelphia: J. B. Lippincott Company, 1909.
National Geographic Magazine: December, 1912, March, 1913.

Morocco
Meakin, Budgett.   The Moors.   London: Allen and Unwin, 1902.
Tilke, Max.   Oriental Costume.   New York: Brentano, 1922.

Netherlands
Edwards, G. W.   Holland of Today.   New York: Moffat, Yard and Company, 1909.
Jungman, Beatrix.   Holland.   London: A. and C. Black, 1907.
Meldrum, D. S.   Home Life in Holland.   New York: The Macmillan Company, 1911.
National Geographic Magazine: January, 1915, September, 1916.
Semple, Miss.   The Costume of the Netherlands.   London: Ackerman, 1817.

Norway
Jungman, Beatrix.   Norway.   London: A. and C. Black, 1905.
National Geographic Magazine: February, 1917.
Tönsberg, N. C.   Norske Nationaldragter.   Christiania: 1852.

Palestine
Grant, E.   The People of Palestine.   Philadelphia: J. B. Lippincott Company, 1921.
Neil, James.   Everyday Life in the Holyland.   London: Cassell and Company, 1913.
Tilke, Max.   Oriental Costumes.   New York: Brentano, 1922.

Persia
De Warzee, Dorothy.   Peeps into Persia.   London: Hurst, Blackett, 1910.
Lory, E. and Sladen, D.   Queer Things About Persia.   London: E. Nash and Grayson, Ltd., 1907.
Ridpath, J. C.   Great Races of Mankind.   Cincinnati: Jones Brothers, 1893.
Sykes, Ethel.   Persia and Its People.   London: Methuen and Company, 1910.

Plays and Pageants
Barton, L.   Historic Costume for the Stage.   Boston: W. H. Baker and Company, 1935.
Chalmers, Helena.   Clothes On and Off the Stage.   New York: D. Appleton and Company, 1928.
Chubb, P.   Festivals and Plays for Schools and Elsewhere.   New York: Harper and Brothers, 1912.
Evans, Mary.   How to Make Historic American Costumes.   New York: A. S. Barnes, 1942.
Grimbal, E.   Costuming a Play.   New York: The Century Company, 1925.
Haire, F. A.   The Folk Costume Book.   New York: A. S. Barnes, 1926.
———.   The American Costume Book.   New York: A. S. Barnes, 1934.

MACKAY, C. D. COSTUMES AND SCENERY FOR AMATEURS. New York: Holt and Company, 1915.

NORTHRUP, B. AND GREENE, A. HISTORICAL COSTUME PLATES. New York: Teachers College, 1925.

SELNER, E. HISTORIC COSTUME PLATES. Worcester: *School Arts Magazine.*

SMITH, MILTON. PLAY PRODUCTION. New York: D. Appleton and Company, 1928.

YOUNG, A. B. STAGE COSTUMING. New York: The Macmillan Company, 1927.

Poland

HOLME, CHARLES. PEASANT ART IN RUSSIA. London: "The Studio," Ltd., 1912.

ZIENKOWICZ, LEON. LES COSTUMES DU PEUPLE POLONAISE. Paris: 1841.

Portugal

BRADFORD, WILLIAM. SKETCHES OF COSTUME IN PORTUGAL AND SPAIN. London: J. Booth, 1812.

National Geographic Magazine: November, 1922, November, 1927.

RACINET, A. LE COSTUME HISTORIQUE. Paris: Firmin-Didot et Cie., 1888.

Quaker costume

GUMMERE, A. M. THE QUAKER. Philadelphia: Ferris and Leach, 1911.

McCLELLAN, E. HISTORIC COSTUME IN AMERICA. Philadelphia: McCrae Smith Company, 1910.

Rome

HARPER, DICTIONARY OF CLASSICAL ANTIQUITIES. New York: Harper and Brothers, 1896.

HOPE, THOMAS. COSTUME OF THE ANCIENTS. London: Bulmer and Company, 1841.

JOHNSTON, H. W. PRIVATE LIFE OF THE ROMANS. New York: Scott, Forsman, 1903.

METROPOLITAN MUSEUM OF ART. DAILY LIFE OF THE GREEKS AND ROMANS. New York: Metropolitan Museum, 1924.

NORRIS, HERBERT. COSTUME AND FASHION. London: J. M. Dent and Son, 1925–27.

WILSON, L. M. THE ROMAN TOGA. Baltimore: The Johns Hopkins Press, 1924.

Roumania

CLARK, C. U. GREATER ROUMANIA. New York: Dodd, Mead and Company, 1922.

HAIRE, F. H. THE FOLK COSTUME BOOK. New York: A. S. Barnes, 1926.

OPRESCU, GEORGE. PEASANT ART IN ROUMANIA. London: The Studio, Ltd., 1929.

Russia

CHALIF, L. H. RUSSIAN FESTIVALS AND COSTUMES FOR PAGEANT AND DANCE. 1921.

HOLME, CHARLES. PEASANT ART IN RUSSIA. London: The Studio, Ltd., 1912.

HUBBARD, M. AND PEEK, E. NATIONAL COSTUMES OF THE SLAVIC PEOPLES, New York: Women's Press, 1921.

National Geographic Magazine: July, 1913, November, 1914, September, 1916.

PERLBERG, H. C. HISTORICAL RUSSIAN COSTUMES. New York: H. C. Perlberg, 1923.

Serbia

DURHAM, M. C. THROUGH THE LAND OF THE SERB. London: E. Arnold, 1904.

TILKE, MAX. COSTUMES OF EASTERN EUROPE. New York: E. Weyhe, 1926.

Scotland

McIAN, R. R. COSTUMES OF THE CLANS OF THE SCOTTISH HIGHLANDS. New York: F. A. Stokes Company, 1845.

MACKAY, J. G. THE ROMANTIC STORY OF THE HIGHLAND GARB AND TARTAN. Stirling: E. Mackay, 1924.

STUART, J. S. S. COSTUMES OF THE CLANS. Edinburg: J. Menzies, 1845.

South America

FORREST, A. S. A TOUR THROUGH SOUTH AMERICA. London: Paul and Company, 1913.

GIAFFERRI, P. L. FEMININE COSTUME OF THE WORLD. Paris: Editions Nilsson, 1926.

SPICER, D. G. LATIN AMERICAN COSTUMES. New York: Hyperion Press, 1941.

Spain

National Geographic Magazine: August, 1924.

BELL, G. F. G. SPANISH GALLICIA. New York: Duffield and Company, 1923.

PALENCIA, ISABEL DE. THE REGIONAL COSTUMES OF SPAIN. London: B. T. Batsford, Ltd., 1926.

WILLIAMS, LEONARD. THE LAND OF THE DONS. London: Cassell and Company, Ltd., 1922.

Sweden

ALFBILDNINGAR AF SVENSKA NATIONAL DRÄKTER. Stockholm: P. B. Eklund, 1907.

HOLME, CHARLES. PEASANT ART IN SWEDEN, LAPLAND, AND ICELAND. London: "The Studio," Ltd., 1910.

National Geographic Magazine: October, 1928.

PHILIP, J. B. HOLIDAYS IN SWEDEN. London: Skeffington and Company, 1914.

STEVENI, W. B. UNKNOWN SWEDEN. London: Hurst and Blackett, 1925.

WISTRAND, P. G. SVENSKA FOLKDRÄKTER. Stockholm: 1907.

Switzerland

BAUD-BOVY, DANIEL. PEASANT ART IN SWITZERLAND. London: "The Studio," Ltd., 1924.

HEIERLI, J. DIE SWEIZERTRACHTEN. Zürich: Polygraphisches Institut, 1896–1900.

REINHARDT, J. C. COLLECTION OF COSTUMES SWISSES. London: 1830.

Textiles

COLE, ALLEN. ORNAMENT IN EUROPEAN SILKS. London: Debenham and Freebody, 1899.

CRAWFORD, M. D. C. HERITAGE OF COTTON. New York: Fairchild Publishing Company, 1948.

FLEMMING, ERNEST. ENCYCLOPÆDIA OF TEXTILES. London: E. Benn, Ltd., 1928.

GLAZIER, RICHARD. HISTORIC TEXTILE FABRICS. London: B. T. Batsford, Ltd., 1923.

HUNTER, L. L. DECORATIVE TEXTILES. Philadelphia: J. B. Lippincott Company, 1918.

PRIEST, A. AND SIMMONS, P. CHINESE TEXTILES. New York: Metropolitan Museum of Art, 1931.

RODIER, PAUL. THE ROMANCE OF FRENCH WEAVING. New York: Frederick A. Stokes Company, 1931.

VON FALKE, OTTO. DECORATIVE SILKS. New York: W. Helburn, 1922.

Tibet

LANDOR-SAVAGE, A. H. TIBET. New York: Harper and Brothers, 1905.

Turkey

GARNETT, LUCY. THE TURKISH PEOPLE. London: Methuen and Company, 1909. TURKISH LIFE. New York: G. P. Putnam's Sons, 1904.

SHOBERL, F. WORLD IN MINIATURE. London: Ackerman, 1827.

TILKE, MAX. ORIENTAL COSTUMES. New York: Brentano, 1922.

Turkestan

CURTIS, W. E. TURKESTAN, THE HEART OF ASIA. London: Hodder and Staughton, 1911.

SCHUYLER, EUGENE. TURKESTAN. New York: Scribner, Armstrong and Company, 1877.

TILKE, MAX. ORIENTAL COSTUMES. New York: Brentano, 1922.

Underwear

HOLLIDAY, R. UNMENTIONABLES. New York: R. Long and R. R. Smith, 1933.

United States

EARLE, A. M. TWO CENTURIES OF COSTUME IN AMERICA. New York: The Macmillan Company, 1903. HOME LIFE IN COLONIAL DAYS. New York: The Macmillan Company, 1902. COSTUME OF COLONIAL TIMES. New York: Charles Scribner's Sons, 1894.

HOES, R. G. CATALOGUE OF AMERICAN HISTORICAL COSTUMES. Washington, 1915.

LESTER, K. M. HISTORIC COSTUME. Peoria: Manual Arts Press, 1925.

McCLELLAN, ELIZABETH. HISTORIC DRESS IN AMERICA. Philadelphia: McCrae Smith, 1910.

PARSONS, F. A. THE PSYCHOLOGY OF DRESS. New York: Doubleday Page and Company, 1920.

SINGLETON, ESTHER. SOCIAL NEW YORK UNDER THE GEORGES. New York: D. Appleton and Company, 1902.

WARICK, E., AND PITZ, H. C. EARLY AMERICAN COSTUME. New York: The Century Company, 1929.

WHARTON, A. H. SOCIAL LIFE IN THE EARLY REPUBLIC. Philadelphia: J. B. Lippincott Company, 1902. COLONIAL DAYS AND DAMES. Philadelphia: J. B. Lippincott Company, 1895.

Wales

National Geographic Magazine: February, 1914, April, 1915.

RHYS, J. AND JONES, D. B. THE WELSH PEOPLE. London: E. Benn and Company, 1900.

TOPICS FOR CLASS DISCUSSION

PART ONE

THE HISTORIC DRESS OF THE ANCIENTS, THE FRENCH, THE ENGLISH, AND THE AMERICANS

CHAPTER I

1. The relation between Egyptian religious beliefs and the preservation of records of their everyday life.
2. The effect of climate on the dress of the Egyptians.
3. Possible reasons for the few changes in women's dress.
4. The effect of religious belief on the choice of textile fibers, employed in Egyptian dress.
5. Egyptian hair dressing compared with that of the French in the eighteenth century.
6. Cosmetics and the care of the body as practiced by the Egyptians.
7. Examples of Egyptian influence in modern dress.
8. Color in Egyptian jewelry.
9. Color in ancient Persian dress as shown in illuminated manuscripts.
10. Similarities in old Hebraic costume and that of the modern Bedouin.

CHAPTER II

1. Contrasts between the dress of the Cretans and the Greeks of the classical period.
2. Greek dress as an ideal for modern designers.
3. Greek fibulae and modern dress fasteners.
4. The laws of proportion as exemplified in Greek costume.
5. Greek drapery as found in modern dress.
6. The sources of our knowledge of Greek dress.
7. Recent excavations as sources of information of customs and costumes of the ancients.

CHAPTER III

1. Comparison of the methods of arrangement of the *toga* and the *himation*.
2. Dress as an indication of citizenship in ancient and modern times.
3. Reflections of Roman footwear in present day sport sandals.
4. The fabrics employed by the Romans.
5. The increase in luxury and extravagance in dress as coincident with the expansion of the Roman Empire.
6. Roman dress as modified by contact with other peoples.
7. Evidences of Byzantine dress in that of modern ecclesiastics.
8. Mosaics as illustrative of early Christian dress.
9. Purple as a significant color with the Romans.

CHAPTER IV

1. Striking differences in the costumes of the Greeks and the Gauls.
2. Evidences in early French dress of Byzantine influence.

332

3. Wars as disseminators of ideas of dress.
4. The use of heraldic devices in moyen âge costume.
5. Possible reasons for the use of fur in the costume of the Middle ages.
6. Class distinction as expressed in dress during the Middle Ages.
7. Military reflections in civilian dress.
8. Sources of information regarding costume ot this period.
9. The effect of increasing trade and the opening of new trade routes on French dress.
10. Tapestries of the fifteenth century as records of costume.
11. Gothic architecture and contemporary French dress.
12. Sumptuary laws of the Middle Ages.
13. The pretensions of the wealthy bourgeoisie in matters of dress.
14. Italian fashions of the late fifteenth century and their influence on French dress.

Chapter V

1. The effect of international marriages of rulers on dress of the period.
2. The changes of silhouette during the sixteenth century.
3. How the personalities of rulers affected dress.
4. The importation and use of lace in France during the Renaissance.
5. The establishment of the silk industry in France.
6. Materials used in the decoration of sixteenth century dress.
7. The relation of neckwear to hair dressing.
8. The effect on home industries of the royal encouragement of extravagance in dress.
9. The policy of Colbert relating to the establishment of the lace industry in France.
10. Reflections of Spanish court fashions in those of France.

Chapter VI

1. The fabrics employed in seventeenth century dress.
2. The evolution of the coat of Louis XIV.
3. The influence of favorites of the king on French styles.
4. Children's dress in the seventeenth century.
5. Records of costume of the period; the engravings of Bosse and Callot: famous painters of the period.
6. Changes in neckwear of men during the seventeenth century.
7. The advent of ribbon as an important trimming in costume.
8. The leadership of Louis XIV in matters of dress.
9. The backgrounds against which the costumes appeared: houses and furniture of the period.
10. Textile designs of French silks of the seventeenth century.

Chapter VII

1. Characteristic colours of the costumes of the eighteenth century.
2. Textile designs of the eighteenth century compared with those of the Renaissance.
3. How costumes influenced furniture design.
4. Accessories of eighteenth century costume.
5. The silhouette of the woman of the time of Marie Antoinette compared with that of the time of Catherine de Medici.
6. The unhealthful head-dresses of the time of Marie Antoinette.

7. The influence of the English in matters of dress in the later years of the eighteenth century.
8. The Revolutionary costume as a reaction from the extravagances of fashionable France from the time of Louis XIV.
9. The importation of Indian prints and the establishment of factories for the printing of cottons in France.
10. The results of the Revolution as seen in the industries relating to the manufacture of accessories of costume.
11. The influence of artists on the mode.
12. The expression of political opinions through the medium of clothes.
13. The effect of the invention of textile machinery during the eighteenth century on the costumes of all classes.

Chapter VIII

1. Indications in the costumes of the Empire of suggestions gleaned from the East.
2. The policy of Napoleon in his encouragement of extravagances in dress.
3. Healthful features of Empire dress.
4. Self trimming as the dominant form of decoration on the dresses of the period of the Restoration.
5. The principles of design as applied to the costume of the Restoration.
6. Characteristics of the costume of the Second Empire.
7. Famous French women and their contributions to the modes of their day.
8. The breaking down of class distinction in dress.
9. Results of the invention of the sewing machine.
10. The results of machine inventions in the textile industry.
11. The changes brought about in women's dress by the introduction of sports.

Chapter IX

1. The effect of the World War upon the dress of women.
2. The evolution of the corset from the sixteenth to the twentieth century.
3. The ready-to-wear clothing industry of to-day. Its effect on individuality in dress.
4. Why all women dress alike.
5. Evidences of eighteenth and nineteenth century styles in the dress of to-day.
6. The dress of modern business women.
7. The effect of modern transportation facilities and heating systems in houses and office buildings on the dress of modern women.
8. Costume fabrics of to-day: how they compare with those of the sixteenth century and the Empire.
9. Leading French and American designers of to-day.
10. The influence of the radio and moving picture on women's dress.

Chapter X

1. Foreign influences affecting the dress of the English during the Middle Ages.
2. English commerce and English dress.
3. Distinctive head-dresses of English women during the Middle Ages.
4. The use of embroidery in English dress.
5. The furnishings of castles and manor houses as a background for the costume.
6. Monumental effigies and sepulchral brasses as sources of information regarding English costume.

7. English costume as described in the "Canterbury Tales."
8. The part played by the Crusades in English dress.

Chapter XI

1. Women's head-dress as shown in the drawings by Holbein.
2. The English sumptuary laws.
3. The development of the ruff and hoop.
4. The eccentricities of Elizabethan costume.
5. The influence of the Tudor monarchs on dress.
6. The effect on English dress of the settlement in England of the Huguenots.
7. English fabrics of the sixteenth century.

Chapter XII

1. The sobering influence of the Cromwells on English dress.
2. The dress of the Cavalier contrasted with that of the Puritan.
3. Children's dress as depicted by famous artists of the seventeenth century.
4. French inspiration for the modes of the reign of Charles II.
5. The influence on dress of the foreign-born queens of England.

Chapter XIII

1. Color in men's dress during the period of the Georgian rulers.
2. Exaggerations and eccentricities in masculine styles as expressed by the Macaronies.
3. Comparison of French and English fashions in women's dress during the nineteenth century.
4. The influence on English fashions of the French Revolution.
5. English dress as described in the literature of the period.

Chapter XIV

1. Contrasts and similarities in Puritan and Virginian dress in the early years of the Colonial period.
2. Religious beliefs of the Colonists as affecting their dress.
3. Home manufacture of clothing by the Colonists.
4. The characteristics of early Quaker dress.
5. How Continental fashions reached the Colonists.
6. The social backgrounds of the different groups of Colonials.
7. The sartorial results of increased communication facilities between the various colonies.
8. The financial status of the Colonists as affecting their clothes.
9. The laws of old New England relating to dress.
10. Social backgrounds of the early Revolutionary period.
11. The dress of the Dutch settlers as described by Washington Irving.
12. French and American styles immediately following the American Revolution.
13. Fashion magazines of the Republic.
14. The lack of strictly national costume in the United States.

PART TWO

NATIONAL COSTUME IN EUROPE, NORTHERN AFRICA, ASIA AND THE AMERICAS

Chapter XV

1. Moorish influences that are found in some costumes of Spain.
2. Characteristics of Spanish dress.
3. The shawl in Spanish feminine dress.
4. The survival of moyen âge modes in some French peasant head-dresses.
5. Color and decoration in peasant costumes of Western Europe.
6. Aprons of Western Europe.
7. The distinctive dress of various religious sects.
8. Geographic conditions as determining factors in various peasant modes.
9. Changing standards of dress among the peasant classes of Europe.
10. Social significance of world-wide fashions and uniformities in dress.

Chapter XVI

1. The variety of caps in the Netherlands.
2. The importance of jewelry and buttons in peasant dress.
3. The plaid of the Gaul in ancient France and the tartan of the Scotch.
4. The hat of the Puritan as the ancestor of the Welsh woman's hat.
5. Native materials employed in the dress of the Lapps.
6. Climate as a determining feature in national dress.
7. The decorative fastenings of national costumes as inspiration for modern costumes.
8. A comparison of the corselet as worn by Swiss and Scandinavian women with that worn by the women of Central Europe.

Chapter XVII

1. The survival of Byzantine head-dresses in those of modern Russian ones.
2. The use of leather as decoration in Hungarian and Czechoslovakian costumes.
3. The characteristic use of sheepskin in the costume of Eastern Europe.
4. The importance of the sash or belt in men's dress.
5. The distinguishing feature of Moslem women's dress.
6. The Turkish domination of many of the costumes of Southern Europe.
7. The use of hand woven materials in Slavic dress.
8. Masculine headgear in Eastern Europe.
9. The use of coins as decoration.
10. The use of beads in Balkan and American Indian costumes.
11. Factors making for the disuse of many of the native costumes in Europe.
12. Racial characteristics as expressed in dress.
13. Occupations as influential factors in dress.
14. Typical motifs found in the embroideries of the Czechs, the Roumanians, and the Bulgarians.
15. Materials employed in the decoration of Slavic costumes.
16. Colors typical of different nationalities.

Chapter XVIII

1. The part played by climate in Oriental dress.
2. The religious beliefs of the Orientals as reflected in their dress.
3. The position of women in the East and its effects on their dress.

4. Native materials of the Arabs.
5. Modern Egyptian dress compared with that worn in the time of the building of the pyramids.
6. The character and color of Arabian dress.
7. The importance and significance of jewelry in the costume of the Oriental woman.

CHAPTER XIX

1. The variety of arrangements possible with the draped garments of the East.
2. The various methods of obtaining pattern on fabrics as employed by the Orientals.
3. The significance of embroidery in Chinese costume.
4. The use of semi-precious stones in Chinese jewelry.
5. The prevalence of silk in the costumes of the Chinese and Japanese.
6. The power of custom in Chinese costume.
7. Cold weather costumes of the Chinese.
8. The extensive use of cosmetics by the women of Asia.
9. The superstitions of the Koreans in regard to the head covering of the men.
10. The significance of color and pattern in the materials used in the kimonos of Japanese women and children.
11. The foot covering of the different Orientals.
12. The materials used by the natives of the islands of the Pacific.

CHAPTER XX

1. The importance of skins and furs in early American Indian dress.
2. Native dress materials of the Arctic regions.
3. Factors instrumental in the preservation of the manner of dress of the Eskimo.
4. Feathers as distinctive ornamentation among the American Indians.
5. Spanish fashions in Mexico and South America.
6. Wraps and hats as distinctive of South American costumes.

APPENDIX

A—SUGGESTIONS TO TEACHERS

Historic Costume for Teachers.—The broad, far reaching subject of historic costume offers to teachers and students material that is so diversified and rich that they are at times embarrassed by the necessity of choosing a very small amount that can be best fitted into the limits of a crowded school curriculum. The easiest solution to many is the omission of all matter pertaining to that subject—dress—which has for centuries received a large share of the attention of men and women of all sections of the world, and of all stages of civilization, and has affected their social, industrial, and economic life in large measure. The courses of study dealing with textiles and clothing until recently have, on the whole, made but scant mention of the historical material relating to this subject and have neglected a very rich, cultural foundation to that very practical study. The teachers of costume design have been wise enough to utilize this field for the enrichment of their courses but many times have not availed themselves of more than a very small section of the entire subject. French and English historical costumes have usually been drawn upon for suggestions for the student of design, while the wealth of suggestion offered by national and peasant dress, by armour as worn in Western Europe during the Middle Ages; by textiles, laces, and accessories; by the furs and skins as utilized by the peoples of northern American and Eurasian countries; by the embroideries of the Asiatic and Central European peoples; by the garments worn by the civilized races of northern Africa; even by the cut of monastic and ecclesiastical garments of present and past vintage—all these have been largely neglected. Yet all are exceedingly rich in suggestions for details and should be frequently drawn upon by teachers of design who endeavor to discover and cultivate originality and independence on the part of their students.

This applies likewise to those in charge of clothing classes who desire to break away from the old treadmill of pure construction

338

and open to the young student and prospective teacher ways and means of developing resourcefulness, originality, and confidence, as well as introducing them to cultural material of absorbing interest in itself, and helping them to enrich their own teaching. The young teacher should learn how much costume has meant in the lives of earlier generations as well as in her own; that dress has been more than a mere feminine whim—an important factor in the industrial, economic, and social as well as artistic life of countless peoples; that the changes of fashion are especially influential in the lives of all present-day Americans, making or imperilling the livelihood of an enormous mass of the population of the country in which she lives. She should know that with a richer economic and industrial life the generation to which she belongs has been freed from the restrictions that applied to the dress of members of various ranks of society until comparatively recent times; that with the possible exception of differences of texture and quality, the girl or woman of "limited income"—sometimes very limited—may have the same number, design and colour of clothes and accessories as the girl or woman of larger means.

In the study of the healthful features of modern clothes, the young teacher in training should be led to understand the arduous road by which these new features have been attained, and to see for herself what must have been the effect of the numerous articles of clothing, the confining corsets, and the distorting shoes of many earlier periods upon the bodily health of men, women, and children. These, by force of contrast, drive home to all the advantages of the simple, healthful, non-restricting garments of recent times, or show wherein the present-day scientific enlightenment has not yet been able to overcome many failures to break away from antiquated ideas which are still clung to by a few. In short, historic costume as a background subject may be utilized to evaluate the worth and progress of much of our present-day health teaching in matters of dress. Concrete illustrations of how this may be handled in a class of prospective teachers are offered as follows: The topic before the class may be "good posture helped or hindered by the clothes we wear." Corsets and shoes may be the two articles of the wardrobe used to illustrate the point. Each student may be asked to collect pictures of these articles as worn now, and as worn in other periods of history—pictures of Indian moccasins, Greek sandals, the tiny shoe for the footbound woman of old China, the long pointed-toed shoe of the fifteenth century, the very high heeled shoe or slipper of the lady of the court of Marie Antoinette, and the thin, heelless slipper of the Empire. The footwear of peoples of other lands of today offers interesting contrasts to those examples of shoes, and to our own; the wooden sabot of the Hollander; the straw sandal of the Spaniard, the leather, curling-toed slipper of the Turk, the *zori* and *gheta* of the Japanese, are just a few of the modern shoes that can be studied in relation to the matter of posture and foot health. Some very forceful, telling lessons may be derived from such a collection as the above, even from pictures, though better, naturally, from a collection of the real shoes themselves.

While the above is suggested for classes of student teachers, such a lesson, very simply carried out, can be most effective for younger students of the high school or grades, and while suggested primarily for Home Economics students, it will be interesting for students of physical education and supplemented by exhibits, posters, and an assembly presentation, may start a movement for shoe hygiene throughout a whole school.

A similar method could be used in a child study or children's clothing class. The pre-school age child who is occupying the attention of educators today has not always been as healthfully, simply clad as at present, and indeed is wholesomely clad in only a few countries of the world today. As an appreciational background, a brief study of how the little child is clothed in other countries may be profitably made, particularly for those who are to teach in sections of the country with a large foreign-born population. Pictures and clippings on the bulletin board may be used very effectively when but little class time is available for such a study.

In classes which deal primarily with the problems of clothing selection, for either adults or children, historic costume offers very rich material for illustration. A collection of Old World caps and bonnets, or good reproductions of the paintings of such masters as Gainsborough, Holbein, Watteau, or the drawings of Dürer, have much to emphasize points of contour, line, and the relation of the hat to the dress and silhouette for a group making a study of the selection of hats. In addition they strengthen the acquaintance of those same students with the works of famous artists. Examples of this type of illustration in conjunction with pictures of modern hats will certainly give the young student a broader point of view than may be obtained from the use of modern examples alone. Other pictures, wisely selected, may be as successfully used in the study of necklines, hairdressing, and silhouette especially.

Home Economics teachers in sections of the United States where there are large settlements of citizens born in other countries have a very wonderful opportunity to do worthwhile work, not only for the new citizens themselves, teaching them the best that the new country has to offer, but also for the community at large. This teacher, touching as she does on the personal home life of the children, can readily win her way into the understanding of and acceptance by the older people, encouraging them in turn to offer the best of what their own old-land home life may contribute to the new. These housewives are proud not only of the national dishes they can so skillfully prepare, but also of the brilliant, attractive dresses that they have now given up in the new land. One clever clothing teacher in charge of the apron table at a school fair used as a background decoration for the aprons made by her own classes the brilliant-hued, embroidered and elaborately patterned aprons contributed for the occasion by the mothers of her young students, and as a result won hearty support for her work from parents and the public generally.

Another interested teacher included in a style show of dresses made by the school children, dresses of the various nationalities represented in the school population with most gratifying results of increased interest and coöperation on the part of the foreign born parents. A somewhat similar idea has been carried out in several colleges with a large number of foreign born students. Dressed in the native costume of their country they have staged entertainments for their American school fellows to the great interest and appreciation of the latter.

For the teaching of decoration in clothing, the embroidery on the garments worn by peoples from the Central European countries has a wealth of material for study, inspiration, and adaptation in simplified form for the garments of children or adults. The various books in the "Peasant Art" series, the National Geographic Magazine, A Magyar Nép Müvészete, as well as the colored plates of Bossert's Book of Ornament, are excellent for material of this type. Plates showing the batik *sarongs* of the Javanese and the silken tie-dyed turbans of the East Indians may be drawn on for designs for batik and tie-dye scarves or other accessories of modern dress. The embroidered caps of the Czech woman and the similarly decorated aprons of the Swedish woman can be most pleasingly adapted into pocketbooks to accompany summer frocks. The fastening devices employed by the Chinese, the Japanese, and the Magyar peoples are most suggestive for adaptation to modern American costumes and are very helpful illustrative material in all clothing design or construction classes.

For an advanced student interested in draping on the dress form there is no more profitable method of study, in addition to ample experimentation with a wide variety of materials and textures, than a careful analysis of the ways old masters have handled materials, either in painting or in sculpture. The possibilities offered for varied and fine line, and space division in the classic Greek *chiton* and *himation* as represented by the old master sculptors should be called to the attention of all such students and presented for their careful study.

In high schools where the custom exists of having the various departments take charge of certain programs on assembly days the clothing group has a splendid opportunity of presenting an educational program in which historic costume is used incidentally in coöperation with the history, literature, or geography classes or to show the development or present significance of certain features of costume. In illustration of the latter idea it is suggested that in connection with an informal showing of simple sport frocks made in a clothing class, there may also be shown the costumes worn for tennis, swimming, bicycling, and golf about twenty or more years ago. This could be done by means of pictures and a reflectoscope, or better still, from the point of view of group participation, by having some students appear in costumes made of inexpensive material like those worn when those sports were first generally indulged in. Such costumes could be borrowed or rented, in some instances.

In some schools it may be desirable to develop the subject of historic costume in a very logical systematic manner, while in others more effective results can be attained by selecting topics very closely related to the work under consideration in other courses.

When the systematic approach is followed it is advisable that the students be urged to read as widely as time will permit of general history and literature. Historical novels have been found to give a very attractive background for those students whose knowledge of history needs to be brushed up but who do not have a great deal of time for careful reading. Since the World War caused so many changes in the boundaries and territories of Central and Southern European countries many students need the aid of a map in their study of peasant and national costumes. The map helps also, in the understanding of the influence of geographical position on the clothing of various nations.

The instructor who has on file in her classroom a diversified collection of photographs or sketches of the costumes of various peoples in different historical periods should find coöperation with the instructors and students of history, literature, and geography a very helpful and simple matter as the newer methods of the presentation of those subjects, particularly history and geography, more and more stress an understanding of the life and customs of the people concerned.

There are many ways in which historic costume may be presented and utilized, and probably as effectively as any indirect method, is the use of the bulletin board either in the classroom or in the corridor of that part of the building where the clothing and costume design classes are conducted. Clippings of modern costumes placed beside illustration of historic ones from which the modern dresses were designed; a photograph of the scene in a current play or moving picture in which period costumes are shown; and photographs of the costumes of the natives of a foreign country where some national personage is visiting are all of interest to the general student body, and of particular interest to those students who have had their attention directed along those channels in classes. To hold attention it is necessary that the clippings on the bulletin board be changed rather frequently, and if possible, that students be urged to contribute.

Illustrative Material.—Many teachers feel that little can be done with this subject of historic costume because their individual schools cannot afford an elaborate collection of expensive books. An abundance of beautifully illustrated books owned by the school is naturally very desirable but by no means absolutely essential as in most progressive city libraries there is available for the use of schools and teachers a constantly growing collection of pictures which can be borrowed on a regular library card in the same way that a book is borrowed. These pictures, gathered from old books, and current magazines are usually of convenient size for class use and pleasingly mounted. There is as a rule no charge for their use. For a very small fee—usually just the transportation charges— many large museums send to schools a collection of pictures, slides, or mounted examples of textiles that are suitable for the purpose. In but few cases is it wise when writing to a museum or a library for illustrations to ask for pictures or slides of costumes. In most instances the classification is made on the bsais of paintings and sculptures, so that pictures of the works of artists that depict costumes should be asked for. The stills of a motion picture with an historical setting serve as excellent illustrations of costumes usually. As a rule the authenticity of the costumes may be relied upon as most of the important moving picture producing companies have very competent people in charge of those properties and very adequate libraries of authentic books on costume.

For a very moderate sum an excellent collection of reproductions of paintings and sculpture illustrating costume may be obtained from firms handling pictures for school use. Hand-books, catalogues, and bulletins published by museums and art galleries are on the whole inexpensive and contain very good illustrations. Many museums sell post cards and small prints. The following list is of firms and museums from which photographs at varying prices may be obtained.

Alinari, 8 Via Nazionale, Florence.
American Museum of Natural History, 77th Street and Central Park West, New York City
Anderson, D., Via Salaria 7a, Rome
Art Institute, Chicago, Ill.
Braun, A., Dornach, Alsace, France
Bibliothèque Nationale, Paris
British Museum, London
Brown and Company, Beverly, Mass.
Brown-Robertson Company, 424 Madison Ave., New York City
Curtis and Cameron, 12 Harcourt Street, Boston, Mass.
Detroit Publishing Company, Detroit, Mich.
Druet, E., 20 Rue Royale, Paris
Essex Institute, Salem, Mass.
Field Museum of Natural History, Chicago, Ill.
Giraudon, A., 9 Rue des Beaux Arts, Paris

Hanfstaengl, F. Herzog, Rudolfstrasse 1, Munich
Hispanic Society of America, Broadway and 156th Street, New York City.
Les Archives Photographiques d'Art et d'Histoire, Palais-Royal 1 bis, Rue de
Valois, Paris
Louvre, Paris
Metropolitan Museum of Art, New York City
Museum of the American Indian, Heye Foundation, 155th Street and Broad-
way, New York City
Museum of Fine Arts, Boston, Mass.
National Gallery, London
National Portrait Gallery, London
Perry Pictures Company, Malden, Mass.
Raymond and Raymond, 40 E. 52nd Street, New York City
Roig, Casa, Calle de San Augustin, 13, Madrid
Seemann, E. A., Leipzig
United States Museum of Natural History, Washington, D. C.
University Prints, Newton, Mass.
Victoria and Albert Museum, South Kensington, London
Wallace Collection, London
Worcester Museum of Art, Worcester, Mass.

Illustrated magazines are another source of comparatively inexpensive illustrative material for historic costume. Most schools
today have in their libraries current magazines as well as bound
copies on file. If not in the school library they will most certainly
be found in the public library. Some, like the International
Studio contain excellent reproductions of the paintings of the
masters, in color, which faithfully reproduce the costume of the
period. Others, like The National Geographic Magazine, might
well be used as an illustrated text on national and peasant costume
of present times. Such magazines as the following will be found
very helpful in the study of costume:

Asia, The International Studio, Travel, The Theatre Arts, The
National Geographic Magazine, Peoples of All Nations, and Arts
and Decoration.

It is important to remember that as large a number of the
illustrations as possible should be in color. Colored prints are
generally more expensive than those in black and white, but are
almost necessary to give students a clear idea of the quality of
color used in the costumes of the various periods. This factor of
color adds to the expense of costume books and makes the latter
unobtainable for many schools. For that reason it is all the more
advisable that many colored prints—even small ones—be in the
school collection.

For their preservation, good illustrations should be mounted on fairly heavy cardboard with generous margins, and for the convenience of all members of the school staff using them, filed according to a suitable system. Many schools find the classification according to countries the most desirable one with the sections devoted to France, Germany, England, Italy, Spain, and the United States subdivided according to centuries.

The size of an illustration naturally enhances or detracts from its value for class use. As the large prints are fairly expensive, where there is a reflectoscope to be used by all instructors the smaller prints are just as valuable as the larger ones. Slides are also desirable but too limited and expensive as well as fragile to be very generally employed.

Books for Costume Study.—The instructor in this subject is certainly assisted in her teaching by the existence of a good library. Costume books because of their necessarily abundant illustrations are costly, and some of the older ones with beautifully colored illustrations are out of print and consequently almost unobtainable by the average school. Where these are present in the public libraries of large cities, in schools of art and architecture connected with a university or college, the instructor and her students usually have access to them. The state libraries are as a rule willing to send for short periods of time the costume books of their collections to schools within the state. Where only a very limited sum is available for the purchase of books by the school it will be found more advisable to secure one or two books which illustrate the costumes of all peoples and all periods even if they have no text, than to have a few books dealing only with French, English, or American dress. Such general books (see page 323 in the bibliography) can be of use to teachers of other subjects than historic costume needing such material, as well as for pageants and design, and may be supplemented by the encyclopædia to be found in every school library.

For teachers of very young children, such books as the following which deal clearly and simply with the dress of little children of other countries will be found very helpful.

Chance, L. M., Little Folk of Many Lands
Fairgrieve, A., Children of Many Lands
Headland, I. T., The Chinese Boy and Girl
Miller, O. T., Little People of Asia
Milne, L., Little Folk of Many Lands

Perdue, H. A., Child Life in Other Lands
Perkins, L. F., The Dutch Twins, The Eskimo Twins, The Japanese Twins

The books listed under plays and pageants in the bibliography may be found in most public libraries, and are just a few of the many suggested for those in charge of the production of school theatricals or pageants.

Firms making slides:

Chicago Slide Company, 6 E. Lake Street, Chicago, Ill.
Keystone View Company, 219 E. 44th Street, New York City
National Geographic Society, Hubbard Memorial Hall, Washington, D. C.
Underwood and Underwood, 242 W. 55th Street, New York City

Museums with lending collections:

Art Institute, Chicago, Ill.
Metropolitan Museum of Art, New York City
Museum of Fine Arts, Boston, Mass.

INDEX

348